TEN
MEDIEVAL STUDIES

George Gordon Coulton, English historian and noted authority on medieval history, was born at King's Lynn in 1858
and died in 1947. He studied at Cambridge and Heidelberg.
During his lifetime he was lecturer in history at Cambridge
where he was an honorary fellow of St. Catharine's College,
professor and fellow at St. John's College, and Rhind lecturer
at Edinburgh. Among his many books are ART AND THE
REFORMATION, CHAUCER AND HIS ENGLAND,
FIVE CENTURIES OF RELIGION (4 vols.), LIFE
IN THE MIDDLE AGES (4 vols.), MEDIEVAL
THOUGHT, and INQUISITION AND LIBERTY
which is soon to be published as a Beacon Paperback.

TEN
MEDIEVAL STUDIES

By G. G. COULTON

BEACON PRESS   BEACON HILL   BOSTON

First published in 1906
First Beacon Paperback edition published in 1959 by arrangement
with the Cambridge University Press.

Library of Congress Catalog Card Number: 59-6388

Printed in the United States of America

PREFACE TO FIRST EDITION (1906)

THESE essays, mostly reprinted from the Reviews, are intended to defend the moderate Anglican position against the misrepresentations of writers who disparage modern civilization in comparison with a purely imaginary and unhistorical idea of medieval life.

The author attempts to show how much is lost, even from the purely picturesque point of view, by thus sacrificing plain truth to false sentiment; for we shall never see the great men of the past in their full greatness until we realize the difficulties under which they lived and worked. Although the Studies are necessarily controversial to this extent, they are written *entirely from orthodox pre-Reformation sources*, no others being quoted except here and there in corroboration of facts already established: since the curse of Church history is the too frequent habit of writing from second-hand or partisan documents.

As the plan of these pamphlets renders it impossible to give a crowd of references which would only weary the general reader, the author is glad to give a definite guarantee of his good faith by offering four pages in each pamphlet to any competent critic who will undertake to convict him of serious error. If his statements are inaccurate, he thus undertakes to supply their refutation at his own expense. He has already made a similar offer in vain to many Romanist controversialists, including all the writers of the Catholic Truth Society; and he now repeats the offer, in order to enable the general reader to realize how strongly Anglicanism is supported on many important points by the most incontrovertible medieval testimony.

PREFACE TO SECOND EDITION (1915)

THESE papers, though occasional and to a great extent controversial, have one general purpose in view—to justify the main trend of modern culture. Strongly as the author sympathizes with the triumph of medieval over classical civilization, he is equally convinced of the necessity of outgrowing the Middle Ages. St Augustine had to combat a formidable reactionary party which attributed all the evils of the fifth century to Rome's abandonment of her old gods; we, in the twentieth century, have still to combat a similar reaction towards institutions which have lost the universal obedience which they once commanded. Whatever may be our attempts to solve the riddle of the universe, whether in the religious or in the secularist sense, much must depend upon the appeal to history. To a great extent, our theory of life and our hopes for the future must be based upon the facts of the past; and any falsification of those facts must therefore, in the long run, impede true social progress. Opinions will always differ widely and legitimately; but many facts of history might be established with practical certainty, if only we were willing to take a little more trouble. The difference between a Roman Catholic, a Protestant, and an agnostic is often even more philosophical than historical. And those differences could be far more tolerantly discussed if only all parties could agree more nearly on matters of ascertainable fact: the widest dividing gulf is the suspicion, on one side or the other, of careless mis-statements, or even of literary dishonesty.

This is the main reason for a second edition of these essays; though the author, when the question was raised early in 1914, had decided against republication. In the first edition, he merely exposed such mis-statements of Abbot Gasquet's as came directly in his way. To these exposures, though supported by unexceptionable

documents of the Middle Ages, the Abbot never directly
replied; and now he publicly claims his promotion to the
Cardinalate as an Apostolic testimonial to his historical
scholarship.[1] To abstain from republication might therefore have encouraged the impression, openly expressed in
many quarters, that the Cardinal's main contentions are in
general based upon actual documentary evidence, and that
the points on which that evidence fails him are few and
negligible. The author has therefore added to this new
edition a rough list of such blunders and mis-statements
of facts as he has noted during a far from exhaustive study
of the Cardinal's books and of their professed sources.
These fifty-four pages of criticism may enable students to
realize the true meaning of Cardinal Manning's famous
dictum, that the appeal to History is a treason and a heresy;
or again of Cardinal Newman's despairing answer to the
suggestion of founding a Catholic Historical Review.
"Who would bear it?" wrote Newman: "unless one
doctored all one's facts, one would be thought a bad
Catholic". In short, just as these *Studies* were first
printed because some plain protest seemed necessary
against the habitual distortion of historical facts by
Ultramontane writers, who profess to rely upon actual
documents, so they are now reprinted because that protest
seems still necessary, and because the author's silence, in
the face of claims recently made by, and in behalf of, the
new Cardinal, might seem like allowing judgment to go by
default.

The English official historian seems sometimes a little
excessive in his disregard of the general public. Even our
professors had not always realized, until a few months ago,
how successfully the ideas of millions can be moulded by
the steady influence of teachers who preach plausible
untruths systematically *ex cathedra*; and, in this direction,
Ultramontanism has exploited our indolence as steadily as
Imperialist Militarism. It was of the Ultramontanes that

[1] See Appendix II (in third edition, no. III).

Pascal complained "they find it easier to produce monks than reasons"; and the same Pope who promoted Abbot Gasquet to the purple had previously put Loisy and Duchesne upon the Index. Here, in a nutshell, is the key to the furious anti-clericalism of France, Italy, and Spain; it is the inevitable reaction of a long-poisoned public opinion. Moreover, even our official historians are more truly products of contemporary public opinion than they themselves always realize; for they pick up many of their ideas in Clubland, which in its turn owes them to the man in the street. English historians of the highest rank have lately lent themselves, whether through neglect or ignorance, to the comedy of exploiting a political honour as proof presumptive of historical accuracy. They have looked aside from the high interests entrusted to them, and have publicly condoned, in their own domain of History, what would never have been forgiven by men of equal distinction in the domain of Natural Science. If any zoologist of repute had based an important theory upon the alleged total absence of *felidae* from the fauna of Borneo, and if another zoologist had replied by producing thirteen visible and tangible specimens of different *felidae*, there might indeed have been much curious speculation concerning the causes of the original error. But one thing is certain; the peccant theorist would never have dared to republish, without a single word of apology, his original mis-statement of fact, and his original theories based upon that falsehood. Or, even if it were remotely conceivable that he should have done so, we may at least feel assured that his speculations would have been tabooed in all serious scientific circles until he had repented and made public amends. If, moreover, for political reasons, some Prime Minister had presently raised him to a peerage, certainly the President of the Royal Society, with two other equally distinguished scientists, would not have joined a committee formed for the purpose of offering him a public testimonial. In the realm of Natural Science, public opinion is too strong and too healthy to permit such things; and, if it be true that History cannot purge herself of her own dross by the same straightforward methods, then History is irrevocably doomed to that hopelessly inferior rank to which too many readers are already inclined to relegate her. Let us, however, have faith in the ultimate victory of the public conscience. A century hence, the facts to which I am here calling attention will very likely seem almost incredible—almost as incredible as it seems to us that Pitt should have been the first Paymaster who refused to enrich himself by robbing the army officers of £30,000 a year. But, in the meantime, it is difficult to trace any definite and immediate sign of an awakening conscience. We can scarcely assert that the tone of literary morality is higher in this field than it was fifty years ago; and this is my main reason for deciding upon a republication which might otherwise have been postponed altogether.

One essay has been omitted, because I have since published its contents in *From St Francis to Dante*; another has been added in its place (No. 2). Minor alterations have been made to bring the essays up to date, and small slips have been corrected. My inferences from Bishop Nicke's visitations (p. 3) were vehemently attacked at the time by a Roman Catholic theologian in a letter to a common friend; but I was not permitted to publish this, and in fact his severest criticisms rested upon certain popular theories, as to the nature of medieval visitation documents, which are now abandoned by the majority of competent students.[1] I have, however, revised Nicke's evidence in the light of these criticisms, and find that I had rather understated than overstated my case. On no other point, so far as I am aware, have my facts been

---

[1] See my article on *The Interpretation of Visitation Documents* in the *English Historical Review* for Jan., 1914. Mr R. C. Fowler, of the Public Record Office, had already expressed much the same conclusions in his preface to Baldock's Register, which I ought to have noticed in my article; and three other editors of visitation documents have since written to assure me of their full agreement.

questioned, though a good many scholars may disagree
with my deductions.

Appendix I[1] is designed to raise my criticisms as much
as possible out of the sphere of scattered detail. The piece-
meal character of the papers here reprinted might otherwise encourage the notion, expressed by the late Mgr
Benson, that I am a pedant who has found a few mistakes
in Cardinal Gasquet's work, and who cannot look beyond
these small flaws to the main issues involved. I contend,
on the contrary, that we have here one of the broadest and
most vital of historical issues. Is History to be written
without documentary references, or even with indefensibly
false references, by authors who are under every personal
and professional temptation to see only one side? or, on
the other hand, must we not all gain by submitting our
prepossessions to the wholesome pressure of outside
opinion, by giving full and accurate references, and by
imitating at least the formal honesty of the children of
this world, who know that their whole public credit
depends upon the soundness of their business vouchers?
I have therefore put together, in this Appendix I, a rough
list of nearly 200 blunders and mis-statements noted during
a perusal, sometimes cursory and sometimes detailed, of
most of the Cardinal's books. The list could probably be
made far longer if this were worth while; but for most
readers it will probably suffice as it stands, and will tell its
own tale plainly enough.

[1] In this third edition, Appendix II.

PREFACE TO THIRD EDITION

MORE than one correspondent has pressed for this republication of the first series of my Medieval Studies; and the same reasons which decided me in 1915 seemed equally cogent in 1930; see Appendix 1. The opportunity has been taken to add three Studies from my second series, which had also fallen out of print.

G. G. C.

CAMBRIDGE
Sept. 1930

CONTENTS

[1] For the numeration of this essay, see page 189.

TEN
MEDIEVAL STUDIES

THE MONASTIC LEGEND[1]

"To manipulate ancient writings, to edit history in one's own favour, did not appear criminal [in the 'Ages of Faith'] if the end in view were otherwise just and good."

Dr W. Barry (*Papal Monarchy*, p. 133).

THE very thoroughness of the Reformation is, in one sense, its weakness. Modern morals are already so far removed from the medieval, that Anglicans are ready to disbelieve the most undoubted scandals of the past; and modern tolerance listens candidly to the misrepresentations of writers whose shrift in pre-Reformation days would have been short. In the face of opponents who devote their lives not only to exposing the real faults and foibles of the Reformers, but also to raking up scandal against them from the most tainted sources, one is driven sometimes to the pertinent retort that, even if all these things were true, matters were incomparably worse in the "Ages of Faith". But the very strength of this argument from the point of view of historical truth makes it very difficult of use in modern society; just as, in good company, the very grossness of a man's defects may save him from the obvious retort which would crush him at once among his own class. Thus, the modern Romanist controversialist finds a real protection, for a time at least, in the very unsavouriness of certain chapters of medieval Church history. Cardinal Gasquet—I name him as the most brilliant writer on the particular subject with which I propose to deal—has argued for the last twenty years, with very considerable show of historical apparatus, that the Dissolution of the

---

[1] This essay was severely criticized by Mr Egerton Beck in *The Month* for August 1921. This led to a correspondence in *The Tablet*; Mr Beck refused permission to reprint his letters, but mine are printed in the fifteenth of my *Medieval Studies* (2nd series), entitled "More Roman Catholic History."

Monasteries was an act of unredeemed iniquity, and that
the blood of these innocent men is still on our heads.
Many students who are convinced of the contrary have yet
been reluctant to enter upon a somewhat invidious discussion; and, meanwhile, the Cardinal has found his
strongest ally in the comparative decency of modern
society. That which, before the Reformation, was proclaimed daily without reserve—by sinners with wanton
laughter, and by saints with bitter tears—is too shocking
to be lightly believed by men who know what their own
clergy have been for generations past, and who have never
seen the monastic system at work except under the safeguards afforded by modern laws and modern publicity.
If we may believe a certain section of the press, Cardinal
Gasquet has been lecturing in America with conspicuous
success on the innocence of the medieval monks and the
sin of their suppression. He is apparently about to repeat
these lectures in England: it is, therefore, time to abandon
the attitude of distant scepticism, and to look closely into
arguments which, if sound, would call for an act of
national repentance.

Six years ago, in going through a course of Roman
apologetics, I came upon Cardinal Gasquet's book. It
struck me from the first page as extraordinarily inconsistent with original documents; and one point specially
arrested my attention. The Cardinal claims that "anything
like general immorality was altogether unknown among the
Religious of England. This much is clearly proved by the
testimony of the acts of Episcopal visitations...".[1] I read
this with some surprise: for I knew a little of English
visitation acts, and they seemed to me to point clearly to
the opposite conclusion. It was necessary, therefore, to
make sure, first of all, what were the documents to which
he appealed in support of a statement which, if correct,
might almost have spared him the trouble of writing all

---

[1] *Henry VIII and the English Monasteries*, I, 38. My quotations are
from the 3rd edition, 1888.

the rest of his book. I therefore expressed my doubts by letter to him, pointing out that his mere general reference to "the Episcopal Registers" or "the Acts of Episcopal Visitation" was no reference at all; and begging him, therefore, to supply this grave omission by letter. To save him trouble, and for the sake of a clear understanding, I enclosed a list of the score of volumes containing episcopal visitations which I knew to be accessible to the general student, requesting him to initial those upon which he could rely as supporting his statement, and to draw his pen through those for which he could not answer from personal study. At the receipt of my letter, he was unfortunately under the doctor's orders; but when I repeated my request six months later his answer was final. It amounted to a confession that he had forgotten the very names of the books on which he had professed to base the most sweeping and vital statement, perhaps, in his whole history.[1] His book had, indeed, surprised me at first by the easy familiarity which it claimed *en bloc* with documents so bulky, and so laborious to study, as the episcopal registers: all the greater, therefore, was my surprise to find him now pleading that, without much search among his notes, he could not even *name* such of these twenty volumes as he had studied and could safely appeal to. In this embarrassment, I was driven to make what I could out of the Cardinal's footnotes. I found that the episcopal acts are, in fact, quoted somewhat sparingly —far less freely than many other books of infinitely less historical value. Some of the references, being to volumes still unprinted, are difficult to verify; but, fortunately, by far the most important are to books which, though still in manuscript when he wrote, have since been printed. These are, firstly, the Exeter registers, to which one very confident appeal is made, though apparently at second-hand; and secondly, the Norwich visitations of Bishop Nicke, to which

---

[1] I have these letters by me, and will gladly print them with the Cardinal's leave.

he thrice appeals for confirmation of some of his most sweeping statements.[1] This simplifies the problem a good deal. In the days when the learned Cardinal did know which registers he had or had not read, he appealed specially to the records of Exeter and Norwich, as proving (1) the methods of visitation, (2) the fact that there was "nothing like general immorality" in the monasteries, (3) that, for any grave breach of the Rule, punishment was stern and unsparing, such as the instance which he quotes in full from a York register.[2] Here, then, is a plain issue, which I will test first by Nicke, from whose "two valuable volumes" he claims support in the most emphatic words. "Nothing like general immorality" is, of course, a somewhat vague plea: we find, for instance, an earnest and learned Roman Catholic apologist in France congratulating himself that the thirteenth-century visitations of Rouen show no more than thirty-three unchaste nuns out of a total of 373, or 9 per cent.[3] Cardinal Gasquet, however, has evidently a far higher ideal of monastic chastity; for he claims that the registers give us a picture very different from that of Henry's visitation, which, after all, accused scarcely more than 3 per cent. of immorality.[4] Yet, on Nicke's first visitation of his diocese, in 1514, he found nearly double of that percentage suspected by their fellow-monks or nuns of immorality. The arguments which fill nine-tenths of the Cardinal's two bulky volumes are meant to prove that the reports of Henry VIII's commissioners are too bad to be credible. In the course of these arguments he appeals confidently to the support of certain episcopal visitations, still in manuscript, but well known to himself. When these are printed, it transpires that they yield a

[1] Of the six Exeter volumes only the least important had been published when Cardinal Gasquet wrote.

[2] *Henry VIII and the English Monasteries*, I, 36 note, 334 note: cf. 355.

[3] E. du Méril, in *Soc. des Antiq. de Normandie*, 1847, p. 125.

[4] I, 352. Elsewhere the Cardinal reckons the total of monks, friars and nuns at 8000 (II, 323). Assuming that figure, the 250 cases reported give us 3·1 per cent. The numbers in Nicke are 332 monks and nuns, with twenty cases of immorality, *i.e.* 6·1 per cent.

statistical result far less favourable than Henry VIII's![1]
And the most inexplicable error is still to come. We are
twice referred to Nicke for proof that grave faults were
vigorously punished.[2] Yet (to take one grave fault only)
Nicke found thirty-three monks or nuns suspected of
incontinence by their fellows. In fifteen, at least, of these
cases, either a child had been born, or Nicke's injunctions
show that he held the charge to be founded. Yet he records
only two punishments; though in one other case, which was
already ancient history, we hear that the prior himself had
"corrected" it at the time. Of the two punishments
recorded, one was inflicted upon an unchaste nun, and
runs as follows: "The Lord Bishop...enjoined on the
Lady Agnes Smyth that she should sit for a whole month
below all the other nuns, and should repeat during that
period the whole Psalter seven times over". The other
offender was the Prior of Walsingham, who had habitually
embezzled moneys, stolen jewels and plate from the
treasury, committed manslaughter on a peasant, and
exalted John Smyth's wife to a quasi-official position as his
own helpmate. The bishop ordered the summary dismissal
of Mrs Smyth, and within six weeks he had prevailed upon
the prior to resign his office, *under assurance of "a competent annual pension" for the rest of his life*. Again, the
Prior of Aldby complains to Nicke against the system of
banishing "incorrigible" monks to the smaller priories,
where they spent their days in dicing and indiscipline.[3]
There are several complaints against drunken monks, but
none are punished—indeed Dr Rashdall has pointed out
that drunkenness was not recognized as a punishable offence
by the medieval Oxford statutes. The gravest peculations
and betrayals of trust are recorded without punishment.

[1] The later visits show considerably less; but there are many obvious
reasons why a first visit should show a worse record than others.
After all, Henry's also was a first visit.

[2] I, 36 note, 334 note.

[3] Pp. 197, 265. *Cellulas* is used here, as sometimes elsewhere, in
the sense of *cellas*.

An excellent case is that of Wymondham in 1514. The late abbot had peculated; the present abbot had not rendered his accounts. The prior had broken open a chest and abstracted documents without the abbot's leave; had tried to kill two fellow-monks with a sword; had thrown a stone at another in the abbot's presence; had not been to confession for nine months. When threatened with my Lord Bishop's displeasure, he had said: "tell my Lord both and my Ladie, for I care nott"; the sting of which lay no doubt in the fact that Nicke's own morals were in evil repute among his contemporaries. The night services were often neglected, the choice books and ornaments were out of repair: other books had been stolen. There was no schoolmaster. Some monks had broken the cloister bounds. One was a drunkard, had openly denied the resurrection of the dead in the flesh, absented himself from matins, and was suspected of adultery. Another's cell was frequented by "suspected women"—two married, and two of the widow's daughters from the abbey dairy. Another was grievously suspected of adultery. One of the confessors had broken the seal of confession, and the prior complained that his attempt at reform had caused the monks to "blaspheme his name in public places without the monastery". This would seem a sufficiently heavy bill of offences for a community of eleven monks; I here subjoin, word for word, all the notice the bishop takes of it. "The Lord Bishop enjoined *that henceforth no layman should be admitted to any office within the aforesaid abbey until he had first pledged himself to keep faithfully the secrets of the abbey.* He further enjoined that he (the abbot) should elect another monk in the prior's place within a month. After which injunctions and the aforesaid evidence taken, my Lord concluded his visitation for this time." The deposed prior was succeeded in that office by one of the worst sinners of a previous visitation (p. 161). I must beg the reader to note the words I have italicized, for I shall recur to them. In the meantime I only wish to point out how these manuscript volumes, when printed, contradict Cardinal Gasquet flatly by showing an impunity almost incredible to modern readers; yet (as I am ready to prove, if necessary) absolutely normal in the Middle Ages.

So much for Nicke's evidence: now for that of the Exeter registers. Cardinal Gasquet argues, with an emphasis which may seem even exaggerated, that the Black Death of 1349 dealt a blow to the monasteries, materially and morally, from which they had not yet recovered at the Dissolution (1, 7). Therefore, in choosing the first twenty-one years (1327–48) of the register of Bishop Grandisson, perhaps the greatest of all the medieval Bishops of Exeter, I am choosing a field which ought to be eminently favourable to Cardinal Gasquet. How far this is so, the reader may judge from the history of three monasteries which I find extracted in my notes.

(1) ST JAMES'S PRIORY, near Exeter. In 1334 (p. 279) the prior of this house, William de Bittendene, is stigmatized as "oftentimes convicted of embezzlement and fornication, and lately refusing to allow himself to be visited...pretending himself exempt", in spite of documentary evidence to the contrary. The priory was waste, the church in ruins, and divine service had ceased. The bishop excommunicated him and tried to sequestrate the revenues of his priory. In 1335 he was "wandering about the country, having let loose the reins of honesty and utterly cast away the modesty of his monastic profession", and the bishop therefore writes sadly to the prior of the parent house of St Martin, "Would that you would send some good man to rule the said house: for this person fears neither God nor man, which is a blot upon the honour of monasticism and justly offends God's majesty". In 1338, however, William was still prior, and the bishop wrote of his past "enormously dissolute life" without implying any present amendment. Next year we find him again as prior, and noted among the clergy who have not paid the last tax to the Pope. There is no record of his being deposed (pp. 71, 279, 289, 305, 745, 883).

(2) TAVISTOCK ABBEY. In 1328 Grandisson wrote to the Pope, his good friend and patron, "God is my witness that I lie not: the Abbot of Tavistock in my diocese, a native of Aquitaine, now promoted by your Holiness through the deceit of others, hath since his first arrival held himself aloof from all religion and all worship of God". This was Robert Bonus, who had previously been Abbot of La Réole in Gascony. The bishop, out of reverence for the Pope and his noble French friends, had first "coaxed him gently to myself" and then, when kindness failed, had threatened his own wrath and the Pope's; but both alike in vain. Bonus had already begun to waste the abbey revenues, and "in a fit of drunkenness, had almost slain" a young French squire of his own retinue. Grandisson, though a man of noble birth, high attainments, great force of will, and special favour with the Pope, was quite unable to enlist the help of the Papal court. On the contrary, in 1333 he had to justify himself to some of the cardinals for such pressure as he had dared to bring upon Bonus, over whose morals he thinks it better to draw a veil, "out of reverence to your Paternity and to his Order". "In these days especially, wherein the wickedness of the human race is increasing", it is almost impossible for a prelate to do his duty without incurring slander: he therefore prays his friends at the court to credit no reports of his alleged indiscretions, or illegalities, until at least they have heard his own version of the matter. How little he deserved such accusations, his own letters to the erring abbot prove only too clearly. As early as 1328, he found himself compelled by popular outcry to come and visit the abbey: but, the abbot having put in the usual plea of exemption, he offered to waive his episcopal rights, and come informally as a friend. It was only in 1333, when both cajolery and threats had proved unavailing, that the bishop proceeded to sequestrate the revenues of the house, whose abbot, "wasteful not only of goods but also of his own fame, is leading and is wont to lead a life detestable to God and man, publicly and daily eating flesh in Lenten-

tide without reasonable cause, and damnably committing very many other enormous offences which we pass in silence through reverence for the monastic order and profession ". He "has notoriously so dilapidated and consumed the monastery's property that it is now brought to the disgrace of almost irreparable ruin", and that "some monks of the convent have needed to be sent wandering abroad to beg for their bare daily livelihood". Therefore, "lest the wickedness of this his obstinacy and dilapidation escape utterly unpunished", since he has already scorned our mandate of sequestration and excommunication, we commit to the Abbot of Buckland and certain other monks the duty of seeing our orders strictly obeyed. Moreover, since he has set us at nought and refused to appear before us, we hereby depose him (pp. 97, 98, 109, 395, 405, 703–6, 717) at the end of the year 1333.

Nor was this the end of troubles at Tavistock. The prior and monks put the choice of a new abbot in the bishop's hands, and the latter chose John de Courtenay, whom he had before selected as one of those who were to enforce his sentence against the late abbot. Grandisson, in his joy at getting rid of Bonus, described his new choice as "a man recommended by many virtuous gifts": but he was soon bitterly undeceived. Only five years later, he finds the abbey again bankrupt and suffering from "certain proved faults both in the Head and in the Members, which we, willing to spare your reputation, have thought best to pass over in silence for the present". He cuts off the abbot from all share in the money affairs of the house, banishes him from the precincts until the debt shall be paid, orders him to abandon his unmonastic foppishness of dress, and directs that one of his fellow-monks, "recommended by his honesty and cleanliness of life," should be always in attendance on him as chaplain, and sleep in his chamber. Meanwhile he is to have, for his own and chaplain's support, a pension of 120 marks—or about £1600 a year of modern money—the rest of the monks being put off

with 100 pounds a year between them, and burdened with
the payment of all corrodies and liveries. Seven years
later, in 1345, Grandisson visited the abbey, and found
"very many faults; some of which—to say nothing for the
present of the greatest and most grievous—we set forth
clearly to you". The abbot has again relapsed into secular
finery, and has imitators among the monks; three of them
have "frequently offended hitherto by casting off their
monastic habit". Nearly all the monks ate forbidden flesh
in their own cells. The abbot had been proved to "consort
day and night with secular persons, even of suspected
morals, in damnable contempt of our former mandates":
on which account the bishop again directs that a monk of
acknowledged purity of life should act as his chaplain, be
always with him, and sleep in his chamber. The monastic
moneys were wasted on a pack of hounds, and two of the
monks had been guilty of embezzlement. In 1348 again
the abbot, "defamed by many excesses and crimes well-
known to you and to the whole convent," has not only for
many years wasted the abbey property; but, "finding no
more moveable goods wherewith further to satisfy his
pleasures", has begun to sell and alienate even farms and
rents. The beautiful buildings were falling to ruin; and
the monks were as deformed in inward religion as was
their abbey in outward aspect. The bishop therefore decrees the abbot's suspension. He is no longer to enjoy
his liberal pension, but "removing all his costly retinue
and all hunting dogs whatsoever" to live in common with
the rest of the monks. A few months afterwards came the
Black Death, and we hear no more of John de Courtenay
(pp. 887, 889, 996–8).

(3) BARNSTAPLE PRIORY. This was a cell to St Martin
des Champs at Paris. In 1332 the prior was John de Sta
Gemma, who preferred Paris life, and did not reside, "to
the grave peril of the souls committed to his charge, and
as a pernicious example to very many others". The bishop
therefore sequestrated the priory revenues to compel his

return, and took proceedings against one John of Paris who had intruded himself as prior during the real prior's absence. The Prior of St Martin, instead of sending the latter back to his work, appointed in his stead one John Soier. Grandisson then wrote to St Martin's, begging earnestly and almost humbly that this appointment might be quashed:

otherwise, we beg you not to take it ill even if we freely use our right of reforming those points on which, with bitterness of heart, we perceive the said priory [of Barnstaple] to need reformation. For we must tell you truly that Bro. John Soier, your monk and presentee, is said, as one who is prodigal both of his reputation and of his salvation, to have lived in Wales a life so enormously dissolute (even begetting a family and bringing it up notoriously at the expense of church goods, and likewise publicly defamed of the vice of simony recently committed here at Barnstaple for the aforesaid reasons, and suspected of future embezzlement), that he himself should rightly fear to climb to the high post of prior of this monastery, and we must fear to admit him against our own conscience.

The protest was utterly unavailing: and one of the strongest bishops, in perhaps the most independent of all great European countries, found himself compelled to accept this ruffian as prior of Barnstaple! In 1334 Soier died, but that brief space of two years had sufficed to justify all the bishop's fears. In protesting against the Prior of St Martin's sudden recall of the new prior after only a few months' residence in England, Grandisson writes: "If you often acted thus, the priory would be ruined and all observance of religion dissolved....For the present income, and even all that will come in for a long time hence, will scarce suffice for the bare necessities of the prior and his monks at that house; since his accursed predecessor (I say it with shame) together with one John Colecote his abettor, have inhumanly dealt the priory almost irreparable harm".

Let me point out here the full significance of this evidence. Cardinal Gasquet appeals to the Exeter registers to prove two main points (1) "the graver irregularities which are recorded against the Religious after the most searching scrutiny, made by the bishops or their commissioners, are after all few and far between"; and (2) "the extreme punishment with which such irregularities were visited proves that, so far from not being heeded, the moral reputation of the monastic and conventual establishments was considered of the first importance". Let me take those two points in order.

(1) The *rarity* of immorality in the diocese cannot possibly be proved from the episcopal registers: *for the registers do not contain any full accounts of monastic visitations*. It is most important to insist upon this point, since it is almost always blinked by apologists.[1] The actual visitation records were written in separate rolls or books which have seldom survived and still more seldom been published.[2] *The bishops' registers themselves contain only here and there a few extracts from, or allusions to, these records, in cases where the gross scandal of the offence, or the sinners' contumacy, rendered the usual summary proceeding unavailing, and necessitated special and repeated attention from the bishop himself.* Even in these cases, the misdemeanours are constantly veiled in a cloud of phrases, to avoid scandal. They therefore no more present a full record of serious monastic offences than the *Journals* of

[1] An *Athenaeum* reviewer, who seems to be responsible for several articles containing *obiter dicta* in defence of monastic morality, has apparently at last begun to realize this truth. (April 22, 1905, p. 490.) This may be connected with the fact that I pointed it out a year or two ago in a letter addressed to the editor, begging the reviewer at about the same time to jot me down on a postcard (without prejudice to his anonymity) full references to a manuscript which he cited as proving monastic innocence. I received no reply to my request for this reference: but my trouble has not been wasted if I have at last made him understand that the registers do not profess to record visitation *comperta* with any completeness.

[2] Nicke's and Goldwell's visitations are of this kind: and Cardinal Gasquet evidently recognizes this, though only dimly (p. 36 note), and without realizing the crucial importance of the difference to his argument. (See, for a fuller discussion of this question, my article in the *English Historical Review* for January, 1914.)

the House of Lords present a full record of the offences of British subjects.[1] If I am right in this assertion—and I offer Cardinal Gasquet the chance of contradicting me within the covers of this very pamphlet, besides the fact that here at least I have on my side a determined defender of monastic morality—then it shows sheer ignorance of the true facts to speak of the silence of the registers (where they are silent) as proving the innocence of the monks. The registers can at most offer us only records of a few cases (not necessarily even the worst), and leave us to infer vaguely from these samples what the batch was like.

(2) This brings me to Cardinal Gasquet's second contention—that the Exeter registers prove "the extreme punishment with which irregularities were visited". On the contrary, they entirely agree with that of Nicke in proving exactly the opposite. This exceptionally strong and determined Grandisson, with his exceptional influence at the Pope's court, is obliged to accept a notorious adulterer as Prior of Barnstaple without hint of his punishment, and is quite unable to bring to justice the equally notorious Prior of St James's, or even to get rid of him from his priory. It costs him a struggle of five years to get rid of Bonus, and he has scarcely less difficulty with Courtenay!

Here again the very strength of my case is, in a measure, its weakness. Is it credible, the reader may well ask, that a writer of such reputation can have referred the unsuspecting public so confidently to manuscript sources which

---

[1] This accounts for the striking fact that the worst cases are to be found in the registers of the strongest and best bishops. Grandisson's gives us a far worse picture of clerical morality than that of his predecessor Stapledon or his successors Brantyngham and Stafford, who were all three great ministers, busy to their finger-tips with State affairs, and compelled to treat the government of their diocese as a secondary matter. Stafford, the best of them, spent scarcely more than half his twenty-five years' episcopate in active episcopal work. Abuses which such men winked at or compounded with, Grandisson fought against with all his might; and hence his register shows us more immoralities than theirs, though nobody who knows the character and work of the four bishops can doubt that the diocese was in a far better state of discipline under him.

contradict him so flatly on such simple issues? I cannot say
how far it is credible, I only say that it is true, and that I
will willingly affirm its truth by the one guarantee in my
power—by offering to put myself in the pillory if I am wrong.
Before publishing this pamphlet I will gladly allow Cardinal
Gasquet eight pages in it for any denials or explanations
which he would care to see printed within the same covers
as my criticism. If he takes me at my word, my readers
will know that they have both sides of the question before
them. If, however, he declines the challenge, I may here
refer by anticipation to two articles in the *Church Quarterly*
for October, 1900, and January, 1901, in which he is proved
to have supported his theories on the Old English Bible
by mis-statements and omissions only a few degrees less
inexplicable than these which I here expose.[1]

Having thus dealt with what are really the Cardinal's
most important witnesses, I will review very briefly the
abundant evidence which proves that Henry's condem-
natory report was substantially correct. I say *substantially*,
because I have little more belief than Cardinal Gasquet in
the *unsupported* evidence of Henry's commissioners. The
King found in the monasteries one of the most serious
hindrances to his political schemes. He dreaded their
power and coveted their money; therefore he appointed
commissioners to make out a case against them. In this
he simply followed the precedents of medieval justice; for
Cardinal Gasquet entirely blinks the fact that Henry was
a true child of the Middle Ages. The injustice with which
he carried out his designs was incomparably less revolting
than that with which a fourteenth-century King and Pope
suppressed the Order of the Templars. The barefaced
dishonesty with which he pocketed the spoils compares
favourably, after all, with that of the Popes for a good
three centuries before the Reformation. During these

[1] I need hardly say that neither the Cardinal nor any of his supporters
has taken me at my word. The Cardinal consoled himself with throwing mud at me in the preface to his next edition, while carefully
avoiding every issue of historical fact.

three centuries, the Pontiffs had regularly squeezed vast sums out of Europe for the Crusades, and had spent them as regularly on personal wars, personal luxuries, or personal vices. Still, the fact remains that Henry's injustice and cupidity were very great. Cardinal Gasquet easily proves thus much; and, indeed, it had been clearly proved before him.[1] But here, on the very threshold of the real question, nearly all his arguments stop. Yet the real question is far more important than that on which he spends nine-tenths of his arguments. For three centuries and more before the Reformation, public opinion had discussed the merits and demerits of monastic life. Does the public judgment of those three centuries show us a state of things compatible with modern civilization? or does it show us the monks so idle and useless on the average, so depraved in many instances, that few people would wish to see them among us again at this moment, in the same state in which the Dissolution found them? That is the real question, and that is what Cardinal Gasquet has made no serious attempt to answer. He blinks the obvious fact that, from the date at which Dissolution first became a burning political question, evidence *on either side* must be received with the greatest caution. Nearly all his witnesses are as *ex parte* and as untrustworthy as the commissioners themselves. An old man (name unknown), who just remembered the Dissolution as a boy—another later and equally anonymous author, many of whose statements are so patently false that I can only wonder how the Cardinal dared to print them— these are two of the main pillars of his great fabric.[2] Apart

---

[1] Even Fuller and the Whig Burnet, in the seventeenth century, disclose much of the truth; and in modern times the point has been laboured at great length, and with ample evidence, by Blunt, Brewer, and Dixon. A clear and popular abstract of Brewer and Dixon would quite suffice to correct Froude's exaggerations: by taking a line midway between Froude and these critics, we should come very near to the truth.

[2] (1) The *Rites of Durham* is a little book by an anonymous hand, of which the earliest manuscript dates from half-a-century after the Suppression. It describes the monastery and church of Durham

from the registers which he misquotes so incredibly, he makes scarcely any pretence of bringing historical evidence for the condition of the monasteries during the four centuries preceding the Reformation. In his introductory picture, he skips from St Anselm in the early twelfth century to an anonymous reactionary of the late sixteenth. What theories could not a future historian maintain about the England of 1905 by this simple method of judging it from two documents dating respectively from A.D. 1600 and 1950!

Moreover, even within the narrow and vicious circle to which he limits his enquiry, he shows strange ideas of evidence. To take a few instances: one of his trump cards is the formal compliment paid to the greater monasteries in the preamble of the bill which dissolved the smaller houses. Has there ever been an age in which a statesman's formal utterances in one year's Parliament could not be turned against him some other year? Again, while justly

Cathedral, chiefly from the point of view of a ritualist and antiquary, referring only incidentally to the monks' morals, etc. It remained in manuscript during the years when its publication might have provoked flat contradictions from others who also remembered the monastery in their youth; and, when finally unearthed and printed, it was at once attacked (rightly or wrongly) as apocryphal and legendary. (2) The Cole manuscript is equally anonymous and obscure; its author, I believe, does not even pretend to have seen most of what he describes, and tells us definitely that for a knowledge of the monks' morals and usefulness he was dependent on his father's report (II, 321). It was apparently never published, even partially, until Henry and the dispossessed monks had been more than two centuries in their graves. Yet these are documents on which Cardinal Gasquet lays special stress, to the exclusion (as will be seen) of the most definite and irrefragable evidence. Moreover, the author of the latter manuscript at once puts himself out of court by asserting that the cottages of England had increased *fivefold* in the sixty years following the Suppression: a statement which Cardinal Gasquet renders still more absurd by italicizing the word *towns* and laying stress on it in its modern sense of boroughs and market-towns. To a sixteenth-century writer, as to modern villagers, the term *town* includes even hamlets. On this blunder he founds what, to many readers, would be one of his most telling arguments. It is not enough for him to build upon such worthless hole-and-corner documents; but he must also misread them in order to get the results he needs.

reprobating the alleged indignities offered to nuns by Henry's commissioners (and this is one of his strongest points, though the assertion rests only on the word of two bitter partisans, of whom one was not even a contemporary), he ignores the fact that the very best of medieval visitors permitted themselves on similar occasions liberties which are absolutely revolting to modern ideas. He accepts, whenever they suit his purpose, statistics which are demonstrably wrong by at least 4000 per cent. (I, 2—II, 504). He misapplies to the sixteenth-century monks a testimonial which Professor Thorold Rogers does indeed give to those of the thirteenth century, but expressly refuses, on the very same page, to those of Henry VIII's reign in whose favour Cardinal Gasquet quotes them![1] Again, Cardinal Gasquet imputes the miseries of modern England to the

---

[1] I will give the quotations here, since they exemplify clearly in a few lines the Cardinal's habits of literary dishonesty—it is impossible to use a milder phrase. In a chapter designed to set forth the harm done to England by the Suppression, he writes (II, 496): "In strong contrast with the caricature drawn from the imagination of novelists, who at best clothe the cloistered life with a poetic unreality, the description given of it by a deeply-read writer of modern times may here be quoted. 'The monks', says Mr Thorold Rogers, 'were the men of letters in the middle ages, the historians, the jurists, the philosophers, the physicians, the students of nature, the founders of schools, authors of chronicles, teachers of agriculture, fairly indulgent landlords and advocates of genuine (sic) dealing towards the peasantry'". Here, as often, he gives no reference; but his allusion is evidently to the following passage from Thorold Rogers' Six Centuries of Work and Wages (p. 362): "These monasteries were in the zenith of their reputation during the first half of the thirteenth century, when they had, it would appear, been stimulated to a beneficent activity by the rivalry of the two new orders of preaching friars, those of Dominic and Francis. They had, to be sure, the fatal gift of wealth, but they seem to have used their wealth well. They were founders of schools, authors of chronicles, teachers of agriculture, fairly indulgent landlords, and advocates of generous dealing towards the peasantry". But, only eleven lines lower down, Professor Rogers goes on: "It is not easy to understand how these monasteries declined in character and usefulness till they came to the condition which is described so indignantly by Gascoigne— a condition which renders probable the charges which Henry the Eighth's commissioners made against them. But many causes appear to have contributed to the result". The italics are mine: the quotation needs no further comment.

Dissolution, without pausing to consider what was the state of the working classes in all countries where the monasteries were spared until the French Revolution. He takes care to name religious houses where Nicke's visits give a better result than those of Henry's commissioners, but suppresses the cases in which Nicke corroborates or even outdoes the others in blame. But perhaps his weakest and most dangerous argument, though one of his most frequent, is to emphasize the very grossness of this or that accusation made by the commissioners, and then to work upon the modern sense of decency. "Can you, as English gentlemen, believe this to be true?" To the credit of modern Anglicanism, that has proved one of his most effective arguments, as I know by experience. Yet, however successful such an argument may be with candid modern opponents, it would have been simply laughed out of court in the Middle Ages. Of all these cases which the Cardinal seeks to discredit as inherently improbable because they shock nineteenth-century minds, there is not one which cannot be paralleled and outmatched from the most unimpeachable medieval sources. For instance, one of Cardinal Gasquet's strongest points is that so many of the accused monks and nuns were afterwards pensioned. Yet the reader has already seen how Bishop Nicke pensioned the adulterous, thieving, and homicidal Prior of Walsingham: how the scandalous Abbot of Tavistock was allowed, for himself and for his private chaplain, not much less than all the other monks together received for their needs and for those of their corrodians; and far worse cases might be quoted. A century earlier, Balthasar Cossa, chamberlain to Pope Boniface IX, scandalized even the people of Rome by more shameless immorality than any that Henry's commissioners record; and the Pope found no better remedy than to create him Cardinal and send him as Legate to Bologna. Here he outdid even his previous enormities, and was presently raised to the Papacy. Anyone who has been impressed by Cardinal Gasquet's argument *ex incredibili* should read the catalogue of the crimes with which he was charged by the Council of Constance.[1] What is more, the cases which Cardinal Gasquet tries to put out of court as too impossible to be believed can all be matched from these very visitations to which he has appealed as proving the contrary! He finds inherent improbability in the statement that the Prior of Crutched Friars was found in gross misconduct at eleven o'clock on a Friday in Lent: yet we find an orthodox and irreproachable visitor accusing a monk of Wendling of adultery "not only in the holy time of Lent, but also in Passion Week".[2] The Abbot of Langdon was accused of incontinence and drunkenness; to which Cardinal Gasquet objects that "if Layton's accusations were true the abbot could have been got rid of without expense and without the scandal of proposing to place such a man in cure of souls". Yet neither Nicke nor Grandisson, as we have seen, could get rid of worse offenders without expense: and in pleading the improbability of Layton's story, Cardinal Gasquet simply supplies another proof that he does not know his own documents. Again, in the case of the Abbot of Wigmore, he claims that "the accusation of murder is absurd on the face of it, and may be dismissed". Yet Nicke's Abbot of Walsingham had murdered a peasant: Grandisson's Abbot of Tavistock had tried to murder his squire: and the registers give no hint in either case of what we should consider a fit punishment for such an offence. Eudes Rigaud, a far stronger prelate than either, was entirely unable to prevent his subordinate Bishop of Lisieux from giving a canonry in that cathedral to a nephew who was "ill-famed of homicide" (p. 61). Nobody who had really faced the facts of the Middle Ages could appeal

---

[1] Lea, *Celibacy*, p. 344. A case even more shocking, perhaps, is to be found lower down on p. 431.

[2] Brit. Mus. MS. Add. 4934, p. 82. Cardinal Gasquet is at present editing the register from which Peck made these extracts: I am not aware that he refers to it in his *Henry VIII*, but it was well known and easily accessible then.

to impunity for a proof of innocence, as Cardinal Gasquet more than once does.

Nicke, for instance, found the Prior of Eye in 1514 "suspected" with Margery Bery, for whose son he had built a house. In 1520, at the same monastery, Margaret Verre, who may or may not be a different person, "is dwelling with the prior and lives suspiciously". There is no record of punishment in either case. The reader will remember how the bishop's injunctions for Wymondham, which I italicized, show far more solicitude to avoid scandal outside the monastery than to inflict punishment inside; and we find that even the most energetic and saintly prelates of the Middle Ages left the plainest immoralities unpunished whenever they could thus avoid a public scandal.[1] As a far more accurate scholar than Cardinal Gasquet has pointed out (in speaking of the constant abuses revealed by visitations of the Wells, Ripon, Beverley and Southwell chapters), even the frequency and gravity of the accusations are far less significant than the impunity of admitted guilt. "Next to contumacy," writes Mr A. F. Leach, "revealing the secrets of the chapter or the Vicar's Hall to the laity seems to have been the most heinous crime....Only two of the innumerable cases are actually suspended for sexual misbehaviour....We can only conclude that neglect of duty and sexual immorality

---

[1] Cf. the following extract from the register of Archbishop Eudes Rigaud, the friend of St Bonaventura and one of the most determined medieval reformers, whose contemporaries surnamed him "the Pattern of Good Life". He is visiting a chapter at Pontoise. "Richard de Triguel is accused of sin with a certain prostitute; yet there was no great scandal: we warned him to desist. Again Master Robert is accused with the gardener's daughter, and has but lately had a child by her, but the scandal is not great: we warned him to desist. Moreover, he behaves improperly in going barefooted outside his door to a certain workshop where women of ill fame are often congregated: we warned him to desist from such behaviour" (p. 42). This hushing-up spirit is constantly traceable in the visitation records, and damages them very seriously as witnesses for the defence. When the register of one of the strongest prelates in the Middle Ages reads like this, how can we argue from the silence of bishops who scarcely ever lived in their dioceses, or whose own lives were immoral?

were so common that they were never punished, except when some public scandal was created by them."[1]

That is the real clue to the visitation records which have come down to us. Religious houses had, even at the crown of the Middle Ages, such good reason to dread lay criticism, that nothing might not be pardoned so long as scandal could be avoided. Even St Bonaventura, and at least one archbishop worthy to be placed by his side in Dante's heaven, felt this as strongly as it was felt by inferior men. For, of all Cardinal Gasquet's mis-statements, perhaps none is so hopelessly inaccurate as his repeated assertion that the Middle Ages did not accuse the monks, and that their evil repute dates from Henry VIII or later. This assertion sums up the whole object of his two bulky volumes, and I must contrast it very briefly with notorious facts.

On the one hand, the ascetic writers assure us emphatically and repeatedly that immorality will ensue in monasteries if the monks cease to work hard, are allowed pocket money, gad abroad, or eat flesh except with the utmost parsimony. On the other hand, we know that not one only, but all of these relaxations were rather the rule than the exception in the sixteenth century. The desperate efforts made to prevent the monks from possessing private property testify not only to the serious bearing of this point on convent morality, but also to the irresistible growth of luxury and indiscipline. Innocent III, among his other reforms, decreed that the "proprietary" monk or nun should be buried like a dog in a dunghill, as a token of the soul's certain damnation. Torquemada gravely asserted that a Religious committed mortal sin by merely claiming a book as his own, except by a mere slip of the tongue. No clause of the Benedictine Rule was more explicit or hedged round with greater safeguards; yet Dr Kitchin points out how the Winchester monks had their regular pocket money or private incomes; and to Nicke

[1] Introd. to *Southwell Visitations* (Camden Soc.), pp. 75, 85, 89.

they clamour again and again for the money which, if he or they had taken the Rule seriously, was the wages of death to their souls. Again, in the matters of labour, of strict attendance at the services, of wandering outside the walls —in all those safeguards of monastic morality, the Rule was equally relaxed. The Carthusians alone (I believe) kept to the original Benedictine Rule about flesh; and they alone have been able to take for their motto with some real truth "Never *re*formed, because never *de*formed". Henry's commissioners, therefore, only professed to find in the monasteries that which monastic disciplinarians had prophesied as certain.

Again, medieval literature simply swarms with tales of monastic immoralities—not only or mainly, as Cardinal Gasquet asserts, of a ribald character and imported from the East—but solemnly told in solemn works of theology written by monks or friars. I believe it might be safely asserted that such stories, told to point a moral in religious books, outnumber those told in jest by medieval satirists. Moreover, very definite and almost unquotable attacks on monastic morality are made in the thirteenth century by Roger Bacon, St Bonaventura, and his fellow-cardinal Jacques de Vitry; in the fourteenth by Merswin, Gower, Langland, St Catharine of Siena, and Wycliffe; and in the fifteenth by Gerson, one of the reputed authors of the *Imitation of Christ* and the greatest churchman of his age. Of these nine, Wycliffe is far from being the most emphatic. Jacques de Vitry stigmatizes the monks, before the Franciscan reform, as "keeping an outward show of piety but denying its inward virtue... disobedient, murmurers, backbiters, bearing Christ's cross unwillingly, unclean and incontinent, walking after the flesh and not after the spirit". Turning to the nuns, he asserts that a girl's virtue was safe among none but those of the Cistercian Rule (*Hist. Occ.* cc. 4, 15). The learned Gower, who hated Lollardy and chose to spend his last years within the priory of St Mary Overy, complained how, "in

some monasteries" of his time, chastity was dead, and
lechery had taken her place; how "very many" monks
(*plures*) went to hell for women, and how nuns were
sometimes seduced not only by their confessors but by
the very visitors who were supposed to guard them[1] (*Vox
Clamantis*, IV, 327 ff., 461, 595: an abstract of these complaints may be found in Morley's *English Literature*, IV,
187). Gerson, among other remarks almost equally strong,
says in one place: "I actually doubt whether boys and
girls do not sometimes learn worse morals...at schools
and among monks and nuns[2] than they would in brothels".
Dr Lea's *Sacerdotal Celibacy* swarms with the most
damaging quotations from medieval sources, and no
Romanist has ever dared to grapple seriously with this
book, now nearly forty years old. I recently pointed this
out in vague and general terms *à propos* of a blunder in
the *Church Times*, and appealed for several weeks to
readers of that paper and of the *Catholic Times* to supply
me with any *contemporary* denial of the numerous and
definite accusations of medieval writers against monks
and nuns. Nobody supplied me with such evidence, and
both papers finally salved their consciences by suppressing
my later letters. So far as I am aware, the orthodox theologians who undertook to refute Lollards with painful
minuteness on other points never dared to assert that the
accusations of widespread monastic immorality were mere
slanders. Gascoigne, though Wycliffe was one of his pet
abominations, agreed with Wycliffe in repeatedly describing the monks as idle, uncharitable, and immoral. He
looked upon them as a hindrance rather than a help to
religious or secular education; and he echoed with even
wearisome iteration Wycliffe's plea for their disendowment.
Over and over again he appeals to the Pope and the Lords
of the Church to acknowledge that the then state of things

---

[1] It is noteworthy that Gascoigne, a contemporary, accuses Archbishop Stafford, while Bishop of Bath and Wells, of having had "sons
and daughters" by a nun.

[2] *In religionum et scholarum contuberniis*, Paris, 1606, II, 629.

was intolerable; and indeed the final crash was only de-
layed for eighty years more. The fact is that, not content
with misquoting the witnesses he brings forward for his
own special plea, Cardinal Gasquet has turned his face
steadily away from all that would have thrown real light
on his subject. To say nothing of the great Continental
visitation records—Eudes Rigaud at Rouen, Busch in
North Germany, Ambrose of Camaldoli in North Italy,
Ninguarda in Bavaria and Austria—he knows nothing even
of English visitations which give the lie to all the main
contentions of his book. He knows nothing of Gascoigne,
though Professor Thorold Rogers refers emphatically to
him in the very passage from which Cardinal Gasquet has
quoted with such signal bad faith. Yet Gascoigne, one of
the greatest chancellors Oxford ever had, supplies by
himself enough evidence to upset the whole apologetic
fabric which Cardinal Gasquet has reared so painfully in
two large volumes. Cardinal Gasquet, for instance, pleads
that the lack of fifteenth and sixteenth century monastic
chronicles points less to the idleness of the monks than to
the "probability that many such monastic records were
destroyed at the Dissolution" (p. xxx note). Gascoigne,
however, tells us plainly:

Formerly the Kings kept, in the monasteries which they
had founded, writers of the books of great Doctors and of
chronicles which recorded the examples of former kings: but
alas! for now books are rather ruined and lost and corrupted
than written afresh among monks! O then, O that Kings and
Lords who have the advowsons of monasteries, moved thereto
by good confessors, would enjoin on the abbots and convents
to keep continually certain writers of [the works of] holy
doctors and men great in science, under certain penalties
imposed by the King or by such Lords! (p. 73; cf. p. 112).

It is hardly too much to say that every argument of any
importance in *Henry VIII and the English Monasteries*
is similarly contradicted by the experience of this distinguished scholar, who in 1450 unwillingly prophesied

much that was verified at the Reformation. Even if
Cardinal Gasquet had not already known that Gascoigne's
Liber Veritatum was one of the most precious authorities
for English life a few generations before the Reformation,
Professor Thorold Rogers's words must have drawn his
attention to it. A single glance at the index would have
shown that it was full of information about the monasteries; a couple of days' work, at the most, would have
shown that Gascoigne, an eye-witness, gives the lie direct
to all these theories of monastic innocence which are, after
all, purely modern.

For I beg the reader to note that every word of my
criticisms rests upon the statements of orthodox and
learned medieval writers, except so far as I quote Wycliffe
on points on which he agrees with the rest. From the
testimony of these contemporaries, it follows that any
attempt to whitewash the monasteries must take account
of the following incontestable facts.

(1) Ascetic writers prophesy intolerable abuses if once
the Religious get into the habit of neglecting any one of
the main outward observances of their Rule. Four of these
main outward observances, at least, were habitually neglected long before the Dissolution—monks habitually ate
flesh, possessed property, had ceased to labour, and went
in and out of their precincts pretty well as they pleased.

(2) Not only satirists and comic writers almost without
exception, but noble churchmen from whom the bitter
confession was wrung by the necessity for reform, accuse
the monasteries of deep unfaithfulness to their religious
ideal, and often lay stress on those very immoralities
which modern apologists ignorantly attribute to Protestant
slanders.

(3) While Lollards and other heretics found one of their
strongest arguments in the accusation of immorality, their
orthodox opponents, replying point by point to heretical
attacks, avoided this particular accusation with the most
significant persistence. What is more, from the thirteenth

century onwards, great churchmen are themselves found complaining that heretics drew their strongest arguments from the frequent immorality of the clergy.

(4) Although we have no diaries or autobiographies of medieval monastic reformers for England, such as those which throw so lurid a light on French, German and Italian monasticism before and after the Reformation, yet even the scantier English official documents frequently show us scandals which would not be tolerated in modern society.

(5) All the countries which did not suppress their monasteries in the sixteenth century have been obliged to do so since, at one time or another. The state of the French and Italian monasteries just before the Revolution was such as no apologist, so far as I am aware, has seriously attempted to defend.[1]

These, then, are the questions which every champion of monastic purity must set himself to answer before he even begins to consider the evidence of Henry's commissioners. Let us set this evidence altogether aside, for good or for evil. Let us take our stand on the years before Henry's visitation, and look back over the available evidence for the preceding three or four centuries of monasticism. We shall then ask ourselves: Why did the Fathers prophesy monastic immorality? Why did medieval saints and sinners, orthodox and heretics, complain of monastic immoralities? Why do the records of visitors reveal gross offenders enjoying absolute or comparative impunity? And then (looking forwards over the next few

[1] See Dom Paul Denis, *Le Cardinal de Richelieu et la Réforme des Monastères Bénédictins* (Paris, 1913), especially Preface, pp. vii, viii, and pp. 163–212. With this evidence from the early seventeenth century, compare the very rare little book published in 1503 by the Abbot of St Sulpice at Bourges under the title of *Reformationis Monastice Vindicie* (Paris, Marnet). This booklet, which throws more light upon monastic conditions, perhaps, than any sixteenth-century document of equal compass, is fully summarized, with copious extracts, in my *Medieval Studies*, No. 11 (Simpkin, Marshall and Co., 2s. 6d. net).

centuries): Why had those monasteries which were spared in the sixteenth century become intolerably corrupt, in the most exclusively Romanist countries, before the end of the eighteenth? These are points with which, hitherto, Cardinal Gasquet has made no attempt to deal, though they stare the historian in the face. His indiscreet and disingenuous advocacy, though disguised under an appearance of candour and commended by an easy style, can only prejudice his clients in the long run. Not until the original documentary evidence has been sifted and summed up by some first-rate historian—and it is a disgrace to English historical scholarship that this and kindred subjects have not yet found special students, but have been left in the hands of writers whose very profession tempts them to subordinate strict truth to "edification"—only then will educated Englishmen be able to render more enlightened homage to the undoubted virtues of the earlier monks, while clearly distinguishing them from those who formed too large a proportion of the communities suppressed by Henry VIII. Nothing is so wasteful as untruth, even in the holiest of causes: and the rancorous anti-clericalism of modern France, Italy, and Spain is directly traceable to the incurable propensity of the Romanist clergy, medieval or modern, "to edit history in their own favour", as Dr Barry puts it with characteristic tenderness.

It only remains for me to mention a popular book on *The English Monasteries* (reprinted from a series of anonymous articles in the *Church Times*), which, with much show of evidence from the registers, relies almost wholly on Cardinal Gasquet for its most important statements. I challenged the anonymous author some six months ago to correspond with me publicly on crucial points on which he seemed to mis-state the plain facts. He kept a discreet silence; but, even now, in case Cardinal Gasquet should decline my offer of eight free pages on this subject, I willingly offer them to the author of *The English*

Monasteries, without asking him to break his resolution of anonymity. Failing him, I am ready to extend the same hospitality to any writer for the Catholic Truth Society; any well-known Romanist apologist like Messrs Wilfrid Ward or W. S. Lilly; or, indeed, anyone else who can claim to have actually studied the visitation records.

P.S. As will be seen from pp. 2–14, it is probable that Cardinal Gasquet knew practically nothing of the Exeter registers beyond the scraps he had read in Oliver. When challenged to produce chapter and verse, he found it safest to fall back on his reputation, leaving the public to take his word against mine for the assertion that the testimony of medieval visitation records is favourable to the monasteries. Let me, therefore, cite two independent witnesses, who have written since Cardinal Gasquet's book was published. Sir George Duckett, writing in 1893, summed up his impressions of a series of Cluniac visitations extending from 1269 to 1529, and embracing England, most of Germany, and part of France. (*Visitations and Chapters General of Cluni*, p. 331.) His judgment runs: "But who, we may ask, after reading these several Reports and Resolutions, forming an endless list of crimes and misdemeanours, which (be it remembered) were never intended to see the light, can for a single moment wonder at the Reformation, or secession from the Romish Church in 1517, or in any way pretend to deny or palliate the state into which religious foundations had sunk in this and every other country at the time of that event? History has handed down to us their state; the foregoing records go distinctly to prove and verify the same. There are some who pretend to deny both, though after such a tissue of excesses and abominations as the foregoing disclose, reading more like extracts from the Newgate Calendar, what other results could ensue but that Reformation?" The second witness, Mr A. Hamilton Thompson, has kindly permitted me to quote from his *Lincoln Visitations*,

now ready for the press.[1] It will be seen that he writes less
dogmatically: not only that he is a better and more judicious
scholar, but his material is considerably smaller than
Duckett's, and seems to show less definite evidence of
monastic decay. Yet, with every wish to do justice to the
monasticism of the fifteenth century, he writes: "No one
can fail to draw the conclusion that in many houses matters
were far from satisfactory. Not merely are there specific
instances, as at Eynsham, Godstow, and Markyate, of
blots upon the fair name of a convent; but in four cases
(Huntingdon, Caldwell, Daventry and St Neot's priories)
the preamble selected for use by Bishop Gray is a sweeping
indictment of a state of utter slackness and degeneracy.
Gray's injunctions to Ramsey abbey were accompanied by
further sealed injunctions, dealing with faults more serious
than he cared to publish; and he also took this course with
regard to the dean and chapter of Lincoln.... But we may
believe that there were monasteries in the diocese, which,
under the headship of capable men, were still instant in
the observance of their religious duties and needed little
correction and few injunctions from the visitor".

I quote these, not to imitate Cardinal Gasquet's habit
of deciding medieval questions by appeals to modern
authors, but to emphasize the absurdity of his claim to beg
the whole question by a single sweeping appeal to the
reader's faith or credulity. Modern historical method
demands that a writer should produce his documents, or
should at least give clear and detailed references.

---

[1] Introduction to *Injunctions, etc., from the Registers of Richard
Flemyng and William Gray, bishops of Lincoln*, A.D. 1420–36 (Lincoln
Record Soc. and Cant. and York Soc.), pp. xi–xiii.

A REVIVALIST OF SIX CENTURIES AGO

THERE is a charming essay on Religious Revivals in Medieval Italy among the old *Cornhill* essays of the late J. A. Symonds. He describes in the first place the "Great Alleluia" of 1233, and the marvellous career of John of Vicenza, under whose influence north Italy seemed for a few weeks to have no business but prayer and praise and religious processions. John and his companion friars healed for a time the most inveterate feuds: city after city surrendered to them at discretion, and allowed its statutes to be made or unmade by these wandering preachers. Vivid as is Symonds's description of the Revival, he yet leaves some of the most curious details ungleaned. The Statutes of Parma, for instance, show us the friars cleansing that great cathedral of the corn which, to the scandal of the more devout, was habitually stored in its nave—just as, in the year after Dante's great vision, a Devonshire parson was found using his church as granary and brew-house combined. Again, the Franciscan Salimbene gives us many curious details of the Great Alleluia, which probably determined his own conversion. Sincere believer as he is, he nevertheless describes with great gusto the ingenious bogus miracles which his great friend Brother Gerard of Modena used to concoct in conjunction with John of Vicenza; and he assures us that many were converted by this means. He also describes how Brother John's head was turned by his success. When the great preacher was shaved during a visit to a Franciscan convent he was naïvely disappointed (it appears) that the Brethren did not pounce on the

---

[1] This paper, from the *North American Review*, June 7, 1907, is here substituted for my original 2nd Study, which is now incorporated in the second edition of *From St Francis to Dante*.

shavings for relics. Such little touches go to explain John's final fall. He demanded to be created Duke and Count of Vicenza, and used his sudden power so recklessly that he was cast into prison, from which he emerged a discredited and neglected man. For the Great Alleluia had died away as rapidly as it rose; and within a few months family feuds and civil wars were raging worse than before.

Symonds describes other similar revivals in medieval Italy—half sincere, half theatrical, but always fierce and short-lived. I propose here to speak of a very different mission-preacher of the same age, the greatest perhaps of all the Middle Ages, the German Berthold of Ratisbon. He, too, produced effects difficult to be imagined in these days of widely diffused education; but in him there was no touch of quackery, and his influence outlasted that of his Italian colleagues. The linden under which he preached at Glatz was still famous in the seventeenth century; and his sermons, printed in modern German as a book of living theology, are in their third edition.[1] Born in 1220 of an upper-class burgher family at Ratisbon, Berthold joined the Franciscans while still a youth, and was the favourite pupil of David of Augsburg, whose writings have often been attributed to St Bonaventura. In 1250 he was already a famous preacher; until his death in 1272 he tramped from town to town, from village to village, like a Wesley or a Whitefield of later days. In this fashion he traversed Bavaria, the Rhineland, Switzerland, Swabia, Austria proper, Moravia, Bohemia, Silesia, Thuringia and Franconia. His fame was great even in Italy, and is enshrined in the early Franciscan chronicles. At this moment, especially, it may well interest a modern reader to get a glimpse of medieval mission-preaching.

Of the effect of these sermons we have very marvellous stories, even when due allowance has been made for medieval exaggeration. The best description of him, as we

[1] Regensburg, Mainz, 1873.

might expect, is to be found in the autobiography of his contemporary Salimbene, who always gives life to whatever he touches:

All who have heard him say that, from the days of the Apostles even to our own, there was never his like in the German tongue. He was followed by a great multitude of men and women, sometimes to the number of sixty or a hundred thousand; or, again, the whole populations of more than one city would come together to hear the honeyed and saving words which flowed from his lips. He was wont to ascend a wooden belfry, which he used as a pulpit in country places: and they who set up the structure crowned it with a pennon, that folk might see whither the wind blew, and so seat themselves as to hear most clearly. And, wonderful to relate! he was heard and understood as well by the most distant as by those who sat by his side; nor did any rise to depart until he had made an end of his preaching. And when he preached of the tremendous Judgment of God, all would tremble as a rush quivers in the water; and they would beseech him for God's love to speak no more of that matter; for it grieved them beyond endurance to hear him. One day, when he was to preach in a certain place, a ploughman besought his master for God's sake to let him go and hear the sermon; but his lord answered, "I myself shall go, but thou shalt go plough in the field with the oxen". So, when the ploughman had set himself to plough in the field at dawn, straightway by a miracle he heard the voice of Brother Berthold preaching, though he was thirty miles distant; and forthwith he unyoked his oxen and let them feed, and sat down to listen to the sermon. And when the sermon was done he ploughed as much as he was wont to plough with a full day's work.

A precious fragment printed in the appendix to the first volume of the *Analecta Franciscana* reports a conversation of Berthold with St Louis and with the King of Navarre. The latter questioned the great preacher about this reported miracle of the ploughman, and Berthold replied:

Good my lord, believe it not, and give no faith to tales of this kind which men tell of me as though they were miracles.... There are certain men who, either for lucre's sake, or for some other vain cause, follow me among the rest of the multitude, and at times invent such tales and tell them to others.

Yet the real wonders he worked led inevitably to such reports. A noble lady had "followed him for six whole years from town to village, with other women that were of her company, yet could never get speech of him in private". At last, when all her money was spent, she was able to see him and tell him of her distress. He sent her to a banker in the town, who would give her (he said) "the money value of one single day of that indulgence for which she had followed Brother Berthold these six years". The banker, contemptuously humouring her fancy, was astonished to find that all his gold was as a mere feather in one scale so long as the lady breathed into the other; "for the Holy Ghost lent such weight to her breath that no weight of coin could balance that scale". He was converted, as was also a robber-knight so notorious that the burghers of the nearest city had adorned their council-hall with a fresco representing him by anticipation on the gallows.

Berthold, like all mission-preachers, especially in the Middle Ages, appealed most constantly to the simple themes of heaven and hell. According to an often-repeated legend, a woman was so overcome by his terrible invectives against her own besetting sin that she gave up the ghost in the middle of his sermon; but his prayers recalled her to life for just long enough to make her confession and her final peace with God. She told the horror-stricken congregation that, out of 50,000 souls which had departed at the same moment with herself, three only had been worthy even of purgatory, and one of heaven; the remaining 49,996 having gone straight down to hell! Something of this vivid imagination may be found in Berthold's sermons even after six hundred years. We see him addressing his vast congregations in the open air. At one moment, speaking of the glory of transubstantiation, he says:

Grant now that our dear Lady St Mary, Mother of God, stood here on this fair meadow, while all the Saints and all the

Angels found room around her, and that I were found worthy to see this sight.... I would rather turn and bow the knee before a priest bearing the Lord's body to the sick, than before our Lady St Mary and all the Saints of the whole host of heaven.

Again, he answers an objection from his hearers:

"Brother Berthold, thou speakest oft and oft of these devils and all their sleights; yet we never see or hear or touch or feel a single devil."

"Lo, now that is even the worst harm they can do thee: for, hadst thou but once seen a single devil in his true form, I should know for certain that thou wouldst never sin more.... If the devil came out at this moment from this forest hard by, and this city that we see before us were a burning fiery furnace heated through and through, then should ye see such a press of folk as never was seen, and such as never shall be seen in this world, and all of them thronging headlong into that burning fiery furnace!"

Berthold's sermons give a gloomy view of society even during the years between St Francis's death and Dante's boyhood. The Pope could make and unmake emperors; cardinals and bishops were among the greatest princes of the day; the parish priest had inquisitorial and disciplinary rights over almost every act of his parishioners, yet the people were not only far more ignorant, but had even less of true religion than to-day. "The laity are evil, the Religious are evil" is a quotation constantly recurring in Berthold's sermons. He finds himself compelled to advise his hearers on delicate points of spiritual relationship arising from the numbers of "parson's children" who were to be found everywhere. "It often happens", he continues, "that a bishop has children, few or many"; yet for two hundred years clerical celibacy had been the strict rule of the Church. He complains that bribery and corruption are as rampant in the spiritual as in the lay courts. In consequence of the depredations of robber-nobles, "in places where there might well be two or three parish priests, there is scarce one; and even he may well be found unlearned". The pagan superstition still flourished which held it an evil omen to meet a priest the first thing in the morning. Berthold alludes to the constant tithe-quarrels; as an English bishop of the same date complains that parishioners, indignant that priests should exact tithes even of milk, revenged themselves by bringing their pailful to church and pouring it on the floor before the altar. The priest himself, again, was often excommunicate, and the whole parish involved with him in mortal sin. Nor, with all his nominal authority, could the parson put down the constant habit of Sunday work, or secure regular attendance at church. "Lo, a stinking goat of a Jew has more reverence for his holy days than thou!" The people's religious education also left much to be desired. "Many rise in the morning without even making the sign of the cross, and very likely reach the age of twenty years without being able to repeat the Lord's Prayer." Many, again, are so ignorant of the creed that they fall a prey to the first doubt suggested by the experience of life: "Ah, God! who, then, are in the right—Jews, heathens, or heretics? I know not how things stand, nor who hath the right faith". Of Bible study in the modern sense there was of course no question, nor would it have been permitted even if it had been otherwise possible. The laity are therefore warned against disputing with Jews: "For ye are unlearned, while they are learned in the Scriptures, and they have pondered carefully how they may persuade you; so that ye will be ever the weaker in faith for that dispute". As St Louis pleaded in the same century, a layman's only valid argument in such cases was "to thrust his sword into the Jew's belly as far as it would go".

But had not the parish clergy strong auxiliaries in the swarms of friars who filled the land? The best influence of the friars was fast waning during Berthold's lifetime, though these new Orders were scarcely half a century old. Too often the friar and the parish priest were at daggers drawn; or heretics carried on their propaganda in the name of St Francis, just as the first Franciscan missionaries had been taken for wandering heretics. Berthold's constant and impassioned warnings show clearly (if we did not know it from other sources) how little the Roman faith could claim to reign unquestioned even during this its golden age. He reckons the heretical sects of his time at "a good hundred and fifty", and appeals to his hearers' knowledge of "how many thousand men are led astray by unfaith". The process of perversion, as he describes it, is simple. A heretic is never converted; his heart is turned to stone; "and just as crystal is petrified water, so are heretics petrified Christians: as little, therefore, as the crystal can ever be turned to water again, so little can a heretic be turned back to Christianity, however fresh and green he may be in his heresy".[1] On the other hand, it is only too easy to make a Catholic into a heretic. The preacher illustrates this through one of his most picturesque, and least accurate, illustrations from natural history. Playing upon the German names for *heretic* and *cat* (*Ketzer*, *Katze*), he says:

No household beast can work so great harm in so short a time as this, more especially in summer: let all take good heed of the cat. She goes away and licks a toad, under some hedge or wheresoever she may find it, until the toad begins to bleed; then the poison makes her thirsty, and she comes and drinks at the same water whereat men drink, and defiles it, so that many a man is sick for half a year, or a whole year long, or even to his life's end; or it may be that he takes his sudden death therefrom. Or again the cat drinks so greedily that a drop falls from her eye into the water, or that she sneezes therein: and he who uses that water must taste of bitter death.... Wherefore, ye folk, drive her away, for the breath that cometh from her throat is most unsound and perilous: let her be driven forth from the kitchen or from wheresoever ye may be, for she is deadly unclean. And thence also hath the heretic his

[1] The contemporary Dominican preacher, Etienne de Bourbon, complains also that heretics too often know their Bible far better than Catholics, and that, while many are perverted from the faith, practically none are ever reconverted. He explains it ingeniously: wine often turns to vinegar, but never vinegar to wine.

name of *Ketzer*, since in all his ways he is like no beast so much as a cat. He goes as demurely (*geistlich*) to other folk, and speaks as sweetly and can bear himself as softly as any cat; and even so suddenly has he defiled men's bodies. He holds so sweet speech of God and the angels, that thou wouldst swear a thousand oaths that he is an angel himself; yet is he the devil incarnate. And he promises to let thee see an angel, and teach thee to see God with thy bodily eyes: yet he hath swiftly parted thee from thy Christian faith, and thou art lost for evermore....Had I a sister in a country wherein were only one heretic, yet that one heretic would keep me in fear for her, so noisome is he. Therefore let all folk take heed of him. I myself, by God's grace, am as fast rooted in the Christian faith as any Christian man should rightly be; yet, rather than dwell knowingly one brief fortnight in the same house with a heretic, I would dwell a whole year with five hundred devils! What, heretic! art thou by chance in this congregation? I pray to Almighty God that there be none here present!

These sermons explain, almost more plainly than any other document, the state of mind which drove honest and good Catholics into such wholesale and systematic barbarities as we can scarcely think of without a shudder. If, even in the Age of Faith *par excellence*, faith was so frail as to be shattered by the least breath, and heresy so strong as to resist all orthodox arguments, then persecution was plainly the only resource of men who denied to the heretic the name of Christian, and looked upon him and his as mere food for hell-fire. Nor does Berthold show us only heresy rampant; he constantly alludes to free-thought also. But for the stern repression of the Jews, he thinks that these might have succeeded in smothering Christianity altogether. Again, men found it hard to understand why Cato should be in hell with Nero: a point which may explain Dante's promotion of the former to purgatory. Again:

Many say, "the man who is used to hell is more at his ease there than anywhere else." That is a great lie; for man can never be used to hell....Some also say—I have heard it even from learned folk—that our Lord makes for many a man some mansion and comfort in hell, that no pain may torment him. That again is a lie and a heresy....Many again preach openly that, whether a man do well or ill, he will be saved if he be destined to salvation; and, however well he do all through the world, he must go to hell if hell be appointed for him.[1]

This, of course, is the predestinarian fatalism which many modern writers imagine Calvin to have invented, though Joinville and Salimbene show us how common it was among the sceptical upper classes in the thirteenth century in France and Italy. But the most popular arguments of medieval sceptics were drawn from the lives of the clergy:

Men say..."we see none that work such evil as the parsons, nor that do such injustice, as may be seen daily: pay no heed therefore to what the parsons tell thee". This is the root of almost all unbelief and heresy.

This brings us back again to the body of nominal believers: yet even here the picture is no brighter. The system of Indulgences was comparatively new, and far as yet from that colossal pardon-traffic which shocked Luther; yet even Luther scarcely spoke more strongly than Berthold:

Fie, penny-preacher, murderer of mankind!...Thou promisest so much pardon for a single penny or halfpenny, that many thousands trust thee and dream they have atoned for all their sins with the penny or halfpenny, as thou pratest to them. So they will never repent, but go hence to hell and are lost forever....Thou hast murdered true penitence amongst us!

Almost equally fatal was the trust in pilgrimages. Many deliberately ran up a long bill of sins in accordance with the devil's suggestion: "put off (repentance) until thou has gained and laid up money; and then do penance bravely with a pilgrimage to the Holy Land, or a Lententide in Rome, or a journey to Compostella". Moreover, the pilgrim's extravagance often reduces wife and child to poverty; though he himself "gorges himself so that he

---

[1] Compare *Moral Ode* (E.E.T.S.), vol. XLIX, p. 62, lines 134 ff., and vol. XXXIV, p. 166, lines 133 ff.

comes back far fatter than he went, and has long tales of all that he saw, which he dins into men's ears during service and sermon-time". For the custom which made "Paul's Walk" into a sort of Piccadilly for our Stuart ancestors was simply the survival of a medieval abuse. St Bernardino's sermons show us the churches filled with folk who came in and went out when they liked, and scarcely suspended talk and laughter to doff their hoods for a moment at the elevation of the Host. Berthold returns again and again to such irreverences:

Men talk nowadays in church as if they were at market, each calling across to the other and boasting and telling what he has seen in foreign lands; so that one man may easily trouble six or ten who would gladly be silent....And ye women! ye never let your mouths rest from unprofitable babble. One complains to another of her maid-servant, how greedy she is of sleep and how loth to work; another tells of her husband; a third of her children, how this one is a weariness, and that other thriveth not. To what devil art thou complaining thus in church?

The churchyard was used for fairs and markets, with all their attendant disorders, and for indecent pagan dances that were practised in the Middle Ages on Christian festivals; Berthold tells us that it deserved no longer its old German name of *Friedhof*, or Court of Peace. Nor were these dances the most painful relics of paganism. The Mass itself had become a mere pagan incantation, to all practical purposes, for the majority of the laity. Berthold is preaching reverence for the Mass, and one of the congregation expostulates with him:

But, Brother Berthold, we understand not the Mass, and cannot pray thereat so well as we should, nor feel so great reverence as if we understood it. We understand every word of the sermon, but the Mass we understand not, nor know what is being read or sung; we cannot comprehend it.

The preacher therefore spends the rest of his sermon in giving a rough explanation of the service. No wonder that the holy wafer, the holy oils, the holy water in the font, needed to be kept under lock and key from the common people, who used them as engines of sorcery:

Many of the village folk would come to heaven, were it not for their witchcrafts....The woman has spells for getting a husband, spells for her marriage; spells on this side and on that; spells before the child is born, before the christening, after the christening; and all she gains with her spells is that her child fares the worse all its life long....Ye men, it is much marvel that ye lose not your wits for the monstrous witchcrafts that women practise on you!

Like all medieval moralists, he is never weary at gibing at women's dress:

They take a bit of cloth, and twitch it hither and twitch it thither; they gild it here and there with gold thread, and spend thereon all their time and trouble...they will spend a good six months' work on a single veil, which is a sinful great travail....They itch for praise, and to hear men say "Lord! how fair! was ever aught so fair?" Yet our Lady was far fairer than thou, but *she* was humble withal; so was St Margaret, and many saints more.

"But, Brother Berthold, we do it for the goodman's sake, that he may gaze the less on other women."

To which Berthold answers with the pitiless logic of a man and a bachelor. If the goodman be honest, he will care more for your chaste conversation than for your outward adornment; if he be wanton, all your "crimple-crispings" and "criss-crosses" and gold thread will not avail to fix his wandering eyes. Encouraged by these words of sober reason, a man's voice is raised amid the congregation:

Alas! Brother Berthold,...I have ofttimes besought my wife, first kindly, and then sternly; but she would never leave her follies. I fear to tear one gewgaw from her lest she go and buy another twice as dear, and so my last loss be worse than the first.

The friar's answer, ungallant as it sounds to modern ears,

is the true voice of the thirteenth century, from the king to the beggar, from the moralist to the poet or romancer:

Come, man, take heart of grace; art thou not a man, and hast not a sword by thy side? Wilt thou be lightly overcome by a distaff? Pluck up thy courage, take heart, and tear the stuff from her head, even though thou tear away a hair or twain therewithal; and cast all together into the fire! Do thus not thrice or four times only; then will she leave her follies. Man should be woman's lord and master.

Berthold has his own definite ideas, too, about children. Why is there such mortality among rich folk's children in especial?

Because the baby's sister makes him a mess of pap, and coaxes it into him. Now his little belly is soon filled, and the pap begins to bubble out; but she coaxes it in and in. Then comes his aunt, and does the same. Then comes his nurse, and cries, "Alas, my child has eaten naught this day!" and sets herself to coax the pap in again, as before. Meanwhile the child whimpers and tosses its little limbs.

Don't you know (asks Berthold in another place) how your bodies are made? The stomach hangs in the middle, for all the world like a great caldron; and next it lies the liver, by whose heat the pot is kept boiling. If you fill it too full, what can it do but boil over?—hence come heartburn, fevers, dropsy, and all the ills that flesh is heir to!

An article like this can give only a slight idea of the wealth which Berthold offers to students of the past. There are few works equally accessible and equally rich in hints for the student of manners. The great Revivalist will not teach us pharisaical content with our own civilization; but he may well cure us of impotent hankerings after a dead past.

III

SIDE-LIGHTS ON THE FRANCISCANS[1]

To those who knew and loved St Francis before M. Sabatier's *Life* gave such an impulse to Franciscan literature in England, the satisfaction which they feel in the saint's immense popularity is somewhat alloyed by the regret that this literature should run in so narrow a groove. Even in M. Sabatier's book, the light is concentrated too exclusively on the saint and his immediate disciples. We are indeed reminded, here and there, that the ordinary friar of the next generation was already of a very different type; but the story seldom passes beyond that first small group, and everyone seems to avoid the more complicated and laborious question: "What manner of man was the ordinary friar of the second generation?" And yet, until this question is at least approximately answered, we cannot really understand certain traits in the Founder's own character. Scientific history can never admit Goethe's poetic plea:

> Ich brachte reines Feuer vom Altar,
> Was ich entzündet, ist nicht reine Flamme.

It is the sower's business to look well, not only to his seed, but to his soil; for soil will give the increase only by strict natural law, and a man's disciples are, in a sense, only his own thoughts and deeds writ large.

The medieval reaction of the last seventy years in England is, in many ways, a very curious phenomenon. In spite of the number of fine intellects which have led it, it has been far more a matter of sentiment than of logic. The impression that "they ordered these things better in the Middle Ages" prevails among the clergy in direct proportion to their ignorance of actual medieval life; while most laymen, bred under the tolerant traditions of ten

[1] *Independent Review*, February, 1905.

generations of Protestantism, listen to pleas in favour of
the old religion with the same half-contemptuous sympathy
which they extend to the monks and nuns expelled from
France. The current clerical conception of the Middle Ages
is thus rather the product of a negative subtraction from
modern life, than of a positive synthesis from medieval
facts. It is too often assumed that to repudiate any tenet
current among Nonconformists is necessarily to work
back towards an older and purer Church; that, the less
we sympathize with Bunyan and Baxter, the closer we
must approach to St Bernard or St Bonaventura.

I will attempt here to show how mistaken this assumption is, and what true community of spirit may be found
between the English Puritans and those friars who are
generally assumed to stand at the very opposite religious
pole. If I seem here to lay undue emphasis on the weaker
side of the Franciscan movement, it is only that it now
seems high time to protest against the growth among us
of a Franciscan legend as unhealthily one-sided, in its own
way, as that Napoleonic legend which renders so many
Frenchmen incapable of understanding the real lessons of
modern history. The *Fioretti*, the *Three Companions*, the
Mirror of Perfection, are, in a sense, partisan manifestos,
and give us only one side of the truth. Thomas of Eccleston's idyllic descriptions refer, as he himself plainly tells
us, to an earlier, heroic age, which had already passed
away before he wrote, though this was only some thirty-
five years after the Founder's death. To form an idea of
the average friar, we must look wider afield—to the
miscellaneous notices brought together in Wadding's
collections, to the *Chronicle of the Twenty-four Generals*,
to the *Seven Tribulations* of Angelo Clareno, to the *Chronicle*
of Salimbene, to the early Constitutions of the Order, and,
above all, to the disciplinary writings of St Bonaventura
and his school. The most important of these have been
published in a cheap form by the Fathers of Quaracchi, in
two volumes which cost about half a crown each.

These little manuals aim at presenting complete codes of conduct for novices and full-fledged friars; and one's first feeling in reading them is one of gloom and depression. We are already far, indeed, from the real freedom of St Francis—from that sense of open air and sunshine in God's world rather than the devil's, and from an earth where a man may be cheerful without irreverence to greater realities beyond. The model friar of these books is a slave to the letter of the law in petty things, a man who sees danger and defilement everywhere in the world: in short, a Puritan in the invidious sense of the word. The discipline is the discipline of the quarter-deck: hold your tongue in your senior's presence; avoid addressing him by name if possible, and, in any case, never venture to pronounce the bare name "without the sign of his religious title"; never presume, however well-meaningly, to pat him familiarly on the head or the cheek. Rise up when he comes, and never dare to sit while he stands; put back your cowl when you speak to him; never cross the cloister-garth, while the friars are sitting there, "without due soberness and decency in the disposition of thy limbs and of thy habit". Never "thou" and "thee" the senior brother, except in places where, by the custom of the country, this constitutes no undue liberty.

But these, however petty and un-Franciscan, are among the least tyrannous of the precepts. The rules for religious deportment, as a whole, smack far less of the *Fioretti* than of Praise-God Barebones. The general precepts, it is true, merely inculcate an impossible theory of detachment from the world. "Keep thy heart," writes St Bonaventura, after a passage of great beauty:

Keep thy heart with all diligence, and let it be given up to spiritual exercises only; suffer no images of earthly things to leave their impress thereon, that so it may remain a stranger to all things created, and free to devote itself solely to its Creator.

Yet a detail here and there shows what this theory involves in practice: "Avoid all games, especially with the young...

never speak a word to any man which is not premeditated, ordered, useful, and honest...wherever thou mayst be, avoid all women and beardless youths except for reasons of necessity or manifest profit...never have any spiritual familiarity with anyone, but behave thyself alike to all, so that none may be able to mark in thee any difference or special love for any:...avoid special civilities, friendships, and familiarities". But it is in the more detailed exposition of the same theme by St Bonaventura's secretary Bernard of Besse, and by David of Augsburg, that Puritanism weighs upon us in all its self-imposed gloom. Every speech and gesture and action must be measured and calculated: no spontaneity, no Nature; for Nature is evil.

"Let not novices be easily moved to laughter," writes Bernard,..."tittering in general is a great disgrace to the gravity of a Religious. It is utterly despicable for a man of Religion to titter like a boy. No man of Religion should utter laughter with undisciplined lips, but show with a glad face the gladness of his heart."

There is a true ring of St Francis about this last sentence: but the negative precept far outweighs the positive, as we may read in many other passages, and especially in one which Bernard quotes from his greater namesake:

Trifles among worldly folk are mere trifles, but in the mouth of a Priest or a Religious they are blasphemies. If they are forced upon us, we must perchance suffer them, but never repeat them. To open thy mouth to such things is unlawful; to accustom it thereto is sacrilegious; it is base to be moved to tittering, and still baser to move another.

It must be noted that even the author of the *Mirror of Perfection* cannot quote St Francis's love of cheerfulness without adding, as a warning, that the saint never meant thereby to encourage laughter, which on the contrary he specially abhorred: "for he would that the servant of God should not only not laugh himself, but should not afford to others the least occasion for laughter". That even "we who were with him" could have written these words, shows clearly how rash is the common assumption that the saint's admirable combination of inward fervour and outward gladness was shared by his disciples as a body. Many were fervent in spirit, and many were merry of heart; but the fervent and the merry were soon at daggers drawn within the Order.

It is startling in this context to find an express warning against oaths; but the oath was, in the Middle Ages, as natural a garnish even to the churchman's conversation as it is to the modern soldier's. Not only did Chaucer's Poor Parson incur the suspicion of Lollardy by his protest against profane language; but the same is gravely recorded as a common characteristic of heretics by a thirteenth-century inquisitor. Eccleston, in his catalogue of the extraordinary virtues of the early friars in England, thinks it necessary to enumerate that they gave up all oaths in their speech. The novice, therefore, needs the serious reminder that—

To swear at one time by the Head, at another by the Saints, or in any other fashion, is most unbecoming of a disciple of Christ, Who saith, "Let your speech be *yea*, *yea*; *no*, *no*". Among servants of God, there should be comparison of opinions; but no altercation, which is a perverse thing; especially if the mouth of a Religious be opened with damnable boldness to railing or curses (which, as the Apostle saith, exclude from God's Kingdom); or if he take the Devil's name in his speech, or use it often in common talk.

As Joinville remarked in the same generation: "I never heard [St Louis] name the devil, whose name is much used throughout the Kingdom, which I believe to be far from agreeable to God".

So far, then, so good; though we must remember how strongly all this would smack of the precisian to the worldling of those days, and what sad nicknames the French nobles did in fact give to St Louis for his squeamishness on this and similar points. But readers of the *Fioretti* will be pained to find, not only that the novice is forbidden to jest, but also that he is exhorted to a truly Quakerish avoidance of civil worldly phrases in his letters and his speech. David would even forbid the conventional *How d'ye do?* "wherein is no true care for the health of him to whom they speak". It is true, this may be deduced logically enough from St Francis's scruples about using the name "Good," and the common titles of "Father" or "Master"; and yet the saint himself would scarcely have pushed his logic so far. When once such precepts are codified and registered, and imposed upon a whole Order of men, this can only result in a formalism worthy of the seventeenth-century precisians. Moreover, the novice is bidden to pay the same minute and painful attention to the matter of speech as to its manner: the "D.V." and the perpetual "edification" of the Clapham sect are also the ideal of the model friar.

In speaking of doubtful or future matters let them never speak without qualification, but always add some condition to assertions of this kind; for Religion alloweth not precise words concerning things indifferent. No man living hath it in his choice to say "Yea" or "No" without qualification, concerning things which are yet mere contingencies....When thou art about to go forth among the public, forearm thyself, and purpose firmly in thy mind to abstain from empty words. Provide thyself, before going forth, with some useful matter wherefrom to weave thy speech if need be.

This, it is true, "condemns idle loquacity, not opportune affability"; but the line of demarcation depends so much on the individual mind! Here, for instance, is the talk prescribed to the brethren as they walk two and two:

At that time they should beguile their toil by recounting examples of the Fathers, or any other good examples, which may either kindle their affections or at least instruct their intellect. It is most disgraceful to be unable to pass the time with any but frivolous and fabulous stories. Woe unto those who are silent of thee, O Lord; for the loquacious are dumb!

Again:

Let friars beware of carrying news about, even though it be good and probable. It is unbecoming of Religious to be everywhere carriers of news. The falsehood which is very often in the report itself, or which is brought in by secular men who pass it on, is imputed to its first author.... Let them be honest and serious in their talk, not showing themselves worldly in worldly words, and such as move to laughter. A servant of God should speak of God, to fulfil the Scripture: "if any speak, let him speak as it were the speeches of God": otherwise vain words disclose the vanity of the mind.

The same formality extended itself to prayers: "never pray without sighs" (or groans). The gift of tears in prayer was a frequent and much coveted sign of grace: he to whom it was not vouchsafed prayed to have it; for, after all, this is a Valley of Tears. St Louis bitterly regretted that he could so seldom weep in prayer. The Blessed Umiliana, having lost for a while this gift of tears, nearly blinded herself by putting quicklime into her eyes to provoke the accustomed signs of grace. In spite of St Francis and the *Fioretti*, "God's Minstrels" are now forbidden even the solace of song.

Let them not sing on their way, especially to secular airs, even though the words be good; for layfolk understand the bare sound only. And besides this, it befitteth not a Religious to raise his voice above the ordinary.

A vast amount of early Church music was adapted, like the Salvation Army hymns, from secular music; St Francis once took two lines of a popular song for the text of his sermon; Frate Elia was held to have shown his un-Franciscan spirit by grudging that the saint should sing so loud upon his deathbed. Yet already, in St Bonaventura's days, the Puritan estimate of song is officially ratified. What a gulf lies between this and the holy freedom of the first days, when a scoffing knight was converted by hearing a friar sing as he trudged with bleeding feet through the snow! But those first friars had been real missionaries. What we find now is an Order, very jealous of its honour, and all the more sensitive to the breath of scandal because its decay in real religion and popularity was already only too notorious.

Meanwhile, the more grievously all weightier matters of the law are omitted, the more punctiliously are the tithes of mint and anise and cummin paid. The smallest gestures are prescribed. "It is unbecoming in an honest and humble Friar to put his leg over his thigh, or to cross his feet in public, as he sits." He must utterly avoid all bodily games, as St Bonaventura also commanded. For a friar "to take anyone, without necessity, by the hand or the girdle, to carry idly flowers, fruit, or a staff in his hand, or to twirl the end of his girdle round in his fingers, is not in accordance with seemly behaviour; nay, rather, it is to some extent a token of wantonness". "When they go among the laity, let the modesty of discipline shine forth in their words, their walk, and their habit: let them speak briefly and little, let them cover their head decently, and hide their hands [in their sleeves], utterly avoiding to kiss, or to touch the bare hand of any woman, however nearly related to them." For it would be difficult to overrate the prudery of the model friar, if prudery that may be called which had such real underlying reason. Again and again, in the thirteenth and fourteenth centuries, we find solemn repetitions of the ancient decrees which, for the avoidance of scandal, forbade a priest to live in the same house even with his mother or his sisters. It was one of the distinctive virtues of St Louis of Toulouse that, after his conversion, he dared not kiss even his mother. Bernard of Besse specifies this as dangerous, with much more that is almost equally significant. The Blessed Clara of Montefalcone, a sainted Franciscan nun of the same thirteenth century, is commended for having refused to look at her brother unveiled, though he was himself a friar. She would never show an inch of her naked flesh, even to her doctor: and when once, in sleep, she had thrust one bare foot from under her gown, and her sister had told her of the fact, "she expiated it with many tears as a grievous act of impiety". What most distressed her contemporary, the Blessed Umiliana, on her death-bed, was the thought that the crowd which would come to worship her corpse might kiss her naked feet. To avoid this danger, she caused her shoes and stockings to be drawn on while the breath was yet in her body.

Nor was the model Franciscan behind his sisters in these proprieties.

When the friar washes his feet, he should avoid there, as elsewhere, to show his bare shins; nay, he should, with all the greater diligence, wrap his frock around him: for it is a disgrace for persons of Religion to be seen with naked flesh. Every honest [Religious] is careful that his bare flesh be never seen, save in case of manifest and compelling necessity. We read of St Antony that, when he needed to ford a river, he begged his fellow to withdraw somewhat from his sight, lest each should see the other's nakedness. His fellow withdrew, yet even then he was ashamed when he would have bared himself. And, as he thus pondered within himself, God's power bore him across to the further bank of the stream: for doubtless this honest thought of his was acceptable to the Lord.

It is told of a Dominican and a Cistercian monastery, and I think also of a Franciscan, that the Blessed Virgin came one night into the dormitory to see whether all was well, and was much shocked and embarrassed to find one friar showing his bare shins. Here again we are already far from the childlike simplicity of the first times. In the *Fioretti*, the brethren show no such prudery: Ruffino preaches in a church "naked as he was born, save his drawers only"; and St Francis joins him in the same condition. Juniper is more unconventional still: for the earlier version of the story expressly denies to him even the one scanty garment which the *Fioretti* leaves him; and on at least two occasions St Francis also is recorded to have appeared in public without a single rag of covering. The hair shirt, with which Canon Rawnsley covers him in the bishop's presence, is a mere piece of later prudery. The first free association of penitents and missioners founded by St Francis soon became a religious Order, and must perforce fall in with the old monastic routine, which is admirably illustrated by a story in Caesarius of Heisterbach.

Ulrich, Abbot of Steinfeld...rode abroad one day with one of the youths [who were reared in the monastery]; and, as they talked together, they met a fair maiden. The abbot, of set purpose, reined in his steed and saluted her most ceremoniously: she in her turn stood still, and bent her head to return his salute. When, therefore, they were gone a little further, the abbot, willing to tempt the youth, said: "Methinks that was a most comely maiden". "Believe me," replied the youth, "she was most comely in my eyes also." Whereupon the abbot answered, "she hath but one deformity, namely, that she hath but one eye!" "In truth, Lord," replied the youth, "she hath both her eyes; for I looked somewhat narrowly into her face." "And I", said the abbot, moved to indignation, "will look narrowly into thy bare back. Thou shouldst have been too simple to know whether she was male or female."

The threat was publicly and solemnly fulfilled that very evening; and Caesarius presently goes on to extol the exceeding sanctity of a nun who, having lived in the convent from the age of seven years, "scarce knew the difference betwixt a layman and a brute beast". So St Douceline, one of the most remarkable saints of the thirteenth century, "knew no man by sight"; though, as a Béguine, she moved amongst her fellow-creatures. When a little girl of seven, who was in her Béguinage, looked at some workmen who were employed on the house, the ascetic saint "beat her most grievously, so that the blood ran down her ribs, telling her meanwhile that she would sacrifice her to God". To the strict Franciscans, the other sex existed only as a temptation, permitted by God's inscrutable providence. All their earliest disciplinary writings take up the theme of the monks, their predecessors, that the secular woman is dangerous indeed, but spiritual friendship is even more perilous than worldly familiarity. David of Augsburg describes in four separate places, with great plainness and detail, from his own wide experience, the gradual development of such familiarities from apparent good to open evil. He asserts that "the reverence for Religion (*i.e.* for the Franciscan Order) is made vile through such familiarities, and very many evils come to pass". But (as he complains) it is very difficult to avoid evil companionship: there are so many "by whom men are drawn into sin, not only by their example, but even by their persuasion and derision, and 'the sinner is praised in the desires of his soul'. And this evil conformity is now almost the principal cause why evils are so multiplied in the Church, and spiritual studies have failed in Religion, and many have become backsliders to external studies and business...". There are so many, too, of whom it may be said, after years of religious routine,

He is drawn away little by little from his first fervour, and his desire of spiritual progress grows languid, and there glide into his heart affections for religious women (or *vice versa*, of men), and frequentings of such women: and at last, when all else is extinct, nothing is left but this poor solace, that he can still speak of the spirit; whereby either he sets himself above many who have not felt such spiritual experiences, or he gets for himself a name among religious women, who fancy that he speaks from the abundance of his heart, and is a good instructor in spiritual life and inward devotion. Very many are tossed by this storm of temptation, and few come safely to land.

"Often love, which seemed at first good and spiritual... changes to carnal love": "very many have perished by the sin of lechery". St Bonaventura constantly harps on the same theme. There is no real safety but in flight. As Bernard of Besse remarks, after his warning against touching the hands of, or kissing, even a baby sister: "I can call that man neither chaste nor honourable who abhors not to touch a woman or to suffer her touch. How should it be lawful to *touch* that which it is not lawful even to *behold*." No doubt this is to some extent a piece of religious rhetoric; yet it is impossible to study carefully the records, even of the earliest times, without realizing how fatally the Order was shut out from healthy influence over one half of the world. Even if the Franciscan ideal had been otherwise practicable, it must, sooner or later, have been wrecked on this rock. The friar's reputation was as delicate as that of Caesar's wife; and the satire of outsiders like Chaucer or Langland is abundantly explained by the painful solicitude of all earnest brethren within the Order.

Meanwhile, however, the vast and unwieldy phalanx was attempting to follow in the footsteps of the most spontaneous and unconventional genius of many ages; and with the natural result. St Francis had let the world go by, because he had already in his soul a richer inheritance, the kingdom of God. But, apart from the first band of his personal followers, most friars began at the other end, like most men of any age whose religious feelings have received a sudden and violent stimulus from without. The world seemed to them a positive evil, a Thing to be fought against in much pain of soul and body. In the naïve records of the Mendicant chronicles, we get constant glimpses of a terrible gloom of life. The world was to them, as truly as to Bunyan, a Valley of the Shadow of Death, set off only by the painted mockeries and ghastly gaiety of Vanity Fair. St Bonaventura names, under breaches of the Seventh Commandment, besides "curious gazing on women", "the curious listening to news, or to musical instruments...the sight of fair things, and the contemplation of delectable things with inordinateness of affection". Again, "the desire to see fair things and possess rare things" is, in a nun, "concupiscence of curiosity". The rules drawn up for Franciscan and Dominican Tertiaries —i.e. folk who, without entering the cloister, pledged themselves to lead a religious life in the world under the friars' guidance—forbid attendance at weddings or dances, among other "unhonest" and "worldly" spectacles. It is true, dancing is invariably spoken of as an immoral and dangerous pastime by medieval theologians, and with only too much justification from the manners of the time. The objection to weddings, too, may be partly explained by the not infrequent statutes against the practice of throwing snow, sawdust, and street sweepings on these occasions. But the fact remains, that the strict thirteenth-century friar looked with as little favour as Calvin himself upon the ordinary amusements of his time. The Blessed Salomea, sister-in-law to St Elizabeth, showed her sanctity by keeping away altogether from the festivities of her court.

Moreover, outside the narrow circle of writings immediately inspired by the Founder, there is but little love of Nature in early Franciscan literature. Even the not very frequent tales of love for animals are counterbalanced by others of an opposite sort, as of Brother Juniper cutting off the live pig's foot for a sick friend; of the hawk which God sent to rend sparrows who "presumed" to come into the refectory at Saragossa; of the flies which Benedict XIII cursed away from the convent of Morella; and the swallows which Brother Adam drove away from his sermon. The medieval habit of looking for the devil everywhere in Nature precluded anything like the widespread modern consideration for animals. St Dominic is related, in the Appendix to *Lives of the Brethren*, to have deliberately plucked alive a wretched sparrow which disturbed his preaching, and which he therefore imagined to be the devil, "amid much laughter from the Brothers and Sisters, and awful shrieks of the sparrow". The Marquis de Rambures, in his *L'Église et la Pitié envers les Animaux*, has produced very few examples in favour of his thesis, against the many that could be quoted of medieval indifference to dumb beasts; and the very tone of his quotation from St Thomas Aquinas shows what a gulf there was, on this subject, between the general thirteenth-century feeling and the modern. It is not surprising, therefore, that the general attitude of the friar towards Nature is rather that of the monk, by whom the beauty and variety of the visible world were deemed spiritual hindrances. Life was not worth living, if God had not imposed it on us as the one road to eternal salvation. As St Bonaventura says: "Why do we desire life to last so long, wherein the longer we live the more we sin? the longer our span, the more numerous our faults! For evil grows daily, and good diminishes". David of Augsburg blames worldly folk for mourning when their children die, though it is safer they should die after baptism and before they can lose eternal life by mortal sin, than afterwards at a ripe age; for we know not of what sort they will grow up, and manifold are the snares of sin, from which very few escape.

Berthold of Ratisbon, again, complains how life is a prison, but good men "stand ever at the door of their dungeon. As the imprisoned dog ever stands at the door, whining, scratching, travailing to come forth, so stands the righteous ever at the gate of death".

Another fault generally looked upon as specially characteristic of modern Puritanism—the complacent assurance that one's own clique is in the way of salvation, and that all others are on the broad way to damnation—is not only thoroughly medieval, but specially characteristic of those who had taken religious vows. Pious men in the Middle Ages contemplated with the most Calvinistic complacency the hopeless damnation of the whole non-Christian world, including millions of unbaptized infants for whom Christian parents had shed bitter human tears. Jonathan Edwards's sermon on the doom of unbaptized infants, which is often quoted as a typical specimen of Puritanism, is simply a survival of the Middle Ages. St Bonaventura only voices a medieval tenet, common at least from St Gregory onwards, when he says that "the sight of the pains of the damned heaps up the measure of the accidental joys of the righteous". In the contemporary *Diaeta Salutis*, perhaps falsely attributed to him, the author quotes the Psalms to the same effect, describing with merciless glee how the saints at the Last Day, "shall rejoice in the damnation [of the unrighteous] as it is written 'the just shall rejoice when he seeth the revenge: he shall wash his hands in the blood of the sinner'".

His great Dominican contemporaries, Thomas Aquinas, Thomas of Chantimpré, and Humbert de Romans, write to the same effect. Later on, the saintly Gerson, who has often been credited with the *Imitation of Christ*, speaks with even more ghastly assurance, if possible, on this point. The difficulty is to understand, not how men of these convictions showed such readiness to hew Agag in pieces before the Lord for a question of belief; but rather how they managed so often to rise superior to their creed, and to suffer that men of different opinions should breathe the same air with themselves.

Space fails me for more than a bare enumeration of other equally important points. That "personal assurance of salvation", which to Newman seemed a special characteristic of "the extreme of Calvinism or Methodism", is ubiquitous in Franciscan legends. Again, Bunyan himself never wrestled more bitterly with the problems of predestination than many medieval Religious, to whom Satan would also come as an angel of light, and persuade suicide or homicide as the last stage of religious perfection. No village tabernacle was ever plainer than the first Franciscan churches: St Bernard insists on the most Quakerish simplicity for his Cistercians, and Gerson feared that the images overdid their purpose of stimulating even the grosser minds of the laity. Many Franciscans believed that the saint had forbidden church music altogether. The worst vandalisms of the seventeenth century may be more than matched from the thirteenth and fourteenth; and a long chapter might be written on this one point. Churches were ravaged and ruined wholesale in war; even in peace, corn was found stacked in the Cathedral of Parma, and a Devonshire parson used his nave not only as a barn, but as a brewhouse. Abundant evidence of this kind may be found in Father Denifle's *La Désolation des Églises*, and in the visitations of Dean and Chapter churches for St Paul's, Salisbury, and Exeter. In Italy, tombs were foully desecrated for mere political reasons; and jealous monks not only defaced paintings of St Francis, but tore down the friars' crucifixes, and cast one at least into a cesspool.

In short, the unlovely features of Puritanism are simply such as have attended most great religious revivals. It would be difficult to name any doctrine or practice distinctively Puritan—as distinguished from those common to all Protestants—for which ample authority may not be found among orthodox medieval churchmen. Much of the odium rightly incurred by the zealots of the seventeenth century is simply due to the fact that they were the first party strong enough to enforce, on an enormous scale, that exaggerated and often repulsive other-worldliness, which had for centuries been the ideal of the hermitage and the cloister.

IV

THE HIGH ANCESTRY OF PURITANISM[1]

THE more generally the history of medieval religion is studied, no longer by one party exclusively, but by men of widely different views and sympathies, the more evident it becomes that the lessons of Church history contain correctives for the one-sided tendencies of all religious denominations. Nothing, for instance, has more hopelessly undermined extreme ritualism than the historical researches of the most learned ritualists, who have discovered that the thirteenth-century altar was bare indeed, compared with many which seem quite moderate nowadays; and that (to quote from one of them) "Some pious usages [of later ritual] flow from very muddy sources". We are here on the outskirts of a truth which only wider study will finally establish, but which is dawning more clearly every day, that the pre-Reformation Church resembled modern English religion, with all its cross-currents and tangle of authority and conflict of sects, far more nearly than either Romanists or "advanced" Anglicans care to realize. A man dissatisfied with the modern world, if suddenly set back into his imaginary paradise of the thirteenth century, would find himself still confronted by a great deal which he specially abhors in modern nonconformity; and it would, perhaps, grate on him all the more for being then labelled with the label of the Church. Even Baptists and ritualists are on better terms with each other nowadays than were the parish clergy and the friars of the Middle Ages: and the modern priest, who loses no opportunity of expressing his dislike for Puritanism, little suspects how much Puritanism there was in

[1] *Contemporary Review*, August, 1905.

the highest places during the crowning period of the pre-Reformation Church. St Bernard, St Bonaventura, St Thomas Aquinas go farther sometimes in this direction than a moderate Anglican of to-day would care to follow them: and, in spite of St Francis's own joy in religion, there is a very strong note of Puritanism among the early friars. Even M. Sabatier, with his admirable historical sense, generalizes too hastily in this respect from St Francis and the *Fioretti* to the friars in general. Records older than the *Fioretti*, and of a more strictly historical character, reveal among the early Franciscans and Dominicans a gloom of life, an exaggerated and stereotyped other-worldliness, an indifference or aversion to some of the noblest things in creation, which we are accustomed to attribute too exclusively to post-Reformation religious movements. The evidence which I am about to quote here is, of course, only a small portion of all that might be brought forward. It is taken from some of the earliest and most authentic Franciscan documents—from the genuine writings of St Bonaventura and those by his secretary, Bernard of Besse, and his contemporary, David of Augsburg, which have commonly been attributed to the saint himself—from such early chronicles as Salimbene and "the XXIV Generals", and the similar Dominican "Lives of the Brethren". All these documents, with many more like them, point to the same fact, that much which the modern Anglican brands as distinctively sectarian was thoroughly characteristic of the average friar in the earlier and purer days of the two Orders.

To Newman, for instance, the "personal assurance of salvation" was a special characteristic of "the extreme of Calvinism or Methodism". From a purely modern point of view this idea is natural enough: for it is mainly Calvinists and Methodists nowadays who lay stress on that "conversion" of which the other is a natural corollary. But a wider view of religious history sweeps away this narrow limitation: since to the friar also there came a definite moment of "conversion"; and the friars, too, as Newman would have recognized if their original records had come within his reading, rivalled any Calvinist in the personal assurance of salvation. The ancient *Provinciale*, published by Conrad Eubel, which gives a list of the friaries and of their most noteworthy occupants, contains such notices as, "Bro. Andrew earned, while yet he lived, the assurance of the Crown of Life"; or, "Bro. Rolandino, of Florence, being in prayer, was certified of a Crown laid up for him in heaven": and more detailed accounts of similar assurances are frequent in the early chronicles. Moreover, every separate Franciscan might boast something of the same certitude; for the world was never allowed to forget the alleged promise of St Francis that all who kept his Rule should come to eternal life. If Newman, therefore, could have escaped from his modern world of Calvinism and Methodism back to the Middle Ages, he would have found himself in far closer and more inevitable contact with these self-elected Predestinates, diverting parishioners from his services and offerings from his church; often preaching doctrines which to him seemed rank heresy; no longer to be loftily thrust aside as schismatics, but impregnably entrenched behind the special favour of Pope and people.

Nor was this—which I have taken first because of the importance lent to it by such an authority as Newman's— by any means the closest point of contact between modern schism and medieval orthodoxy. Nothing but a close study of the manuals of conduct written for friars by St Bonaventura and his school can make us realize how little the ordinary conscientious Franciscan retained of St Francis's joy in life, or in how many respects he was enslaved to a formalism worthy of the post-Reformation Puritan. The discipline of the convent (as I have pointed out elsewhere)[1] was the discipline of the quarter-deck: the rules of conduct were precise and narrow. Laughter and play are absolutely

---

[1] See above, pp. 44 *sqq.*

forbidden in these books: beautiful sights and sounds are condemned as savouring of "concupiscence"; the formal religious talk and the "D.V." of the Puritan are inculcated; prayer is to be accompanied by sighs and tears; dances and public festivities are improper, not only for the professional Religious, but for all who wish to save their souls. No right-minded friar will gaze upon a woman if he can avoid it; the very existence of the other sex is a temptation permitted by God in His inscrutable Providence; upon this theme our friars wax as eloquent as the Wife of Bath's husband. That which to modern ideas is most repulsive in Calvinism—the iron logic with which it condemns so huge a proportion of mankind to eternal pain—is simply inherited from medieval orthodoxy. Even Dante dared not save the unbaptized children of Christian parents from hell; while Saints Gregory, Bonaventura, and Thomas Aquinas reckon the sight of the wicked in hell-fire to be one of the joys of the blessed in heaven. To the medieval friars, as to the later Puritans, hell was too often a far more vivid reality than heaven; nor did the elaborate theory of confession and absolution save men from the same blind gropings, the same rash confidence on the one hand or unreasonable despair on the other, which are sometimes spoken of as peculiar to later revivals. David of Augsburg writes of his own time as one might write of the eighteenth century. "Some trust only to God's goodness, dreaming that He will save them even in their sins.... And others again have nought but mistrust of God, dreaming that if they are converted, He will not give them perseverance in the spirit or sustentation for their body." It is very remarkable how many medieval saints—and friars at least in proportion to the rest—are recorded to have fought against despair, or against visible devils, on their very death-bed; St Catherine of Siena is a typical instance. The devil was everywhere—legions of devils, often in bodily form. The Blessed John of La Vernia fought them with his staff as a man drives away flies; it was revealed to another of the brethren that "more than 8000 demons" had been specially deputed to lay siege to a convent manned by only seven friars! The *Fioretti* shows us how difficult St Francis himself found it to expose the wiles of the devil who, in our Lord's shape, had assured the saintly Ruffino that he was destined to damnation. Giles, more saintly if possible than Ruffino, spent long hours of such agony with devils in solitude that "at night, when he went back to his cell, he would say with a sigh, 'Now, I look for my martyrdom'". Saints of the Middle Ages often tortured themselves as much with mysteries of Predestination as any Calvinist of them all. And it was worse still when Satan came in the shape of our Lord or of the Virgin Mary, with all the glory of heaven around him, and unutterable temptations on his lips. It was thus (we are often told) that he was specially wont to appear to "men of singular perfection and of good progress in religion". In this guise he would persuade the friar, crazed with his own doubts and fears and ecstasies, that the last stage of religious perfection was to be found in suicide or homicide. Such stories are frequent everywhere, and two chroniclers tell us of a friar who crucified himself to consummate his Imitation of Christ. In fact, the more careless was the merriment of the great world, the worse were the struggles of those conscientious Religious who retired from it. Behind the bright pageants of the Middle Ages there is a constant undertone of spiritual wailing and gnashing of teeth. Even the tournament, dearest of all to modern romance, was anathema to the religious mind of the thirteenth century.

But a modern partisan of the Middle Ages might plead, " All this is merely a natural cloud cast upon earnest minds by the rough conditions of life in those days; this is only one side of Puritanism. You cannot attribute to the Catholic Revivals of the thirteenth century what to my taste is the most hateful feature of the later Puritan. The friars enjoyed all the rich ritual of the Roman Church, and

they have left us some of the most splendid churches in
Italy. Even if they were Puritan in heart, at least they were
Catholic in eye and ear ". No, not even so were they Catholic
(in the lower sense in which the word is used nowadays
even of a pattern in church-tiles), except so far as they were
false to their first ideal. The thirteenth-century parish
church, to begin with, was bare of ornament in comparison
with even a moderately "high" Anglican church of the
present day. And, beyond this, it is difficult to exaggerate
the extent to which religious revivals of the Middle Ages
revived also simplicity of worship. The early Cistercian
ideal is extraordinarily bare. Mabillon rejects a religious
poem often ascribed to St Bernard "because the Cistercians admitted nothing which was bound by the laws of
metre". St Bernard, in his Epistle to Abbot William,
writes of sumptuous churches and their ornaments in
words which George Fox might have echoed. The pictures
of saints on the walls (as he says) "attracting the worshippers' gaze, hinder their devotions, and almost remind me
of the Jewish ritual". In parish churches, this may pass:
for the bishops, "unable to excite the devotion of the
carnal multitude with spiritual things, do so with material
ornaments". But we monks "who have reputed as filth
all that shines bright or sounds sweet to the ear, what fruit
do we expect from these things? The admiration of fools,
or the offerings of the simple? or, since we are mingled
among the heathen, perchance we have learned their
works and even yet serve their idols?" Nor is such
Puritanism confined to monastic churches; though St
Bernard, as we have seen, would permit pictures and
ornaments to the laity who live on a lower religious plane.
The saintly Gerson shows plainly that he believed true
religion to be imperilled in many ways by the gorgeous-
ness even of the parish churches of his day. "Is it ex-
pedient," he asks, "to have so great a variety of images
and pictures in our churches, or do they not sometimes
pervert many simple folk to idolatry?" His older con-

temporary Eustache Deschamps speaks still more plainly to the same effect.

This feeling that the highest religion is least dependent on beautiful sights or sounds was strong among the early friars. They were Puritanical in the plainness of their services. St Francis expressly forbade the saying of more than one Mass daily in each of their little churches— a prohibition which was neglected almost before his corpse was cold; for more Masses meant more money, as the parish clergy had long ago discovered. The majority of the first Franciscan settlements had no church at all, no singing, and not always even a separate oratory for the daily offices of the brethren. When the early friars were near a town or a village, they heard Mass singly like other folk, at the parish church. But many of them worshipped in a solitude of contemplation which seldom needed any outward forms whatever. The Blessed Conrad of Offida was one of the chiefs of the Spirituals, and is conspicuous in the *Fioretti*. Yet he confessed that, since he had been made priest and sung Mass for himself, he had lost sadly in spiritual consolation. It was no doubt for the same reason that Brother Thomas the Irishman, one of the special glories of the friary at Aquila, "cut off his thumb, lest he should be compelled to take priest's orders". The stricter of the friars had even a definite dislike for Church music; as we have seen that St Bernard thought it wrong for a monk to find actual enjoyment in sweet sounds. "If God," writes David of Augsburg, "took delight in the melody of a voice, then should the mere music of instruments or the song of birds charm Him: for these are sweet enough in their own fashion. Purity of heart, and a mind devoted to Him—these are that wherein He delighteth. The servant of God should not care greatly for whatsoever is indifferent to Him." Roger Bacon expresses his disgust at the "curiousness of new harmonies...and foolish pleasure in manifold songs", which has invaded the Church music of his day. So widespread was this dislike of elaborate music, or of music at all, that Wadding, in the seventeenth century, feels obliged to argue against certain of the Order who believed St Francis and his first companions to have forbidden singing and organs in church, and who therefore "utterly forbid" the same in his own day.

The early taste in buildings was equally plain, not to say sordid. A Carthusian of the twelfth century, rebuking his brethren for having borrowed money to build a fine convent instead of the old mud huts, writes, "These beauties and outward elegancies quickly enervate the manly purpose and effeminate the masculine mind....It better befits a mind intent on its *inward* health, that all *without* should be rude and neglected". St Francis, too, loved mud huts, and even wanted to have the new stone buildings at Bologna and Assisi pulled down. The few friars' churches built at this time, as we know from Angelo Clareno, were extremely small and plain. "Our small churches will preach," said St Francis, "and men will be more edified by these things than by words." The church at Cambridge, as described by Eccleston, would have been almost too miserable for a village meeting-house in our day. The building of fine churches coincides exactly, not only in time but in logic, with the persecution of those brethren who clung strictly to the primitive Franciscan rule. The splendid Basilica at Assisi, with its frescoes by Giotto, was almost as definitely contrary to the teaching and example of St Francis as was the Golden Calf to that of Moses. Thomas of Celano relates how an otherwise excellent friar was damned everlastingly for his share in the construction of these glorious buildings; Eccleston is not certain whether any were absolutely damned, but he knows by revelation that many expiated it bitterly in purgatory. Some of the dearest friends of St Francis were imprisoned for their vehement protest against these and other violations of the Rule: one of them, Caesarius of Speyer, was killed by his gaoler. Such buildings as Sta Croce at Florence were a terrible scandal to the Spirituals,

and St Bonaventura finds in them one of the main symptoms of spiritual decay. A vain attempt was made
to check these "excesses" at the General Chapter of
Narbonne (1260), where it was decreed that the churches
must be as small, as plain, and as cheaply furnished as
possible. Not only were bell-towers forbidden, but even
stained glass, except that the east window might have
figures of our Lord, the Virgin, St Francis, and St Antony
of Padua. Yet even this was a falling away from the first
ideal: for Eccleston tells us how the visitor of the English
provinces (about 1230) "took very stringent measures
concerning the [painted] windows in the chapel of the
Gloucester convent; and deprived a friar of his habit by
reason of a pulpit which he had painted; the same punishment was inflicted on the guardian of the convent for
having suffered such paintings".

Even the iconoclasm of the sixteenth and seventeenth
centuries finds its worthy counterpart in the thirteenth
and fourteenth. Salimbene describes how medieval boys,
like their modern successors, threw stones at priceless
sculptures and frescoes; and how a whole town, in a fit of
passion, would subject its artistic glories to the basest
mutilations and defilements. Not only theologians, but
men of genius like Ruskin and William Morris have helped
to spread false ideas on this point. No more systematic
destruction of ancient buildings was ever carried out than
in medieval Rome; and all careful students of Gothic
architecture know that the builder of the Middle Ages was
pitiless to any older work which stood in his way. The pious
and learned Johann Busch describes with unholy glee,
among his other "reforms" in a conventual church, the
"conveyance" of an effigy which had long graced the
tomb of a mere ordinarily holy bishop, in order that it
might be placed over the bones of a sainted predecessor
who had lain three hundred years under a plain stone.
Nor were even the church buildings and furniture so much
respected in the thirteenth century as in our own. The

Mirror of Perfection tells us how sordid they often were in St Francis's day, and what pains he took to sweep them. Here, again, is Brother Salimbene's description of the Italian churches even after seventy or eighty years of Franciscan influence.

> I have found priests who...when the people communicate, thrust the consecrated Hosts which remain over into clefts of the wall: though these are the very Body of our Lord. And many other foul things they do, and horrible to be told, which I pass over for brevity's sake. They keep their missals, corporals, and church ornaments in an indecent state—coarse, black and stained; tiny chalices of tarnished pewter, rough country wine or vinegar for the Mass. The Hosts they consecrate are so little as scarce to be seen betwixt their fingers; not circular, but square, and all filthy with the excrements of flies. Many women have better shoe-bands than the cincture, stole and maniple of many priests, as I have seen with mine own eyes. One day when a Franciscan friar had to celebrate Mass in a certain priest's church on a feast day, he had no stole but the girdle of the priest's concubine, with the bunch of keys attached; and when the friar (whom I knew personally) turned round to say *Dominus vobiscum*, the people heard the jingling of the keys (p. 215).

This is no exaggeration, for we have the surest documentary evidence to the same effect. Eudes Rigaud, the great Archbishop of Rouen under St Louis, orders church windows to be walled up for economy's sake, in as matter-of-fact a way as if he had been a churchwarden of the eighteenth century. Surviving surveys of churches, appropriated to the deans and chapters of Exeter, Salisbury and St Paul's respectively, show that our English sanctuaries in the thirteenth and fourteenth centuries were often scandalously neglected. The worst part of these dioceses was naturally Cornwall, where the visitation of 1331 shows the following results from the sixteen churches or chapels. At one only "all is in a good state, as it seems, for the present". In three the chancel is more or less ruinous; in eleven the church books and furniture are in a scandalously bad state; in three others "there are practically none of the necessaries for divine service". It is only fair to add that one of these cases was due to a recent sacrilegious robbery. At St Marychurch, in 1301, the parson was found stacking his corn and brewing his beer in the nave of his church, and we find similar corn-stacks in the cathedral of Parma about A.D. 1240. Again, the wholesale vandalism which came in the train of medieval wars can scarcely be realized now. Not only were churches constantly pillaged and destroyed by either party, but they were regularly used as fortresses, in spite of repeated prohibitions. Here they were exposed not only to the ordinary fate of a besieged or captured stronghold, but also to the most reckless treatment from a dissolute garrison, including nameless desecrations which their worst enemies would not impute to the Puritans of the seventeenth century. Details which cannot be quoted here may be found in Sacchetti's Sermons, No. VII. The Hundred Years' War was a disciplined and orderly affair compared with those of Italy and the south of France during the thirteenth century; yet those who would realize how much beautiful architecture perished long before the Reformation should read the terrible array of fourteenth and fifteenth century documents published by Father Denifle, sub-librarian to the Vatican, under the title of *La Désolation des Églises*, etc. Nor was that spirit wanting which thinks to do God service by destroying objects of art which the veneration of one party has rendered odious to their religious adversaries. There was at first a good deal of disbelief in the stigmata of St Francis. Religious rivals who envied the popularity accruing to the Order from this miracle (unique then, though it has become common enough since) were wont to disfigure the paintings in which the saint's stigmata were shown. Again, certain Cluniac monks of the diocese of Agen, enraged with the friars for settling there, broke through the roof and doors of the church during service time, and pillaged the furniture and books; Wadding records several cases of the same kind. Next to the Holy Wafer, no material object was so profoundly revered in the Middle Ages as the crucifix. Yet the Cluniacs who tried to drive the friars from Charlieu did not hesitate to break their crosses; and the Bishop of Piacenza, for a like reason, caused a Franciscan wayside crucifix to be torn up by his clergy and thrown into a cesspool. The lamentable iconoclasm of our reformers was simply a survival from earlier and still more barbarous times; an old leaven of malice working under specially favourable conditions.

St Francis was too beautiful a character to be tainted by the worst faults of his age, and a few of his best disciples kept the true spirit of their master. But the vast majority soon became either men of the world or Puritan ascetics of almost the old pre-Franciscan type. It is painful to note how soon they slid into much of that "holy selfishness" (*sancta rusticitas*) which they themselves so condemned in the older Orders. The Blessed Angela of Foligno is singled out for our special admiration in Canon Knox-Little's *St Francis*. She was the spiritual instructress of Ubertino da Casale, whom Dante names as the typical Spiritual of his day. She was suddenly converted by the preaching of a friar, and "within a few days she profited so rapidly in the school of Christ that she loved nought but Him, and all became vile dross to her in comparison of Him alone. She mourned to be held by obedience to her husband, by reverence for her mother, and by the care of her children, for she would fain have devoted herself wholly to Christ, on Whose love she desired to spend all her care. She besought the Lord with frequent prayers that He would deign to remove all hindrances, both within and without, that her soul might be wholly set on cultivating virtue and on contemplating the mysteries of Heaven; and so it befel that, within a brief space, her mother first, then her husband, and presently all her children passed away from this world". The real sig-

nificance of a story like this lies less in the facts themselves
than in the naïve admiration with which they were passed
from mouth to mouth among the Franciscans, the official
solemnity with which they were recorded for posterity,
and the gravity with which they are reproduced, even in
the middle of the seventeenth century, by so sober a
scholar as Wadding. The pages of Franciscan and Dominican chronicles simply teem with indications that both
Orders were still deeply tinged with the old selfish idea
of life as a sort of jostle for salvation, a religious *sauve qui
peut*. "Be not much disquieted about studying for others'
profit," says Brother Giles in the *Fioretti* (pt v, c. 12),
"but ever study and be anxious about thyself, and do
those things which are profitable to thyself...for it is not
credible that thou shouldest love others' souls more than
thine own" (cf. *ibid*. pt I, cc. 42, 45; and v, 5, and contrast
with Romans ix, 3). The extreme Spirituals, as Angelo
Clareno shows us again and again, were scandalized and
not edified by the extent to which their brother-friars
mixed among their fellow-men. Even Berthold of
Ratisbon, perhaps the greatest popular preacher of the
Middle Ages, is not wholly free from this *sancta rusticitas*;
nor even Berthold's master, David of Augsburg, who
deplores the loss of spiritual fervour which comes from
frequent intercourse with the laity; and who writes in
another place: "Beware lest thou regard or scrutinize
curiously other men's persons, faces, dispositions, dress,
gestures, deeds, words or duties. So far as it pertaineth not
to thee to scrutinize these things for the sake of [spiritual
profit], pass them by and think no more thereon than if
they were sheep or other beasts; let them claim no more
either of thine eyes or of thine heart". Who could imagine,
from a study of the *Fioretti* and kindred records, that such
words had been written by one of St Francis's sincerest
followers, and passed down semi-officially to posterity
among the works ascribed to St Bonaventura!

Perhaps the foregoing considerations may give serious

thought to those who are apt to look upon Puritanism as an invention of the sixteenth century, and to discredit modern religious revivals by comparison with the romantic friar of the *Fioretti*. That charming idyll no more represents the real bitterness of the war against the world in the thirteenth century than Lucy Hutchinson's memoirs show us the bitterness of the seventeenth-century Leveller. A closer study of the real thirteenth century would not be comforting to the well-meaning men who are dissatisfied with their own generation mainly because it is their own. Puritanism, indeed, is not of one time, but of most times, and especially of most religious revivals. Its faults are simply the faults of exaggeration, an exaggerated belief in the value of religious phrases and religious deportment, with an exaggerated depreciation of "the world", in that narrow sense which was of hoary antiquity before the sixteenth century was born. Revivals are nothing if not in earnest; yet the word *earnest* itself has gradually acquired an invidious meaning, so impossible is it to avoid exaggeration, and to fight (where there is no doubt that one must fight somehow) with a pleasant smile on one's face. The Puritanism of the Reformation was simply the strictest and most logical attempt yet made to realize certain thoroughly medieval ideals; its theory had long been the theory of the Religious, but none had yet dared to enforce it wholesale. Charles I, as we know, lost his head simply by trying to realize the ideals which his father had held with equal conviction though with less courage. So the pursuit of an exaggerated and impossible otherworldliness, with all its natural fruits of frequent formality and hypocrisy, has damaged for ever the reputation of that religious revival which for the first time found itself strong enough to force time-honoured ideas for a brief moment upon an unwilling nation.

V

ROMANISM AND MORALS[1]

NEVER was there so great a show of wisdom, nor such restless and world-wide activity in so many branches of study, as in the last forty years...yet never did such ignorance and error reign as now....For more sins sway the world in these days than in any previous age; and sin is incompatible with true learning....Therefore, since men's lives contradict the laws of Wisdom, they cannot possibly understand Her, even though they roll pompous phrases in their mouths, like boys gabbling their Psalms by rote, or like clerks and country priests repeating the Church services—of which they understand little or nothing—after the fashion of brute beasts.

The first sentences, a reader might say, are from Dr Barry's indictment of this agnostic century in a recent number of *The National Review*; the last words are the words of Mr Kensit. Yet in fact the whole quotation is from one of the greatest philosophers of the Ages of Faith, and one of the greatest Englishmen of all times: Roger Bacon. It may be found (with much more to the same purpose) in the beginning of his *Compendium of the Study of Philosophy*, dedicated about 1271 to the reigning Pope. The "forty years" refer, as he expressly tells us, to the Franciscan and Dominican reform; yet, after a generation of that reform, the boasted learning of the thirteenth century was, in Bacon's judgment, rotten to the core. Moreover, he traces its rottenness directly to the wickedness of the age, and asserts that his fellow-students were as definitely inferior to the pagan philosophers in morals as they were in true learning, in spite of the help which professing Christians ought to have found in God's grace, through Baptism and Holy Communion. Nor does he stop short at generalities, but enters into details about

---

[1] *Independent Review*, August, 1905.

professors of Divinity and students at Paris which show
a state of things far worse than anything alleged in Dr
Barry's indictment, though it can be proved to the hilt
from other sources. Not only does this contemporary of
St Thomas Aquinas condemn *en bloc* the learning of his
own age, but he criticizes St Thomas himself in words
which might have been echoed, rightly or wrongly, by
Dr Barry's *bête noire*, Huxley. The Thomist system, he
says, is a magnificent building to the eye; but it rests upon
a Bible misunderstood, an Aristotle misunderstood, and
omits altogether two of the corner-stones of true philosophy—the mathematical and the physical sciences.

How, in the face of these facts, can Dr Barry write as
he does? The question is best answered by another. How,
in the face of the notorious immorality of pagan times,
could Bacon put ancient morals far higher than those of
the Golden Age of Catholicism? The cause in both cases
lies in ignorance of past history. In Bacon's days, the real
knowledge of antiquity was impossible; and Bacon could
no more have constructed a true picture of the age of
Socrates than he could have turned out a modern loco-
motive. In our age, sufficient materials for reconstructing
thirteenth-century life are indeed to hand; but Dr Barry
has not cared to use them. He has chosen to write as an
impassioned advocate rather than as a sober student, even
though he claims, "with past history open before me",
to date his article from "the Palace of Truth". And his
logic is as false as his history. If (as he argues) the moral
decay with which he charges our age is due to a waning
belief in dogma, then the whole history of European
morals since the thirteenth century should show a steady
downward progression. Dr Barry knows very well that
this is not so; for he has written otherwise in his *Papal
Monarchy*. After a survey of thirteenth-century corruptions, which, however imperfect, still shows that he
realizes the civilization of that age to have been lower than
our own, he adds: "We can neither conceive nor imagine

such a time; therefore we shall do well to refrain from judging it". He does not, however, refrain from judging very mercilessly the age in which God has cast our own lot; and I claim the right of speaking here as plainly about the "Age of Faith", as Dr Barry has spoken about the "Age of Agnosticism". For if, during the six hundred years in which the civilized world has adopted an increasingly critical attitude, first towards the Romanist creed, and finally towards all creeds that would confine human enquiry within too narrow dogmatic limits—if, during those six hundred years, morality has not actually gone far backwards, then it is evident at once that something halts in Dr Barry's theory. If, on the other hand, with all our faults, we stand as high above thirteenth-century morality as that age, with all its faults, stood above the ages of Socrates or Marcus Antoninus, then we shall only wonder how a professed student of history can claim historical authority for so strangely unhistorical a theory. As a special student for many years of thirteenth-century life, I know how far even the most plain-spoken historians are from telling the naked truth, which I will try to lay very briefly here before the reader. If Dr Barry believes me to be exaggerating, and will stake his authority on that belief, I will gladly print and publish at my own expense anything which he chooses to write in answer to this article, only allowing myself as many pages of rejoinder as he takes for his reply.

Roger Bacon, though living in the main current of the new reforms, looks upon his own age as utterly degenerate. He hopes—with a hope that is nine-tenths despair—for some *Deus ex machina*, for a Good Pope or a Good Emperor, to reverse the worldly policy of his predecessors. Failing that, he sees no hope but in Christ's sudden coming, to judge a world already brimful of iniquity. He lays special stress on the prevalence of the sins of the flesh. Like all other moralists of his time, he names the clergy as the fountain-head of evil. "Everywhere we shall find boundless corruption; and first of all in the Head....Let us consider the Religious Orders; I exclude none from what I say. See how far they are fallen, one and all, from their right state; and the new Orders [of Friars] are already horribly decayed from their first dignity. The whole clergy is intent upon pride, lechery, and avarice." The same testimony is borne by some of his most distinguished contemporaries. The great Franciscan teacher Adam Marsh is never weary of alluding to "these most damnable times", "these days of uttermost perdition", in which all but the spiritually blind "see plainly that Satan is either already loosed or soon to be loosed". Grosseteste, perhaps the greatest of our medieval bishops, complained before the Pope at Lyons that even the small fraction of professedly orthodox Christians was "almost wholly separated from Christ, and incorporate with the Devil through the seven deadly sins". St Francis, at the very end of his life, spoke of "these times of superabundant malice and iniquity"; and his earliest biographer, Thomas of Celano, complained that the overwhelming majority of thirteenth-century Italians "had nothing but the mere name of Christians to boast themselves with". The same despairing cry is echoed by St Bonaventura, Vincent of Beauvais, Humbert de Romans, Gerard de Frachet, Thomas de Chantimpré, Raimondo da Vigna—to name none but distinguished friars who knew intimately the first few generations of Franciscan and Dominican influence. "The Church", wrote Gerson prophetically on the eve of the Reformation, "is more morally degraded than was the Synagogue at the moment when it was about to be swept away"; "it is consumed by an incurable cancer, and the very remedies do but make it more sick".

"But," it may be said, "these may be only the rhetorical exaggerations of well-meaning men who were carried away by the vehemence of their indignation at certain abuses going on under their own eyes. How utterly false would be an idea of our age gathered by some future historian

simply from Dr Barry's article and other *obiter dicta* of the
same kind."

First, then, I would point out, that *all* my quotations
are from standard books of European reputation in their
time, which have been thought worthy of print whole
centuries after their authors' death; while some have the
authority of Roger Bacon, St Bonaventura, and St Francis
—names that will be great as long as the world lasts.
Secondly, the authors whom I quote had no quarrel, as
Dr Barry has, with the *principles* of their time; they wrote
as professing Roman Catholics to professing Roman
Catholics, and therefore lacked the most powerful of all
temptations to darken the picture. Thirdly, their judgments are abundantly borne out by contemporary
evidence.

"First of all, we shall find corruption in the Head."
The Popes of the thirteenth century were, on the whole,
the best the Church had had for five hundred years, or
was to have for three hundred years to come. Dr Barry
was wise to end his own popular history of the Papal monarchy prematurely at the close of the thirteenth century;
he would have found it difficult to continue it up to the
Reformation. Yet the personal purity of at least three
Popes of the thirteenth century was seriously doubted by
their contemporaries; and Popes lie in Dante's hell like
sheep. The Papal court was then, as always until recent
times, a notorious den of corruption. As one of the few
really good cardinals complained, it had turned the city of
Lyons into one huge brothel during its few years of residence there; and the same evil reputation was enjoyed
by Avignon, Constance, and Rome, during other periods
of Papal residence. The other prelates were just as bad.
Gregory X complained, in 1274, that "they were the ruin
of Christendom"; and only by exerting the whole weight
of his authority at a great General Council did he succeed
at last in deposing Henry of Liège, whose episcopal career
of nearly thirty years would be incredible, but for the

number of parallel instances that might be quoted. Two
abbesses and a nun were among his concubines; and he
boasted of having had fourteen children in twenty-two
months. Yet he was bishop by the special grace of Pope
Innocent IV. The inferior clergy followed suit. St Bonaventura complains of their ignorance, their immorality,
and the dangers of the confessional, in language which
would be treated as bigoted in a modern Protestant's mouth.
Salimbene relates that he has "a hundred times" heard
Italian parish clergy quoting, *as a text from St Paul's
Epistles*, the maxim: "If not chastely, at least cautiously",
to justify their immorality. English cathedrals were partly
built out of the fines of incontinent priests. The contemporary register of Eudes Rigaud of Rouen shows that
about 18 per cent. of the parish clergy in his diocese were
known to him by name as black sheep; yet only here and
there could he get rid of the worst offenders. Similar
registers bear out the bitter complaints of clerical ignorance
formulated by Bacon, Bonaventura, Aquinas, and many
others. In 1222, the curates-in-charge of five out of
seventeen Salisbury Dean-and-Chapter livings were found,
on examination, quite unable to construe a single sentence
of the Mass service which they had mumbled daily for
years. Rigaud's register gives us the results of similar
examinations of priests in Normandy. Gerson, again,
represents the Church as crying aloud to the Pope: "Whom
wilt thou give, out of the whole body of the priesthood,
who is not ignorant of Christ's law?" "Ignorance of God",
writes Dr Barry very truly, "lies at the root of social
anarchy." That is why the Reformation was attended with
so much lawlessness, and the French Revolution with still
more. If the masses are not taught the real Duties of Man,
they will inevitably misbehave when they tardily inherit
the Rights of Man.

For the masses of the thirteenth century stood, as they
stand in all ages, below the clergy. Thousands did not
know even the Lord's Prayer; thousands were never

confirmed, though throughout England the population did
not average five hundred souls to a parish—the population
of an ordinary modern village. The very few who could
read were generally discouraged from reading the Bible
or similarly "high and sacred" books—Cardinal Gasquet's
specious arguments notwithstanding. The failure of the
Crusades was followed by a general outburst of infidelity.
Salimbene tells us how men would refuse charity to the
friars, and give instead to some common tramp, crying:
"Take this, in Mahomet's name, for he is mightier than
Christ now-a-days". With all the priest's inquisitorial
and disciplinary rights over his flock, he could not get
his parishioners to attend at more than a fraction of the
Sunday Mass, or to behave with ordinary decency in
church during even those brief minutes. We have the most
varied and curious evidence to this effect. Dr Barry speaks
of the confusion of modern sects. Is he unaware that the
thirteenth century bred many that were far more absurd
and more indecent than those of the present age? Does
he not know how often even the orthodox were tortured
with deadly doubts, and how (by the confession of contemporaries), in proportion to their longing for God's
presence, they were haunted by visions of the devil?
Suicide, the one crime of violence which was rarer then
than now, was yet far more common in monasteries and
convents, where crazy fanatics were often persuaded that
this, or homicide, represented the last phase of religious
perfection.

For it must be understood that even the slight tendency
of certain crimes to increase in recent years leaves us still
out of all proportion better than our ancestors of six
hundred years ago. I will review briefly all the crimes of
which Dr Barry complains. By two independent calculations, from coroners' rolls of Oxford and Bedfordshire, I
get at the same result—that the percentage of murders and
homicides to the total population of those days was *more
than twenty times* greater than at present. With rape, the

disproportion is greater still; for it was a habitual practice
in warfare, and when was Europe without war? Even
nowadays it is in Romanist countries that gambling
is especially rampant; in the Middle Ages it was far
worse, and rendered even chess a disreputable game. St
Bernardino complains of the horrible blasphemies and
mutilations of saints' images to which the gambling mania
led—far worse than anything known to modern Protestantism. Drunkenness, even without the worst modern
temptation of distilled liquors, was also rampant in the
past; at Oxford, as Dr Rashdall points out, it was not
even an offence recognized by the University authorities.
As to obscenity, I dare not even summarise the testimony
of Thomas of Celano and Gerson, which points to something far beyond modern France and Italy. The life of
St Catherine of Siena shows us an extreme licence of
manners in ordinary middle-class circles. There are few
books of medieval history or fiction, even including the
collections of anecdotes for preachers' use, which could
conveniently be published in an unexpurgated translation. Many songs and parodies written by medieval
clerics, and preserved to modern times in monastic or
cathedral libraries, are far too licentious to be translated
and published in any modern community. The beautiful
poem from which Neale took *Jerusalem the Golden* is in
many parts quite untranslatable. It is very strange that
Dr Barry, a professed medievalist, should not have at
least some inkling of these things; and that he should not
know how little the thirteenth century can be spoken of
as a time of pure and ideal family life, untainted by divorce,
though space fails me to grapple here with a subject which
is complicated by medieval legal fictions.

But (argues Dr Barry) crime has only "changed its
character from violence to cunning, and robs where it
used to commit murder". Even that would be something;
for presumably Dr Barry would readily hand over his
purse in response to a serious request for his money or

his life. But the change is *not* such as he describes; the standard of commercial morality has in fact risen as much as that of general morality. His own *Papal Monarchy* shows that he is aware how scandalously and constantly the medieval Popes embezzled for private purposes the vast sums yearly collected from the faithful of Europe for the Crusades. Swindlers not only wore the Papal tiara in the thirteenth century, but also lived very comfortably everywhere; since the press was non-existent, and the judge who refused a bribe was extolled as a miracle of perfection. Study the story of any religious house of which a full chronicle survives; the chances are that you will find very frequent indications of waste and embezzlement. Preachers and moralists complained, with wearisome and ineffectual iteration, that "in these evil times" a tradesman must cheat or starve. What is more, the pious theft was as definitely encouraged by high medieval moralists as the pious fraud. Dr Barry himself has written of the latter, with a touch of his usual tenderness for the past: "to manipulate ancient writings, to edit history in one's own favour, did not appear criminal if the end in view were otherwise just and good". Salimbene and Cardinal Jacques de Vitry both describe the concoction of successful bogus miracles with no less gusto than real miracles; and St Francis himself began his apostolic career with a pious theft.[1]

Throughout the course of history, no country in which Roman dogmas have been accepted can compare in general morality with the modern Protestant States; and I feel sure that Dr Barry himself knows this too well to risk the comparison of original authorities to which I challenge him.

[1] So at least all the earliest accounts imply most definitely; and the first to deny it, so far as I know, is Wadding, more than four centuries after the event. Moreover, even Wadding argues that the theft (if theft there had been) would have been justified by the saint's piety. Canon Knox-Little is characteristically inaccurate in sneering at this accusation of theft as modern; it is only the unqualified horror of it that is modern.

On one point, however, I am glad to agree with Dr Barry. Neo-Malthusianism is comparatively modern *as a general practice*. It is gaining ground alarmingly in most civilized countries; and I heartily endorse his plea that it is contrary both to natural and to Christian morality. It is a difficult subject to discuss in these pages, though here again I am quite ready to join issue with Dr Barry on neutral ground, and to show by contemporary evidence that no Romanist can afford to throw stones at modern society on this account. I will only point out here, that his indictment is one-sided, since it does not sufficiently allow for the temptations created by the diffusion of medical knowledge and mechanical inventions, just as he fails to allow for the temptations to drunkenness created by the cheapness of spirits. Six hundred years ago, when even educated men imagined the stomach to be a cauldron in which the food was cooked by the heat of the adjacent liver, Neo-Malthusianism was primitive in its methods, and by no means unknown (as I will show Dr Barry, if he cares to ask publicly for the evidence) to convents. Moreover, in an age when war and rapine, famine and plague, thinned off the population far more effectually than any modern practices—when the population of Europe was scarcely one-tenth of the present—a large family was an obvious source of strength; and restriction would have been sheer lunacy, from the most selfish point of view. The very virtues of modern times—our comparative peace, the cleanliness which kills disease germs instead of allowing them to decimate us, our better medical knowledge—have thus created new temptations. All such fresh temptations are merely God's ways of proving and improving the human race. Those who cannot resist alcohol die out, first individually, and then in their descendants. So also with those who cannot resist Neo-Malthusianism. For Dr Barry has entirely ignored the one reassuring side of the problem: that medicine is beginning to preach against the practice as emphatically

as theology. The habits of which he complains began in
and have spread to us from France and Italy. But in France
and Italy, as I know from having seen them, cheap medical
books have for years been sold broadcast, which preach
plainly, not the altruistic "you are ruining the race", but the
more direct "Neo-Malthusianism ruins your own health".
We have therefore here only the same story as with alcohol
—first, rapid diffusion and great abuse, then a gradual return
to the normal state of things, as a later generation learns by
experience, locates the enemy clearly, and is armed to fight
against it. The human race will always leave the bones of
its fallen along its track through the wilderness; but it will
always march on, in spite of reactionary cries.

For Dr Barry's article is hopelessly reactionary. He
must know very well that, six hundred years ago, his own
modern Romanism would on many points have left him
open to the Inquisitor's dismal condemnation: "Recant—
or the stake!" Possibly, however, he does not know that,
in that same age, some of St Thomas Aquinas's characteristic propositions were as publicly and solemnly condemned as Darwin's and Huxley's in ours. In his sneer
at the New Decalogue, Dr Barry shows utter blindness to
the entirely modern virtue of toleration, under shelter of
which he is able to cry aloud among Protestants, to get
full credit from both sides for his real good intentions, and
to influence public opinion so far as his assertions will bear
the light of criticism. He is equally blind to the true significance of the modern faith, not only broader but deeper
than that of Aquinas, which looks upon Romanism as only
one of the best among many creeds, to each of which the
wise man must render its due share of respect. He frankly
confesses his own inability to conceive a religion gradually transcending dogma, just as the Chaldean, who was
accustomed to worship God only in His wonderful stars,
sneered at the Hebrew fools who believed in an invisible
Jehovah; or as the Jew, with his ancient Temple and its
splendid ritual, sneered at the publicans and sinners who

risked a new religious venture in memory of a crucified carpenter. He laments a dead and buried world, as the reactionaries of St Augustine's time lamented a dying Paganism, and exalted purely transitory symptoms of history into proofs that Christianity was leading the world to its ruin. Meanwhile, the future belongs, not indeed to the dummy agnostic whom Dr Barry sets up to knock down again, but to the steadily growing majority of thoughtful men who claim the Pauline right of proving all things, and holding fast that which is good. Such men cling to all that is best in the past, as St Augustine clung to his Virgil and Plato; but they look forward to a far more exceeding weight of glory in the future. For their faces are turned resolutely away from the old Egyptian bondage; and, through all failures and punishments for failure, through fears without and fightings within, they have a steady vision of the City of God.

VI

THE TRUTH ABOUT THE MONASTERIES[1]

IN the *Contemporary Review* for December, 1905, I brought very plain accusations of historical misrepresentation against a number of the best-known Roman Catholic controversialists in England, laying special stress on Cardinal Gasquet's treatment of the monastic question. I offered to print replies from these gentlemen at my own expense: while the columns of the *Contemporary* stood open, of course, to any counter-article: but they have all declined these opportunities. I have indeed received uncomplimentary halfpenny postcards from two of the gentlemen named; and a third person, writing from Gibraltar and omitting to pay the postage, has sent me an anonymous letter beginning "Who the d—l are you?" and continuing in the same strain. In addition to this, Mgr Vaughan and Canon Courtenay have attacked me in the columns of the Romanist *Tablet*, but with gross mis-statements which I had no difficulty in exposing: Father Gerard has again attacked me semi-officially in the same paper, showing again an ignorance of German, and a readiness to make any assertion which suited his momentary controversial purpose, beyond what I had before suspected in him. Indeed, it is not so much their original inaccuracy which marks off certain Romanist controversialists from most other men of equal education and social standing, as their attitude in the face of unwelcome evidence.[2] The editor of the *Catholic Times* (though I am glad to say I did him wrong in accusing him of a third suppression) is still

---

[1] *Contemporary Review*, April, 1906.

[2] I hope soon to reprint my *Tablet* letters for the eyes of a wider public. Father Gerard declines to allow me to publish his replies. [This pamphlet is now out of print; but, as Father Gerard consistently refused to meet me on the ground of historical documents, there was no reason for including it in these *Studies*.]

impenitent in the face of an arithmetical blunder which an intelligent schoolboy would have realized long ago; and he can still see no harm in those cooked statistics of Mgr Vaughan's which, three years ago, filled a more plain-spoken Roman Catholic with "shame and indignation".

It seems worth while, therefore, to supplement my former article by laying before the public a few facts about the monasteries during the last three centuries before the Reformation. This is the more necessary, as I altogether despair now of bringing the Cardinal to an open comparison between the statements for which (while refusing references) he asks the public to trust his unsupported word, and those contrary statements for which I have already given many references, and am ready to give very many more. He evidently realizes that it is safer to suffer any exposures from outside than to expose himself by an attempt to answer them. After all, a commercial bankrupt can live very comfortably on the jointure of his wife; and a controversial bankrupt (as I pointed out in my former article) lives in equal comfort with a powerful and united religious denomination at his back. Moreover, Cardinal Gasquet has at present more encouragement than this: for the lamentable lack of original research in England, of which Professor Firth recently complained, has enabled his theories to gain considerable currency even in what ought to be the most trustworthy quarters. The *Athenaeum*, with its just and world-wide reputation for learned impartiality, has more than once served as a stalking-horse to some reviewer who champions monastic innocence, but from whom I have tried in vain, through the editor, to extract a bare reference which would enable me to verify such evidence as he claims to have found in a certain manuscript at Canterbury. The *Church Times*, again, published recently a lengthy series of anonymous articles, since reprinted in full under the title of *The English Monasteries*, and in part (strange to say!) as a Catholic Truth Society pamphlet; but still anonymously. For this modern theory of monastic innocence runs in curious underground channels! In the first of the *Church Times* articles the author boasts with no uncertain voice of his intimate acquaintance with out-of-the-way medieval documents: yet a sudden fit of modesty restrains him from signing his articles, and from permitting the publisher to reveal the authorship of his book. Stranger still, he allows one of his chapters to be used in aid of the Roman Catholic propaganda; and the Catholic Truth Society, while introducing him to its readers as an ornament of the Anglican Church and of the Society of Antiquaries, still omits to mention his name! Moreover, this Great Unknown fully shares the abhorrence of Cardinal Gasquet and of the *Athenaeum* reviewer for definite references. Whether on his own ground of the *Church Times* or elsewhere, he has consistently declined to produce his vouchers or to face open criticism; and the editor has backed him up by suppressing the two brief letters in which I exposed his worst mis-statements.[1] Meanwhile the book is of course assiduously puffed, and the author's claims to special accuracy are swallowed by those who have no means of checking his statements and are too candid to suspect his tortuous proceedings. What, however, will probably for a few months add still more to the popularity of Cardinal Gasquet's theory is that it has been recently embodied in a novel. Mgr Benson's *The King's Achievement* is simply a romantic paraphrase of the already too romantic *Henry VIII and the English Monasteries*. Newspaper reviewers, who of course are not obliged to be historical students, have hailed Mgr Benson as a serious

---

[1] I had already had a similar experience with the *Church Times*. Having published a gross mis-statement of Lord Halifax with regard to confession, the editor suppressed the second and more conclusive of two brief letters in which I pointed out its glaring inconsistency with known facts. I have heard this policy of suppression deliberately defended by counter-accusations against other religious papers: if it be indeed true that religion has so baneful an effect on journalism, this of itself would go far to explain that decay of clerical prestige which the *Church Times* so frequently bemoans.

student of history: though in fact he has taken all his points blindly and uncritically at second-hand. This is the more disappointing as Mgr Benson is evidently a real novelist, and might perhaps have become a real historian if he had spent some years in the study of actual historical documents. As it is, he has simply placed modern English characters upon a stage, and among scenery, bearing the merest superficial resemblance to the England of Henry VIII. One or two of his figures are charming, though even these plainly owe a great deal to Scott, Thackeray, George Eliot and a whole body of wholesome modern romance, of which it would be vain to seek the counterpart in pre-Reformation times. Whatever Mgr Benson learnt from childhood upwards in the home of a distinguished Anglican divine— whatever pure and noble ideas he has imbibed during his honourable career in this England where the clergy have lived in temperance and chastity for three hundred years, and where the laity in turn have gradually risen superior to their grosser vices of the past[1]—all these things he puts into the characters he loves, making them move like gracious figures of the present amid the coarse society of three hundred and fifty years ago. He betrays scarcely an inkling of what Tudor manners were even at their best: the Paston Letters and the writings of his own Sir Thomas More (to go no further) give the lie to half the implications in his novel. Beatrice Atherton runs about alone, at her own pleasure, like any modern American or English girl; one almost sees her drive off tandem, and turns to find her

---

[1] The thirteenth-century visitations of Rouen diocese show us that the Archbishop knew 18 per cent. of the parishes in his diocese to possess an unchaste priest; though legal difficulties, and the worse problem of finding better substitutes, compelled him to leave all but a few in their cures. In Italy, as St Bonaventura assures us, things were worse. An English visitation of 1498 shows fourteen priests of notorious unchastity in ten deaneries (or scarcely more than half the county) of Norfolk. Many of these were very gross cases indeed, yet none of the culprits were ejected. Reg. Morton (Lambeth) ff. 75 ff. Sir Thomas More, even in the stress of his argument against Tyndall, admitted that clerical unchastity was rife in Wales.

card on the hall-table with "Sesame Club" in the corner.
The book swarms with anachronisms, all the more glaring
for the cheap profusion of carved oak and stained glass
and Wardour Street accessories with which Mgr Benson
loads his stage. Yet one feels that it would have been an
excellent novel if he had dealt frankly with the thoughts
and feelings of modern Roman Catholics, and left the
monasteries alone.

There have of course been many admirable monks and
nuns in all ages: but even as early as the thirteenth century
there were many others who chose monastic life from
motives of selfishness and idleness; and the majority took
their colour from these last rather than from the first. The
evidence of monastic decay, long before the Reformation,
is simply embarrassing in its mass and variety. It will be
convenient therefore if I follow Mgr Benson's lead, and
confine myself mainly to those which he singles out for
our admiration—the Sussex houses and the Cluniac Order,
in contrast to the villainy of Cromwell's Commissioners.
I must, however, again warn my readers that I hold no
brief for Cromwell or his royal master.[1] They carried out
brutally, recklessly, and often dishonestly, a clearance for
which even orthodox Catholics had long since clamoured
in England. Already in *Piers Plowman* (1370) the monasteries are spoken of as deeply decayed and as wasting their
great revenues: and the author breaks out into a remarkable prophecy of their future disendowment by the king.
Gascoigne, the great Chancellor of Oxford (1450), complains even more frequently of monastic uselessness and
waste, and pleads even more strongly for disendowment.
Wycliffe, of course, had said the same: but I quote these
two authors because they were bitter enemies of Wycliffe
and the Lollards. Gower, who also hated Wycliffe, complains of monastic immoralities even more strongly than
the Reformer himself. No more glaringly false historical
statement has ever been made than the assertion that the

---

[1] Cf. *The Monastic Legend*, p. 10.

evil repute of the monks dates from Henry VIII's time. Saints and sinners (as I have shown by evidence which has not been questioned) agreed in complaining of the monks' idleness, extravagance, and immorality: and, so far as I am aware, even the most determined medieval apologists never venture on a serious defence against these charges. That paradox has been reserved for our own days, now that three hundred years of clerical decency have taught even Protestants to stagger at the sordid facts of the Middle Ages, and to admit apologetic arguments which no medieval theologian ever dreamed of pleading.[1]

Respectable English folk, therefore, had long been accustomed to serious accusations against monks and nuns at the time when Cromwell and his agents began to visit. The brutality of those agents is in many cases indefensible; but Mgr Benson has been very badly misled on many points. First, he represents the plunder of the religious houses as having been begun by Cromwell. On the contrary, the story of the monasteries, *as told by the monks themselves*, is frequently a wearisome story of embezzlement and robbery from generation to generation. I will illustrate this here from the real history of Mgr Benson's own Sussex houses and the Cluniacs. The great priory of Lewes, the most important of all the English Cluniac houses, was almost always in debt, in spite of its rich revenues.[2] From 1259 to 1317, for which years we have frequent data, the records show us a state of things almost incredible, if it were not borne out by other Cluniac records and by the financial details of the Norman monasteries in the

---

[1] Here and elsewhere, in arguing from the absence of evidence, I speak of course subject to correction. I only claim to have sought honestly for such evidence, but hitherto in vain.

[2] Even at the Dissolution, after more than three centuries of mismanagement, its twenty-six monks enjoyed a net corporate revenue of £9200 a year in modern currency. Here, and all through this article, I change medieval figures roughly into modern values, multiplying by fifteen in the thirteenth and fourteenth centuries, and by ten in the fifteenth and sixteenth.

thirteenth century. In 1259 Lewes had raised money illegally by pledging three dependent priories, two of which were now falling into ruins. In 1279 it owed £33,000 in money, with a very considerable deficit in farm stock; and the visitors report, "At best it will take upwards of twenty years to liquidate its debts". In 1280 they make a general report that the majority of Cluniac houses in England "are much decayed, both spiritually and financially"—as indeed the details show. In 1290, again, though "all are in a good state spiritually", yet "financial matters are ill-managed in almost all the monasteries, and the houses are much involved in debts". In 1291 "many properties have been alienated to outsiders"; the priory "is so heavily in debt that there is no hope of its future recovery, unless remedy be quickly applied": and a similar report is given two years later, when one of its dependent churches is reported as "on the verge of ruin". Next year the prior has paid off only £500 of the debt: then follow a series of gaps in the visitations owing to the French wars. In 1299 the debts are "very great, and of uncertain extent; wherefore the monastic hospitality and alms have been much diminished, and there are fewer monks than usual". In 1301 the debt has risen (unless there is a scribe's error) to £220,000! In 1306 there were only thirty-three monks: whereas it was asserted that there had once been sixty. In 1314 the debt had fallen again to £30,000. In 1317 it was reported as still very heavy: "every effort must be made to diminish it". Presently came the Hundred Years' War, and the end of English Cluniac visitations. But a document which has survived by chance lifts the veil for one moment about 1330, and shows us a disputed election in the priory, during which one of the parties sacked the refectory, carrying off the great gilt cup bequeathed by Prior Foville, with so many other valuables that Lewes was obliged to beg contributions from all its sister-houses in England to make good this deficit. In 1331, a petition to the king stated that the English Cluniacs had fallen to a third of their original numbers,[1] that they patched up their financial mismanagement by a system of bribery, and that for want of proper visitation "the order of Cluny is come to shame, and none dare speak of religion"—*i.e.* of the proper regular discipline. Lastly, in 1489, Pope Innocent VIII issued a Bull which shows that matters had naturally gone from bad to worse: though here the evils specially complained of are deeper seated than mere mismanagement of revenues.

Take Rusper nunnery, again, of which Mgr Benson draws so touching a picture, and to which he sends his hero's sister as a nun. It is the subject of only five recorded episcopal visits. Yet in 1442 the bishop found that the prioress never accounted for the moneys which passed through her hands, although successive Popes since 1228 had specially insisted upon this obvious safeguard of honesty. In 1478 the equally necessary inventory of the convent goods was equally non-existent. In 1521 "the house was in great decay", and much "burdened with expenses by reason of the prioress's friends and relations who constantly stayed there". In 1527 the house was again "somewhat ruinous"; and, instead of the pretty picture of the inmates given us by Mgr Benson, plain history shows that the dilapidated convent was inhabited only by a prioress and two nuns. It will be noticed that only one of the five visits failed to reveal carelessness or dishonesty, and such other materials as we have for tracing the revenues of this nunnery from 1291 to the Dissolution show them in a state of steady decay. Rusper, however, was orderly compared with the neighbouring nunnery of Easebourne, to which, we take it, the sister of Mgr Benson's hero might just as well have happened to go. Here again the finances show a steady decline during the last two and a half centuries before the Dissolution. We have the details of six visitations. In 1441 the bishop

---

[1] This, like nearly all medieval figures of the kind, is no doubt an exaggeration; two-thirds would perhaps be a nearer estimate.

found that the prioress's extravagance had run the house into debt to the amount of about £400. She was constantly out of her convent, feasted sumptuously wherever she went, and wore a mantle of which the fur trimmings were valued at £50. She "sweated" the nuns, and gave them no money for their work.[1] The bishop therefore took the financial management of the house into his own hands: yet, even so, the debt increased within the next eight years from £400 to £650, while the net income had now sunk to £225 a year. In 1478, it was discovered that the prioress had pledged convent valuables to the extent of £150 for a very disgraceful purpose. In 1485 and 1489 the house was reported to be miserably poor, though it now supported only five nuns instead of ten. In 1521 the cloisters were out of repair, and the prioress never accounted for the revenues: nor had she done so even at the next visit (1524): moreover, it was now discovered that convent goods had again been secretly alienated, under circumstances as disgraceful as in 1478.[2] Mgr Benson takes us, again, to Durford, where he claims special pity for the monks. They were indeed in Cromwell's time "far in debt and great decay": but the nine inmates then enjoyed an income of £980; and, though the abbey had suffered two hundred years before from the ravages of war, the scanty notices we possess point here also to mismanagement as the main cause of their ruin.

The rest of the Sussex evidence I must sum up very briefly. In 1518 the bishop pointed out that six different priories "had suffered great loss and diminished rents" through want of proper custody for the common seal—

[1] As a matter of fact, the nuns were forbidden to receive such private moneys, on peril of their souls; and the mere fact of their making this complaint to the bishop speaks volumes for the degradation of the Benedictine rule.

[2] This is not the place to enter into the *moral* details of the visitations, but any reader who verifies these references in vol. IX of the *Sussex Archaeological Collections*, will understand why the medieval nuns were often spoken of by their contemporaries in language which fair-minded Protestants would hesitate to use nowadays.

or, in plain words, through embezzlement: and they are warned also to discontinue the practice of feeding their hunting dogs on the broken victuals which should go to the poor. In 1478 the monks of Mitchelham were found to have sold the convent jewels to pay for a lawsuit against other monks; the two priory mills were in ruins; the prior had presented his accounts only once in twenty-eight years; had sold books, papers, horses and timber for his own profit, and had embezzled certain sums left for the benefit of the donors' souls. At Sele in 1441 the prior was not accustomed to present his accounts, and had "wasted and consumed the goods of the house". His successor, during fourteen years of office, "devoured" (*i.e.* made away with) "11 sheep, 26 draught oxen, 80 young wether beasts, 80 swine...2 mazers [valuable cups] bound with silver uncovered, together with many salt-cellars, chalices, and cruets of silver, granges full of corn, the household furniture, carts, etc.: besides running the house into debt for more than £2000 and reducing the income to £80 a year". His successor distinguished himself by forging the convent seal and thus alienating some of the endowments to his own profit. The next prior obtained his office by a bribe of £100, and for eight years "wasted the property of the house and allowed the buildings to fall into decay". A dispute over the ownership of the priory lands may palliate, though scarcely excuse, the conduct of these last two priors. The priory of Pynham was sequestrated in 1441 by the bishop until it should free itself from debt. In 1478 its revenues were much diminished, and its buildings, vestments and books utterly dilapidated. In the same year Tortington Priory was also very ruinous. In 1527 other dilapidations of the property had taken place. At Hardham in 1478 the buildings were very ruinous, the prior had rendered no account for more than four years, and the jewels and plate were said to be in the hands of a neighbouring rector. At Warbleton in 1441 the prior was negligent, extravagant, and remiss in rendering accounts: in 1473 one of the monks was accused of having embezzled two gold cups and played fast and loose with the common seal: the buildings were ruinous, and the inmates reduced from five to two. At Boxgrove in 1518 the prior rendered no accounts. The costly jewels given by Rufus to Battle Abbey disappeared within about twenty years, many of them "either lost or fraudulently stolen". The number of the monks there had fallen, between 1100 and 1530, from sixty to seventeen. These seventeen monks, who even then enjoyed a revenue of £8800 net, had allowed their library, one of the finest in the kingdom, to fall into a miserable state.

This then is what can be gleaned from even such extremely fragmentary records as have survived. There were altogether twenty-two houses of monks and nuns in Sussex[1]; the foregoing details give us a glimpse of the commercial morality which reigned in twelve of them. I have been obliged to treat this matter at some length, since there is no other way of expressing the cumulative force of the evidence, and of enabling the reader to judge how far Mgr Benson is justified in representing Cromwell and his agents as the only spoilers of monastic goods. Exaggerated as is the novelist's description of the cartloads of jewels carried to London, there can be no doubt that the Cromwellian visitors did abstract many valuables: but it is equally certain that what was lost in this way bore a very small proportion to the sums wasted and embezzled by the Religious themselves.

But Mgr Benson misrepresents far more cruelly the measures taken by Cromwell to keep the monks within due limits. The accusation originated (I believe) with Blunt, who was not bound to know better. It comes fairly naturally, again, from the pen of Mgr Benson, who is accustomed to the freedom enjoyed by modern English monks, and often sees them wander almost as much

---

[1] This is a very liberal estimate, including four or five houses which had probably practically disappeared some time before the Reformation.

abroad as though they had never taken the vows. But Cardinal Gasquet, as the Head of the English Benedictines, might at least have remembered Clause LXVI of that Rule which even the simplest monk is bound to know almost by heart. The latter part of this clause runs: "The monastery, if possible, should be so constructed that all necessary works...may be done inside the monastery, that the monks be not compelled to wander outside, which is altogether unprofitable to their souls. *Moreover, we will that this rule be often read aloud in the congregation, in order that no monk may excuse himself on the score of ignorance*". Poor St Benedict! Little did he dream that one of his most honoured sons would one day impute to an enemy, as an unpardonable sin, the strict enforcement of this never-to-be ignored clause![1] No incident could better illustrate the fatal dangers of arguing, as so many do, from modern Romanism to the Middle Ages. This clause, of which Cardinal Gasquet seems to know not even the first word, was treated by medieval commentators with all the respect due to its strict wording. Some (*e.g.* St Gregory) would even forbid the abbots and priors to take business journeys, except on rare occasions. Another would refuse to allow any but the maturest and soberest monks to go out, even to visit a dying parent! The commentators enforce these prohibitions with such explicit warnings, and such plain-spoken citations of Dinah and other Scriptural instances, as leave no possible doubt of their meaning. Yet the monastic vagabondage which so scandalized the laity in Chaucer's time was already rife even in the golden thirteenth century. The Cluniac visitors complain of it bitterly, and an Archbishop of York would not even permit healthy field-labour to some monks because it implied occasions of sin. After reading Chaucer's *Shipman's Tale* side by side with Martene's commentary on Clause LXVI, one might well wonder whether historical misrepresentation ever went further than this

[1] *Henry VIII and the English Monasteries*, 1, 256, 264.

modern complaint against Cromwell for enforcing upon the monks one of the most emphatic and necessary provisions of their Rule! The fact that he was able to count with certainty upon their disobedience on this point is adequate proof (if such were needed) of their degradation in Henry VIII's reign.

Space fails me to deal with other gross historical errors in Mgr Benson's work, and these pages are not the place for a full discussion of the darkest side of monastic life. The whole book is (as I have said above) a string of twentieth-century notions thinly veneered with medievalism. His description of life at Lewes Priory is taken (apparently at second-hand) from the Rule and the *Consuetudines*, which is very much as if future historians should try to reconstitute modern English barrack life solely from the Army Regulations and the handbooks of martial law. He knows nothing of the remarkable thirteenth-century "Dialogue between a Cistercian and a Cluniac", which shows the deep decay of strict observance even two hundred and fifty years before the Dissolution. Moreover, even the fragmentary records of the English Cluniacs, though they give us demonstrably only an extremely small fraction of the actual facts—probably not one-tenth or even one-twentieth[1]—are enough to scatter his pious fictions to the blast. Our most direct evidence covers a period of eighty-seven years, from a chance mention by Matthew Paris in 1248 to an equally chance record in Bishop Grandisson's register of 1334. The period covered by these years is one of the most favourable that could possibly be chosen by a defender of monastic morality, since on the one hand the Franciscan reform was still a reality, while on the other the worst decay had not yet set

---

[1] The estimate of the exact value of the evidence is too complicated to attempt here: I hope to deal with it soon in detail. But I have long been trying in vain to induce monastic apologists to discuss it with me. [The subject is partly dealt with in my article in the *English Historical Review* for January, 1914, on "The Interpretation of Visitation Documents".]

in. The period ends (1) before the Black Death, which is asserted by apologists to have shaken the monastic system so badly, and (2) at the very beginning of that long Cluniac anarchy which was brought on by the French wars—an anarchy which finally provoked the censures and inter- ference of Pope Innocent VIII. The statistics which I am about to give are therefore extraordinarily favourable for Mgr Benson, since they represent a time when Cluniac discipline was notoriously far purer than in Henry VIII's reign. The monks who were visited during this period from 1248 to 1334 numbered, at an extreme estimate, 446, or not one-eighth of the monks and nuns at present in the United Kingdom. If therefore we multiply the offences proved against them by eight, in order to bring them into terms of the monks and nuns at this present moment among us, these Cluniac records would give us 152 unchaste inmates, mostly priors of monasteries; forty murderers who together had been concerned in the death of sixteen victims and had slain eight of them within the very walls of the church; twenty-four forgers; sixteen convicted of openly embezzling public moneys, besides countless other less flagrant dishonesties; eight drunken and irreligious priors; sixteen monks imprisoned by the town authorities for other offences; eight who had mutilated monastic servants; eight outlawed ruffians lying in wait on the highways to slay their religious superiors. Moreover, even these figures would need to be multiplied by twenty-two and a half if the monks and nuns were proportionately as numerous in modern England as in Henry VIII's reign. Suppose then for one moment that a Parliamentary enquiry were instituted this very year, and that the Commissioners found records of 4000 such criminals as these among our monasteries during the past eighty-seven years. Suppose moreover that even these records were avowedly extremely fragmentary, and that the Commission calculated them to represent, at the most, only about one-tenth of the actual facts. Lastly, suppose

that we knew the Orders to be already on an inclined plane
on which they would slide lower and lower for centuries
to come—as even the most determined apologists acknowledge that the monasteries did decline steadily from the
thirteenth century to the Dissolution.[1] How many voices
under such circumstances would be raised to defend these
Orders in Parliament or elsewhere? With what feelings
would ordinary respectable folk look forward to the probability that, four centuries hence, plausible Romanist
historians, backed up by enthusiastic and romantic con-
verts, would spread abroad the belief that those monasteries had been on the whole seminaries of virtue, and
their dissolution an act of unredeemed iniquity? For
myself, I feel constrained to apologize to the monks and
nuns now among us for even the momentary use of their
name in connection with facts which can be proved to the
hilt against their medieval predecessors. These whom we
see in modern England are a small minority, living amid
a healthy public opinion, and under a system of law and
police such as no man even dreamt of in the Middle Ages.
Catholicism has long since learned that her only chance of
competition with other creeds lies in real purity of life:
so that, although clerical scandals are (I believe) extremely common in Southern Italy and Spain, the life of
the Romanist clergy in Protestant countries is such on the
whole as to command the respect even of non-Catholics.
I would therefore emphatically disclaim any intention to
hint evil against the monasteries now in England, apart
from the danger lest the convents should become sweating-
houses of cheap and insanitary labour, in the absence of
such proper supervision as our law enforces in the case of
other workshops. But I hope I have here written enough
to show how little historical justification Mgr Benson's

[1] Bishop Nicke's first visitation of Norwich diocese (1514) gives
more than 6 per cent. accused of incontinence; this would make, in
terms of our present population, 4000 unchaste monks and nuns in this
year 1906.

book can claim; since the record of the Sussex houses
in general—and indeed of all the medieval monasteries
in general—is quite as bad as that Cluniac record which
I have just quoted as a specimen. The writings of such
disciplinary experts as Busch, Ambrose of Camaldoli, and
Trittenheim—all of them distinguished monks and heads
of houses—read in some places like an evil dream. The
fact is that, with all his real ability and the engaging
personality shown in his pages, Mgr Benson has written
a novel as false to history as the shilling shockers of our
youth, with their diabolical Jesuits and walled-in nuns.
Nobody in Henry VIII's time, orthodox or unorthodox,
would have recognized his description of monastic life as
even approximately true to the facts of that day. It bears,
in fact, just about the same semblance of reality as the
sentimental pink-and-white plaster statues in a Roman
Catholic religious shop bear to the actual living aspect
of spiritual athletes like St Bernard and St Francis.
Inside and outside the cloister walls, his monks are as
unreal as his heroine.

But he might possibly plead, with Æsop's trumpeter,
that this rôle of historian has only been thrust on him by
indolent reviewers: that he himself is no disciplined unit
in the ranks of original research, but simply a poet whose
mission it is to inspire the fighters with his music. Yet,
even so, it is worth while to remonstrate with him seriously
for this once. After all, the average novel has a wider
circulation than the average history: and I cannot believe
that Mgr Benson would willingly propagate such strange
misconceptions as those which I have here exposed.

[To this Mgr Benson replied in the *Contemporary* for
June; but he has declined to allow me to republish this
reply. The reader must therefore be left to infer its character from my rejoinder here following, which was published
in the July number.]

I willingly recognize Mgr Benson's courtesy and honesty

at the bottom of the hard things he feels bound to say about me, of his silence on what seem to me important points, and of his occasional misapprehensions. The unfair "stab" which he imputes to me lies, not in my actual words, but in his own paraphrase, coloured necessarily by his own feelings. Nor had I any idea of imputing to him the literary bad faith which I do impute to some others; though I own that, if my words conveyed this impression to other minds than his, the blame must lie to some extent with me. But I do not feel that the three particular phrases which he adduces can bear that invidious interpretation when considered in their actual context. Each of them refers plainly not to alleged concealment of facts, but to alleged ignorance. To take his first instance: I speak of him as "cruelly misrepresenting" Cromwell by stigmatizing the latter's order for the enclosure of the Religious as a novel and unjustifiable manœuvre. "It was pretty evident that a rigorous confinement would breed discontent", so writes Mgr Benson, without one hint that such confinement was in fact emphatically enjoined by the Rule to which these monks were by profession pledged; and that disciplinarians had for centuries protested against any relaxation as extremely perilous to monastic morality. I cannot see how this statement—which he does not attempt to justify—can be called any less than a cruel misrepresentation of Cromwell. Yet so far was I from hinting dishonesty on Mgr Benson's part, that I took pains to explain how he had evidently been misled. He saw (I said) modern monks wandering about abroad as if the Rule were non-existent; he had argued, like others, from modern Romanism to the Middle Ages; and he had taken this particular blunder straight from Cardinal Gasquet, who, however, had not the same excuse for ignorance. Both here and elsewhere I tried to show (1) how frankly he had used the novelist's right of taking history at second-hand; and (2) how sadly his trusted authorities had misled him; so that his very success as an artist resulted in the further propagation of false history. I looked upon him as an able and honest counsel whose attorney had primed him with a faulty brief; and his reply has but strengthened this conviction. Although the real point at issue between us is the state of the monasteries under Henry VIII, he seems to treat it sometimes almost more as a personal than as an historical question. "It is myself that is in question", he writes; "we are not discussing the thirteenth nor even the fifteenth century, but the sixteenth", and thus he excuses himself for not having studied earlier documents, while accusing me of "almost incredible" perverseness or "adroitness" in arguing from a complete series of forty reports, of which only seven referred directly to the sixteenth century. Yet I carefully gave all the dates for my readers to judge; nor can I understand why, without vouchsafing further reasons, he dismisses my argument as worthless. It is admitted by both parties in this discussion that the monasteries were purer in the thirteenth and early fourteenth centuries than in the sixteenth. Inevitably, therefore, after exhausting the direct evidence for the sixteenth century, we ask, "What evidence have we for earlier times? Were the monks even then, as a body, such men as we should care to have amongst us now?" I produced statistics from *The Golden Age of Monasticism* which seemed to me to supply a clear negative; but to him this whole argument appears a mockery; apparently because, his own studies having turned mainly on later times, he therefore denies my right to travel beyond his book. Yet I had explained that I criticized this not as a novel, but as an unconscious travesty of historical fact; and he has now no possible right to reject valuable witnesses because they were not of his own calling—to exalt, in short, his own personal limitations into a canon of historical truth or falsehood. Moreover, his own mentor, Cardinal Gasquet, goes back a whole century earlier than I do, appealing for support to those same visitation documents which, when I quote them, Mgr Benson dismisses with loathing as "episcopal police-lists". The real difference here between myself and the Cardinal is that I give my references, while he steadily declines to give his. Nor can he now justify this refusal on the score of dignity; for in the preface to his new edition he steps down from that pedestal to revile me (in the French of Stratford attë Bowe), as a literary ragman. It is this refusal of the commonest guarantees of literary good faith—not, as Mgr Benson asserts, our difference of opinion—which has determined me to pursue this subject so far. Indeed, it would seem almost a counsel of despair which prompted Mgr Benson to waste, in an attempt to prejudge this question, space which would have been more profitably employed in dealing with my facts. He quotes two living historians as regarding the Cardinal's work with such "deep respect" that I have no right to attack it; as if anything could ever be proved if the consent of two men, however eminent, carried a power of tribunicial veto at the bar of history! Moreover, one of his pair is very far from bearing a name to conjure with in this matter; while the other, Dr Gairdner, has volunteered to me the statement that he considers my exposure of the Cardinal "a powerful indictment!"[1] So far, therefore, as Mgr Benson's argument ever had any real force, it now turns against himself.

As for his so-called parallel to my statistics, it is painful to deal with anything so slipshod. With all his licence of choosing a single favourable fortnight for generalization, he still cannot produce anything remotely approaching the percentage of immoralities revealed by Nicke's visitation of 1514 in the Norwich diocese. For a real parallel to my figures he must show, not four criminous clerks for the

---

[1] This letter, written by Dr Gairdner to stop the use of his high authority in support of arguments which have not always his approval, was published, with his permission, in *Church Bells* for May 12, 1906. [Before his death, Dr Gairdner went still further, and wrote to me expressing great surprise at Cardinal Gasquet's attitude towards historical facts; see pp. 43–4 of my *Medieval Studies*, No. x, "Monastic Schools in the Middle Ages".]

whole country during one particular fortnight, but over seventy-five in a single diocese like Norwich, within a space of three years.[1] He knows very well that he would need not only great diligence, but exceptional good fortune to produce even one-tenth of this proportion after years of patient study; and it is a pity that he did not work out his own figures, instead of satisfying himself with the most superficial pretence of an argument to throw at me. As a further radical difference—if such were needed— a criminous clerk is ignominiously ejected in these days; before the Reformation, ejections for unchastity were not only comparatively rare, but practically unknown for a first offence. As for his claim of imitating my methods in gratuitously multiplying the recorded figures by four, this is an admirable instance of the misconceptions resulting from those hole-and-corner historical ideas which prevail in his own communion. I have no mere surmises, but definite evidence to show that a large proportion of cases have been omitted from many of the medieval documents by which, in default of others more complete, I support facts already gleaned from fuller sources. I have repeatedly challenged discussion on this point with Cardinal Gasquet, Father Gerard, and the anonymous F. S. A. who writes alternately for the *Church Times* and for the Catholic Truth Society; indeed, I repeated this challenge in a footnote appended to the very statistics at which Mgr Benson carps. They persistently refuse this discussion, finding it safer to throw mud at me from the comparative security of a preface, a Romanist journal, or an anonymous article; and meanwhile their wilful silence enables Mgr Benson to write as if the reasons which I have vainly offered to his own champions were as empty as these mockeries which he flaunts in parody of what he calls "my methods"!

[1] He generalizes from four cases: I from twenty. His figures would work out at only 104 cases in a year out of 24,000 clergy: mine are twenty in three years out of 332 monks and nuns. I work this out in my *Monastic Legend*.

Wherever else he seems to make a real point against me, it is, I cannot help thinking, by misunderstanding my words. In one case this was no doubt partly my fault; I should either have been more explicit about his alleged anachronisms or have left them alone. I never dreamed of blaming him for not adopting bastard linguistic archaisms, or for keeping Tudor vermin out of sight. I referred chiefly to his importation of deeper modern refinements into those times; to the implication of his whole book that Tudor Catholicism had all the virtues and *inward* qualities of modern society, with something more. Nobody could guess from his book how brutally girls were often maltreated, and how hard they found it to escape obscene talk even in the best society—as Sir Thomas More not only complains, but shows by his own example. Mgr Benson refuses to believe in the word of a man like Layton because he tells Cromwell "some tales [of monastic vice] to make you laugh". Yet More tells, with great circumstance and most undeniable relish, quite unnecessarily, a monastic story more unsavoury than any of Layton's; a story, moreover, sufficient in itself to disprove Cardinal Gasquet's assertions of the strict discipline exercised by conventual visitors (More's *English Works*, pp. 1035 and 154). On this, and similar vital points, the novelist antedates by centuries the progress of inward civilization. Moreover, he spends more than a page in disproving an assertion which I never made. When I complain of his letting his heroine "run about *alone*", it is no answer to confront me with quotations which either ignore the crucial word here italicized, or definitely show (as two out of his four do) that the ladies had in fact attendants waiting on them. I know very well that Tudor ladies enjoyed more freedom than their ancestresses, or than Italian ladies; but I believe such freedom to have been far, at its best, from the "almost Victorian" liberty which Mgr Benson asserts them to have enjoyed; nor can I believe that a self-respecting girl like Beatrice would have gone alone to interview her *fiancé* in his own rooms. But I am told that I err in supposing her to have been unattended on that occasion. I have just re-read the chapter (pt. II, c. ix) and feel sure that the author, on re-reading it himself, will admit my impression to have been pardonable, if not correct. Meanwhile, if he will produce evidence rebutting my criticism as it stands, I will acknowledge my error as publicly as I asserted it.

Of his other criticisms I can only say that they seem to me to repose, partly on misreading of my words and partly on his own unfamiliarity with the facts of history. I did not, for instance, say that "if Religious are rich, it must be through oppression or greed", nor can I even guess at the words which he read in this sense. What he says, again, in excuse for their failure to keep accounts and inventories, simply proves how little he has read of papal, conciliar, and episcopal injunctions. I could point out as many mistakes of this kind as there are pages in his article, and am willing to do so in any paper he chooses, under criticism from him or from the Cardinal's earlier champion, Father Gerard. He will no doubt brand me here again with the invidious title of "controversialist", yet I am in fact as hard-worked a professional man as himself, and controversy has brought me, as probably it will always bring me, pecuniary loss without any corre-sponding public gain. For the last ten years I have been working at a book on medieval life which I hope to publish now in a few weeks. In this work I have found myself confronted at every turn by what seem to me the reckless, and sometimes even deliberate, misrepresentations of Romanist apologists. That is why I have stepped aside to clear the ground of weeds to which more distinguished scholars have neither time nor inclination to stoop. I have always offered to print replies at my own expense; and, if I had nothing but controversial tricks to help me, I should long ago have been made mincemeat of by Father Gerard, who has probably written two or three hundred pages of polemics to one of mine. As it is, Father Gerard has steadily declined to face my evidence from pre-Reformation documents, even in the comparative safety of the *Tablet*, which could not print some of my most important proofs.

Moreover, Mgr Benson seems curiously unable to realize how far his own book is merely destructive, or how much he and his own friends depend on "peering through the keyholes" of history, on ferreting out evil from a king's private love-letters, and on studiously blackening men and women who are as silent and helpless now, and who once suffered as cruelly, as any monk or nun. All this is the nemesis of an old evil tradition which has allowed men to use tricks for The Cause which would be reprobated in private life, with the result that Church history cannot yet be written, on either side, with the same judicial calm as other histories. No judge can sum up from concealed evidence, and the "confidence trick" has no more place in history than in law. So long, therefore, as one side deliberately rests on alleged favourable evidence from the episcopal registers, so long must others emphasize even to weariness the damning evidence which those books undoubtedly contain. The workaday Present always cuts a poor figure beside the meretricious fancies of the Past, and it is only fair to remind Mgr Benson that nearly one-third of St Augustine's *City of God* is devoted to purely destructive criticism of the polytheism which many of his contemporaries longed to have back again. So we also can never realize fully the spiritual possibilities of the age in which we live, unless we make these periodical clearances of interested mis-statements which would persuade us to hark back to the past.

P.S. The above was already in type when I saw in the *Guardian* (June 6, p. 937) a quotation from Newman which cuts one knot that had hardly seemed worthy of unravelling at the expense of a couple of pages. Having no time to verify it at the British Museum, I give it here simply on the high authority of the *Guardian*, which quotes it from the Roman Catholic *Month* (January, 1903): "Nothing could be better [Newman wrote] than an historical review. But who would bear it? *Unless one doctored all one's facts, one would be thought a bad Catholic.*" Compare the words I have here italicized with Mgr Benson's complaint (p. 827) that my attitude shows me to have "already decided that no Catholic priest could be anything but a falsifier of history". Even if I had not already exposed Romanist falsifications wholesale, with plain chapter and verse, and without eliciting any real evidence in their favour, I should now only need (1) to collocate Newman's words with the undeniable fact that Cardinal Gasquet is far from "being thought a bad Catholic", and (2) to draw the obvious deduction that the very completeness of Mgr Benson's good faith has helped to make him the unconscious mouthpiece of that "doctored history" for which he is proud to own his debt to "the greatest Roman Catholic historian of our day".

VII

RELIGIOUS EDUCATION
BEFORE THE REFORMATION[1]

BOTH Roman Catholic and High Church papers have lately attempted to contrast the present state of religious education with what they imagine it to have been before the Reformation. There are few more tempting fallacies than that which Sterne has good-humouredly pilloried for all time in his "They order this matter better in France". Whatever seems amiss in the world in which our lot is cast, we are quick to imagine some golden world in which all was the opposite of this ungrateful present. The fitness of things seems to require it, and we feel that there ought to be—that there *must* be somewhere—historical evidence for it. It may therefore be worth while, at this particular moment, to confront this fond dream with the real facts, especially since plausible attempts have been made, in the name of serious history, to misrepresent those facts. The editor of the *Catholic Times* quotes Cardinal Gasquet as establishing the existence of a pre-Reformation England in which education was all that it should have been, and all that it now, alas! is not! One of his correspondents, bolder still, has gathered from the same historian that there was "an age when there would have been no difficulties over an Education Bill, a time when the Church had it all its own way, and yet the Bible was taught...when such immense portions of Scripture were committed to memory, and that by Catholics". Such grotesque travesties of the actual facts are current not only among those who have most temptation to see one side of the question alone, but even among moderate Anglicans. They have been so often

[1] *Contemporary Review*, October, 1906.

repeated, supported with such a specious show of serious evidence, and suffered so contemptuously or so supinely by those who are best qualified to contradict them, that many well-read men accept them now almost without question. Yet this theory that the pre-Reformation times were an age of thorough and widespread religious instruction not only breaks down under any fairly wide view of the actual documents, but is contradicted (as I hope to prove) even by those apologetic writings of Sir Thomas More, on which, by means of partial quotations, it has been mainly built.

Let me begin with the golden thirteenth century. At the Provincial Council of Oxford, in 1222, Stephen Langton enjoined, "Let the archdeacons at their visitations see that... the priests can rightly pronounce at least the formula of consecration [in the Mass], and that of baptism, and that they clearly understand the meaning of these two formulas". This injunction (which was repeated in a later Council of 1237) reveals an abyss of clerical ignorance at which we may well stagger. In an age when the Bible was in Latin, all the Church services in Latin, and only a small fraction even of popular religious books could be obtained in the vulgar tongue, it was necessary for the Provincial Councils to take elaborate precautions for ensuring that parish priests knew just enough Latin to pronounce, and understand, two every-day formulas of half-a-dozen words each! Nor are we left to the inferences, however inevitable, drawn from these injunctions; for we have on record the actual examination, in this same year, 1222, of a number of curates who had long served Dean-and-Chapter livings of Salisbury. The curate of Sonning, who had been four years in priest's orders, was asked to construe the first words of the canon of the Mass—*Te igitur clementissime Pater*—"We pray Thee, therefore, most merciful Father", etc. The report is,

He knew not the case of the word *Te*, nor by what it was governed; and having been bidden to look closely what part

of the sentence could most properly govern *Te*, he replied:
"*Pater*: for He governeth all things". We asked him what
clementissime was, or what case, or how it was declined: he
knew not. We asked him what was *clemens*: he knew not.
Moreover [he knew no music and] knew by heart no part of the
divine service or of the psalter. Moreover, he said that it
seemed to him indecent to be examined by the dean, since he
was already ordained....He is sufficiently illiterate.

The rest tried to concert a "passive resistance" to the
examination, and for a while refused to answer: but at
last their conspiracy broke down, and it is registered that
the curate of Hurst, six years a priest, "is young, and
knows nothing". The curate of Erburgefield, four years
a priest, was also examined in the canon of the Mass,
"and he knew nothing, either of reading or of singing".
The curate of Sandhurst had been four years there, and
"could give no answers" to the same simple questions.
The curate of Ruscombe, nearly ten years a priest, "knows
nothing". It must be borne in mind, firstly, that this
Latin of which the five curates could not even stumble
through the first line is the essential and most solemn
portion of the Mass, and could almost be learnt by heart in
a single day by one who really knew Latin: and secondly,
that no measures were taken to get rid of any of these
priests. It is possible that for Dean-and-Chapter livings
curates were hired in the cheapest market, as was notoriously the case with monastic livings: yet even so it is
startling to find five such incapables in seventeen churches.
The contemporary register of Eudes Rigaud, of Rouen, one
of the greatest of medieval prelates, gives almost equally
startling results. One candidate, set to construe and parse
three verses of the Bible (Heb. iv, 13–15), thought *aperta*
("opened") was a noun, imagined that *compati* ("to be
touched with") had something to do with "opening",
and parsed "without" as a causal conjunction. As he was
also "ill-famed of quarrelling and incontinence", the
archbishop decided not to admit him to the coveted

benefice. Another cleric, having to construe *annuus*
("annual"), dimly thought that it meant "often", and,
when asked "how often?" replied "daily". A third,
whom the archbishop found "unable to read properly or
to construe", promptly gave notice of appeal to the Pope!
We get similar evidence again from Germany in the
fifteenth century. Johann Busch (*de Ref. Mon.* I, xiv) tells
us how he held an archidiaconal visitation at the important
town of Halle, and found one incumbent who, even with
a little friendly help and after mature consideration, could
not name the simple words of consecration of the Mass,
"This is My Body", or "This is the Cup of My Blood".
He offered, however, to find them in the Missal: but when
a book was brought he pointed to the wrong place: though
he proved able to read through the essential portions of
the Mass "after the fashion" (as Busch puts it) "of
secular priests".[1] Busch consulted with the doctors as to
the validity of this man's consecrations; they agreed to hope
for the best, but took the precaution of exchanging the holy
wafers which he had on hand for a fresh batch consecrated
by a more trustworthy colleague. Of one other obvious
precaution—getting rid of the ignorant priest—there was
no question. As St Bonaventura had said two hundred years
before, "If we do get rid of them, how shall we get any
better to fill their places?" For, while sinners mocked at the
ignorance of the clergy, saints and philosophers lamented
alike the magnitude of the evil and the difficulty of reform.
Scholars too often went up to the medieval universities
(as Dr Rashdall points out) without enough Latin to follow
the lectures properly; nor was there any definite theo-

---

[1] It is obvious how far these fragmentary indications from orthodox
sources go to corroborate Tyndale's "I dare say that there be 20,000
priests, curates, this day in England, and not so few, that cannot give
you the right English unto this text in the Paternoster, *Fiat voluntas
tua, sicut in coelo et in terra*, and the answer thereto": and the record
of Bishop Hooper's visitation in 1552 which showed "scores of clergy
who could not tell who was the author of the Lord's Prayer, or where
it was to be found". *Tyndale's Works*, III (Parker Society), p. 75
and note.

logical training for the ordinary student.[1] Moreover, large
numbers of the parish clergy had never been to a university at all. The episcopal registers supply the most curious
evidence on this point, showing that there were two dis-
tinct categories of parish clergy. On the one hand were
the beneficed clergy, who generally belonged to the rich
and influential classes, and of whom about 75 per cent.
had been presented with livings not only before they had
taken holy orders, but even in their youth or their boyhood.
The first act of such clerics, on receiving their benefices,
was often to go to the university. On the other hand were
the poor curates, who might or might not have studied,
but who were generally doomed to vegetate on the lowest
wages, while the fruits of their parishes were mainly consumed by absentees.[2]

In a Church where the rectors were often schoolboys
and the first requisite for a curate was that he should
be cheap and unambitious, it was unlikely that any high
standard could be maintained, even in such learning as
was otherwise possible under medieval conditions. "There
are", writes St Bonaventura, "so many inexperienced
clerics that, even if they be well taught in grammar and
other knowledge, yet where one hundred or more rectors
and vicars are gathered together, there are scarcely any
who have in fact enough knowledge of the Scriptures to
manage either the souls committed to their care, or other
things necessary for salvation." He speaks here specially
of Italy, and says that things were better in France and
England. But St Thomas Aquinas, writing at Paris,
complains of "the inexperience of many priests, who in
some parts are found to be so ignorant that they cannot
even speak Latin, and among whom very few are found who

---

[1] *Universities of Europe in the Middle Ages,* II, 701. Dr Rashdall
adds: "It is necessary to assert emphatically that the 'religious education' of a 'bygone Oxford', in so far as it ever had any existence, was
an inheritance not from the Middle Ages but from the Reformation".

[2] I hope to explain this in detail, with statistics from the registers
on some future occasion.

have learnt Holy Scripture". Roger Bacon, writing about
the same time in England, and wishing to give an instance
of mere parrot-learning, says "just as boys gabble through
the Psalter which they have learnt, and as clerks and
country priests recite the Church services, of which they
know little or nothing, like brute beasts". Gerson, at the
beginning of the fifteenth century, speaks equally strongly
and far more frequently on this subject. He contrasts what
he calls the restless and ill-digested Scripture studies of
the heretics with the supineness of even "great prelates",
who neglect "the wine of sacred wisdom" and cry, "What
is this ye say to us of faith? It is enough that we are
Christians, in good simplicity: that is enough; for he who
pries into majesty shall be oppressed by its glory; and there
is no need to seek things so lofty for us". Again he asks,
"Are all ecclesiastics bound to study God's Law? It would
seem so...yet on the other side it may be argued that to
assert this is to place by far the greater part of ecclesiastics
outside the way of salvation, and to assert that they are
doomed to damnation". He speaks of the lamentable
lack of religious books of any kind among the parish clergy,
and complains that there was no organized attempt to
multiply good writings against the rising tide of infidelity:
to this supineness, and to the ignorance of the beneficed
clergy, he attributes a great deal of what he calls the
notorious decay of the Catholic Church. Finally, complaining somewhat rhetorically in the person of Holy
Church to the Pope, he cries, "What priest wilt thou give
me who knoweth God's Law!" (vol. I, p. 349 C. *De Laud.
Script. Consid.* X–XII; vol. I, pp. 204 A, 268 A, 349 C; vol. II,
552 A; cf. I, 205 F, 208 C, 339 A–C). Nor were the monks
better than the parish clergy in this respect. Popes and
prelates alike, when providing that the Monastic Rule or
other similar injunctions should be read aloud, ordained
that these should be read not only in Latin but also in the
vulgar tongue: and it was taken as quite natural that the
most pious lay-brethren could not follow the sense of the

Nicene Creed during Mass. The friars did indeed revive the study of the Bible among the clergy: but they did little to spread the knowledge of the actual text among the laity, who were fed almost as much on glosses and pious embroideries as on the plain facts of Scripture history. Even the famous *Meditations on the Life of Christ*, once attributed to St Bonaventura, and now traced to one of his disciples, alloy the Gospel story with a good 20 per cent. of sheer romance, based upon the author's own surmises of what might have happened, or on revelations vouchsafed to "a holy brother of our Order". These additions, it need hardly be said, mostly tend to give the Virgin Mary a prominence or an authority which the Evangelists have neglected to give her. Chaucer's keen eye noted this habit of the friars, and he shows us too how much more the popular mind was attracted by these apocryphal legends than by the bare truth. His clerk, Nicholas, speaking to the carpenter about Noah's flood, has no doubt that the latter will specially remember the least Biblical feature of that event as conceived in the later Middle Ages—the refusal of Noah's wife to embark, until she has drunk one more pot of ale with her jolly gossips ashore!

Nor are the instances which I have hitherto quoted rare and exceptional; the evidence of clerical ignorance all through the Middle Ages—and, unfortunately, for a generation or so after the Reformation—is overwhelming. When Dean Colet, in 1509, complained that all applicants were admitted indiscriminately to Holy Orders, so that the Church swarmed with "a multitude of unlearned and evil priests", he was only repeating, almost in so many words, what the Bishop of Mende had said to the Pope at the Council of Vienne in 1311. Moreover, both Colet and the bishop lay stress on the fact that laws had been frequently enacted against these abuses, and that the Church needed no new legislation, but simply courage to enforce time-honoured and repeatedly-enacted laws. For, by a

strange perversion of history, one of the plainest proofs
of medieval religious ignorance has been distorted by
modern apologists into an argument for religious knowledge. If council after council, thundering against the
"dumb dogs that bark not", enjoined that the clergy
should at least be competent to read and speak Latin, and
should give at least a certain minimum of elementary
religious instruction from the pulpit, surely common sense
would suggest that the very repetition and emphasis of
such injunctions pointed to something wrong in practice.
Yet Mgr Vaughan, in his *Faith and Folly* (p. 4), undertakes
to prove by "the following indisputable authorities" that
the Church has always fostered learning. He then proceeds
to give bare references, without quotations, to five Church
councils, the references themselves being full of blunders
and evidently copied from some French book. The ingenious student who manages to verify these references
will find them of this following type: "Henceforward let
no Bishop be suffered to confer deacon's or priest's orders
on an illiterate man; and let any such, who may already
have been ordained, be now compelled to learn.... What
doth he in the Church of God if he be not skilled to read?"
Cardinal Gasquet, again, in his *Eve of the Reformation* and
his essay on *Religious Instruction in England*, hardly comes
any nearer to the real point. His references to episcopal
registers are not accurate; and, even if the facts were as he
states them, they prove no more than that medieval villagers
were generally as unwilling as modern Irish villagers to
bring formal accusations of ignorance or neglect against
their priests. On the other hand, like Mgr Vaughan, he
relies mostly on the repeated injunctions of councils, and
the repeated attempts of prominent Churchmen to
encourage systematic teaching on the part of the parish
clergy, without realizing that the very multiplication of
such injunctions, in the absence of direct evidence that
they were obeyed, tells heavily against his own case.
Gerson, indeed, twice mentions such injunctions, but only

to imply that they were very imperfectly kept (II, 552 F and *De Laud. Script. Consid*. XII). And indeed we have the most definite evidence that this theoretical system of instruction was even less realized in practice than the average of medieval theories. Bishop Haymo of Hythe, founding an almshouse in 1337 for the special benefit of men of good position who had come down in the world, made it a *sine qua non* that they should know the Lord's Prayer, the Ave, and the Creed; and we have many other indications to show how necessary his stipulation was. Berthold of Ratisbon, a mission-preacher of European fame, complains more than once that children reach the age of seven, fourteen, even twenty, without even learning their Lord's Prayer; and the same complaint was made by others, in those ages when the clergy exercised the most despotic disciplinary powers over their parishioners. Again, the fifteenth-century translation of the *Gesta Romanorum*, published by the Early English Text Society, shows the grossest ignorance of the Bible—texts from the Apocalypse, Ezekiel and Canticles are quoted as from the Gospels; two from the Gospels and one from Job are attributed to St Paul; Genesis is confused with Psalms, Isaiah with St James; scraps of the Fathers are palmed off as Bible texts. The Knight of La Tour-Landry, though his book was the most popular educational treatise of the later Middle Ages, and he claims to have written it with the help of two priests and two clerks whom he had in his castle, shows a still deeper ignorance of the Bible. His history of Ruth has scarcely anything but the heroine's name in common with the Scriptural narrative; Boaz is not even alluded to; the whole story is of Ruth's struggle with her stepsons for her late husband's property! A well-known carol of the fifteenth century makes Herod execute St Stephen on the day after Christ's birth. The Franciscan Salimbene (A.D. 1280) bears incidentally the most damning testimony as to the Biblical ignorance both of clergy and of laity in the Italy (and perhaps the France) of his day.

He tells us how he had heard priests quote "a hundred times", *as a text from St Paul's Epistles*, the cynical maxim of sacerdotal conduct, "si non caste, tamen caute" ("if we live not chastely, let us at least sin with caution"). His contemporary Berthold of Ratisbon bears similar testimony in his complaint that "many thousands", persuaded by indulgence-mongers, "falsely believe that they have done penance for all their sins with a penny or halfpenny...and so go straight to hell". The Oxford Chancellor Gascoigne, two centuries later, is still more emphatic on this last subject.

We may glean from many of the medieval preachers a vivid idea of the ignorance and carelessness with which they had to wrestle. Let me quote from Berthold again. Some (he says) have not been seen in church for a month, or ten weeks, or even six months, though the women are better than the men. When they do come,

it irks some to stand decently for a short hour in church, while God is being served with singing or reading; they laugh and chatter as if they were at a fair. They talk in church across from one to the other, and boast and tell what they have seen in foreign lands, so that one may well disturb six or ten others who would have gladly held their tongues....And ye women, ye never give your tongues rest from useless talk! One tells the other how glad the maidservant is to sleep, and how loth to work; another tells of her husband; a third complains that her children are troublesome and sickly!

At this a cry of expostulation rises from the audience:

Yea, Brother Berthold, but we understand not the Mass, and therefore can we not pray as we had need, nor may we feel such devotion as if we understood the Mass. The sermon indeed we can follow word by word, but not the Mass; we know not what is being sung or read, we cannot comprehend it. If it were so that we understood the Mass, then might we pray far better to God and beseech His grace, and have greater devotion in the Mass with prayer and other good things.

Sir Thomas More also (whom Cardinal Gasquet has tried to press into the service of his theory) tells us how little the congregation understood the Mass; and Busch shows the same in describing how, during an interdict, the monks obeyed the Pope by suspending their Masses, without offending the townsfolk who demanded that these should proceed as usual. The brethren had only to ring the bells and play their organ in the choir; and the citizens in the nave were quite happy in the belief that Mass was being said behind the screen. It is indeed difficult to realize how little the ordinary medieval layman really comprehended of the Church services, and how perfunctory was even his personal attendance. From very early times we find complaints that parishioners went in and out pretty well as they chose during Mass. As St Bernardino puts it,

There are many ignorant folk who, when the priest is celebrating, come drunken from the taverns or wait outside the church, talking of their oxen and worldly matters, and even of obscenities; nor do they enter the church until the elevation, at which they gaze in utter irreverence, with their heads partly or wholly covered, and their stiff knees scarcely bowed; and thus—after running noisily to see the Body of Christ, half inside and half outside the church—suddenly, after the barest glimpse of Him, they run off again as hastily as if they had seen not Christ but the Devil!

The same complaint was made at the Council of Cologne in 1536, and repeated only five years later. The Knight of La Tour-Landry, writing for the instruction of his motherless daughters, confesses his own adhesion to that rigorous school which "susteineth that none shulde not speak no manner thing whiles they ben atte masse, and in especial atte the gospelle". Members of the third Orders of St Dominic or St Francis, among other very strict rules of conduct, were pledged not to talk during Mass or sermon. Among the brief and solemn instructions which St Louis gave to his sons upon his deathbed, was the warning to "attend the service of Holy Church devoutly and without jesting talk;...more especially in the Mass when the consecration is made". Nor was this irreverence by any means confined to the laity. A Bull of Clement V (1311) complains that many clergy gabble through or cut short the daily services, "with frequent intermixture of idle, profane, and unhonest discourse"; Gerson asserts that the clergy laugh and chatter during service "like old women at market". More than one set of Cathedral Statutes forbids conversation between clergy at a distance of more than three (or in some cases four) stalls from each other; and in visitations of great churches both in England and in Normandy it is constantly noted that those who should be performing divine service are laughing, talking, or even walking about instead. Moreover, even the most formal offices of religious education were constantly neglected. Sacchetti speaks of "a good many" who did not feel certain that they had been baptized, and consoles them with the assurance that God would take their faith as equivalent to the deed. Gascoigne says that many children died unbaptized through the fault of the monastic clergy. A constitution of Archbishop Peckham (1287) complains that there were in England "numberless people grown old in evil days who had not yet received the grace of Confirmation"; and similar evidence has survived from Germany, Flanders and Austria.

Amid all this negligence and ignorance, religious knowledge flourished only among the unorthodox. We know this on the testimony of their most determined adversaries.

They know the Apostles' Creed excellently in the vulgar tongue,

says Etienne de Bourbon in speaking of thirteenth-century heretics,

they learn by heart the Gospels or the New Testament in the vulgar tongue, and repeat them aloud to each other....I have seen a young cowherd who had dwelt but one year in the house of a Waldensian heretic, yet had attended so diligently and repeated so carefully all that he heard, as to have learned by heart within that year forty Sunday Gospels, not counting

those for feast-days; all which he had learned word for word
in his native tongue, apart from other extracts from sermons
and prayers. I have also seen some layfolk who were so steeped
in their doctrine that they could even repeat by heart a great
part of the Evangelists, as Matthew or Luke, and especially all
that is said therein of our Lord's teaching and speeches; so
that they could repeat them continuously with scarcely a
wrong word here and there. This I say on account of their
diligence in evil and the negligence of the Catholics in good:
for many of these latter are so negligent of their own and their
families' salvation as scarce to know their Pater or their Creed,
or to teach the same to their servants.

Berthold of Ratisbon says the same of the Jews, that they
knew their Bible better than Christian laymen, and were
therefore dangerous adversaries. Gerson also complained
that the neglect of religious education at Christian universities contrasted disgracefully with the careful teaching
given among the Jews (II, 761, 762). At the same time the
Church blindly attempted to right herself by suppressing
these unlicensed Scripture studies, instead of rivalling
them by the thoroughness of her own instruction in
orthodoxy: and even the enlightened and fair-minded
Johann Busch, who would allow the laity some religious
books in their mother tongue, disapproved of "such lofty
or divine books" as a translation of the Communion
service: indeed, finding one in the hands of some nuns, he
committed it to the flames (de Ref. p. 731). Compare with
this the express testimony of Busch's elder contemporary
Gerson.

We do not say that all have a right to possess or read holy
books—especially books whose difficulties need explanation
through other treatises and glosses of doctors—for the common
folk have neither wit nor learning to do thus: but they ought
to seek the law from the mouths of the priests. Yet it seemeth
not right to keep them from moral and devout works which
have neither difficulty nor ambiguity nor absurdity in their
translation, such as are the histories or lives or legends of the
saints, and holy meditations. Translations in [the case of] other
books are rightly blamed, since they offer more occasion for

arrogant error than for humble devotion or salutary learning. (*De Laud. Script. Consid.* XI.)

When perhaps the greatest and best Churchman of the fourteenth century wrote like this, we need not wonder that Tyndale found it easy to persuade men that the clergy condemned his own translation of the Bible mainly because they feared the exposure of their own juggleries with Biblical texts. Cardinal Gasquet's modern apology that only *unorthodox* translations of Bibles were kept from the laity is demonstrably false, and is contradicted even by Sir Thomas More, whom he strangely quotes as the principal witness in its defence.[1] More does indeed give a somewhat qualified denial to such sweeping accusations as those of Tyndale; but he admits that, while heretics spent great sums on the Bible, yet no orthodox printer of his day dared to print any existing version, lest it should be condemned and destroyed by the authorities. He thinks that the Bible needs to be masticated by the clergy before it is fit for the stomachs of the laity. He proposes the most ingenious devices by which the people may read a little of the Scriptures without learning too much. Let the Bible first be translated (he says) under proper authority by some good Catholic. Let each Bishop be provided with copies to lend in his diocese, but with infinite precautions, "to such as he perceiveth honest". At the honest man's death, the Bible must revert to the Bishop, lest it fall into dangerous hands. Moreover, even these honest readers may not always be suffered to study at will: some men are fit to read the Synoptic Gospels, to whom the Bishop would yet forbid St John: to others again he might permit Ephesians, but by no means Romans. It was a pity, thought More, that some such scheme of Bible education

---

[1] "This absolute denial of any attitude of hostility on the part of the Church to the translated Bible is reiterated in many parts of Sir Thomas More's English works." "It has been already pointed out how Sir Thomas More completely disposed of this assertion as to the hostility of the Clergy to the open Bible." (Gasquet, *The Eve of the Reformation* (1900), pp. 243, 246.)

had not been put into practice long ago (*English Works*, pp. 240 ff.).

Indeed, it was even more regrettable than he could have foreseen, dying as he did before the great upheaval. If, from the thirteenth century onwards, the clergy had rivalled or outdone the heretics in Bible study and Bible teaching, there might perhaps have been no Reformation; but the Roman Catholic Church would also have been very different to what we now know under that name. The Church against which the Reformers protested was one in which the laity at large had never known *why* they believed, and seldom even *what* they were supposed to believe. No sooner was full light thrown upon it than it began to crumble away; for the faith of an educated modern Roman Catholic differs in many essential particulars even from that of the learned and candid More. The more violently modern apologists emphasize or exaggerate the unworthiness of the persons and of the methods by which the Reformation was brought about, the more they compel us to seek other than personal causes for a change so sudden and so complete. In proportion as we are forbidden to explain it by the moral strength of the new doctrines, the plainest common sense compels us to surmise some fatal weakness in the old order of things: nor are we left to such surmises alone, for the impartial study of pre-Reformation records shows us fatal weaknesses in every direction. The people at large were not "robbed," as some men would now assure us, of the old faith. That which fell away from them at the Reformation was a faith which, in the true sense, in the sense not only of passive assent but of rational assent, they had never really held.

VIII

PRIESTS AND PEOPLE BEFORE
THE REFORMATION[1]

§ I

IT is difficult for the modern Englishman to realize, even remotely, the power of the medieval clergyman in his parish. Theoretically it was almost unlimited, and practically it was even greater if possible than that which Mr McCarthy reveals in his *Priests and People in Ireland*. In 1287, Bishop Quivil, of Exeter, published a series of diocesan constitutions which not only summarize the most important points of English Church law, but also add very valuable illustrative comments. These detailed instructions, dealing simply with the pressing needs of the moment, and in no way concerned with a distant posterity, throw, perhaps, more light upon medieval parish life than any other document of equal length. Just as the good bishop has no doubt that Jews are born to be the servants of Christians, so also he does not hesitate to remind the laity very plainly of their filial subordination to the clergy, a subordination which aggravates the sin of every trespass upon clerical possessions or privileges.

Unhappy wretches, walking in darkness!...is it not written in the Scriptures[2] "he that stealeth anything from his father or from his mother, and saith, 'This is no sin', is the partner of a murderer"? That man therefore is a murderer who robs Church money by rapine or cozenage. Is it not a plain sign of strange madness when the son seeks to set himself over his father, the disciple over his master! and when they would fain subjugate by unjust obligations him who (as they believe) can bind or loose them not on earth only but also in heaven!

Nor was this mere high-flown theory. Often as the Church maintained her claims against even the great and powerful

---

[1] Reprinted, by permission, from *The Contemporary Review* of June and July, 1907.   [2] Prov. xxviii, 24.

—and sometimes, to her honour be it said, less in her own interest than in that of pure Christianity—still oftener did she assert her rights over the common herd of parishioners. It was punishable to stay away from Mass on Sundays or holy days; to frequent another parish church in preference to one's own; to omit the yearly Easter confession and communion; or to break the ecclesiastical fasts. The archdeacon levied pecuniary fines on the immoralities of the layfolk as well as of the clergy—a system which lent itself to frequent bribery and extortion, as we know not only from Chaucer and his fellow-satirists, but also from the repeated complaints of Church councils. The tithes, again, constituted a land tax, income tax and death duty[1] far more onerous than any known to modern times, and proportionately unpopular. Not only were the farmers and cottagers bound to render a strict tenth of all their produce —theoretically, at least, down to the very pot-herbs of their gardens—but merchants, shopkeepers and even the poorest artisans were by the same theory bound to pay from their personal earnings this same tax of two shillings in the pound.[2] Moreover, the law was pitiless to the peasant. Tithes of wool were held to include even the down of his geese; the very grass which he cut by the road side was to pay its due toll; the farmer who deducted working expenses before tithing his crops damned himself thereby to hell. As Archbishop Stratford complained in the Synod of

---

[1] "A legatee is bound to give tithes on his legacy, even though it have been already tithed by the testator" (*Pupilla Oculi*, a fourteenth-century manual for parish priests, pt IX, cap. 18, sec. al.).

[2] Following St Thomas Aquinas, the Canonists decide that even prostitutes are bound to pay tithes of their sinful earnings, though the Church ought to refuse such contributions so long as they are unrepentant, "lest she seem to share in their sins". When, however, the woman has repented, or if her sin be secret to the world though known to the Church authorities, then the tithe may be taken. The very lepers were bound to pay tithes, with some exceptions; and the beggar was theoretically bound to contribute a tenth of his receipts from alms: though here of course the priest was bound in conscience not to accept it. (Aq. *Summa*, 2a 2ae, q. 87. *Pupilla Oculi*, pt IX, cap. 18, sec. am. *Summa Angelica*, s.v. *Decima*, § 7. Lyndwood, ed. Oxon. p. 195 *b*.)

London (1342), "Men straying blindly in damnable error stumble into the destruction of their own souls, paying [first] the tenth sheaf of their crops for the harvesters' wages, and thus by a false calculation rendering [only] the eleventh sheaf as tithe, contending that they may fairly pay their labourers' harvest wages from the crops before the tithing, and thus setting at naught the precepts both of the Old Testament and of the New".[1] It was further contended that the farmer was bound to cart his tithing-sheaves to the parson's barn; and that the tithe of milk must be rendered in the form of cheese, in which it was most convenient to the receiver. We need scarcely wonder that the laity, thus situated, excogitated many subterfuges of "excessive malice...to the manifest prejudice of ecclesiastical rights and liberties, and to the grievous harm of their own souls", which may be found set out at length in Stratford's constitutions and elsewhere. The most ingenious of these forms of passive resistance was that invented by farmers in Exeter diocese towards the end of the thirteenth century, the golden age of Gothic architecture. "Whereas", writes Bishop Quivil, "the ancient and approved custom in our diocese is that men should bring their tithes of milk in the form of cheese, some men maliciously bring the milk to church in its natural state; and (what is more iniquitous) finding none there to receive it, pour it out before the altar in scorn of God and of His Church." The priest, for his part, had the partial consolation of knowing that such prevaricators of tithes were destined to find their part in hell with Cain, and of proclaiming this solemnly four times a year from his pulpit. Persistent defaulters (of whom many remained even after such general warnings) might be first forbidden the door of the church, and then publicly devoted to the devil in this world and the next by excommunication with

[1] *I.e.* according to Bishop Lyndwood, of Matt. xxii, 21. The whole of this tithe question will be found very fully discussed in Lyndwood's *Provinciale*, ed. Oxon. pp. 185–201.

book, bell and candle, a punishment which often entailed the further inconvenience of imprisonment at the hand of the royal officers.[1] This practice of "cursing for tithes", which Archbishop Winchelsey enjoined upon each clergyman as a sacred duty, in the interests of his brethren of the cloth, was neglected only by a few saintly souls like Chaucer's model priest, of whom the poet writes: "Ful looth were hym to cursen for hise tithes". Wycliffe, of course, emphasised more than once the unbiblical nature of this proceeding; and even the orthodox and anti-Wycliffite Gower cannot help noting the frequent contrast between the hunger of the clergy for tithes and their neglect of parish work.

Nor were the tithes the only burdens of the kind which fell upon the laity. Apart from compulsory rates for maintenance of the fabric and general church expenses, which were perfectly fair and natural at a time when only a very small minority doubted the necessity of such outlays, other less defensible exactions were usual. It was conveniently assumed that even the most scrupulous parishioners must sometimes have failed to pay their full due of tithes; and, as any such retention constituted a mortal sin, the clergy claimed a "mortuary" on the estate of every dead parishioner in the direct interests of his soul.[2] This claim, as regulated by Archbishop Winchelsey in 1305, and repeated by Langham in 1367, was for the second best animal from the stock of anyone who had died possessed of not less than three; the tax might therefore amount to a succession duty of 33 per cent. on personal property, and in some districts it was frankly calculated on that basis. In Brittany, for instance, the clergy regularly claimed a mortuary of one-third of the dead man's personal estate; and the same custom evidently prevailed in some parts of

---

[1] The curse prescribed on these occasions may be found, in all its grisly details, in Myrc's fourteenth-century *Instructions for Parish Priests* (E.E.T.S. 1868).

[2] To realize the jesuitry with which this claim was urged, the reader should refer to Lyndwood, p. 20, note c.

England, as we see from a very interesting case enrolled among the Pleas in Parliament under the year 1330. Thomas le Forter, as executor, had paid what he claimed to be just mortuary on the estate of William le Forter; but the Abbot of Wenlock, as his parson, sued him in the bishop's court for a full third of the dead man's personal property, under the claim that this was the usual mortuary in that place. Thomas obtained a royal prohibition, setting forth that "exactions of this kind are hitherto unheard of by us and the people of our realm, and if they were tolerated in future they would manifestly redound to the oppression of the said realm", and therefore forbidding the bishop to hear the prior's plea. Parliament referred the case to a commission of three abbots, who decided, on the strength of a statute of Edward I, that no royal prohibition could avail to stop proceedings in the bishop's court on a question of tithes or mortuaries; we may take it for granted, therefore, that Thomas was condemned to pay. (*Rotul. Parl.* II, p. 38 *a*.) In most parts of Wales, on the other hand, mortuaries seem to have been unknown; and in some parts of England they were either unknown or considerably lighter than those here described, as appears from a statute of Henry VIII which will presently be mentioned. But, in the large majority of cases, it is plain that the claim was extremely onerous, and that, however strange the very idea of it may be to modern minds, it loomed very large on the struggling peasant's horizon in the Middle Ages. It may be freely granted that the Church was then, on the whole, the best friend the poor man had: she is so still, and so are all the Churches; but, as Ruskin very emphatically pleads in *Fors Clavigera*, we must beware of straining this argument to the breaking point (1871, Letter x); and certainly it should not blind us to many strange and undeniable facts in the past. Imagine for one moment the feelings of a struggling household—one of those large families, working hard day by day to keep the wolf from the door—who formed so healthy a proportion of ancient, as of modern, England. The breadwinner has just been taken, and the outlook would be dark enough in any case; but here comes the lord of the manor to claim for his mortuary (as he often might) the dead man's best beast. Next comes the priest—he who claims to live among his people as a direct spiritual descendant of Christ's Apostles—to take away the second best, in which he has claimed a vested interest from the first moment when the wretched peasant took to his dying bed; and the family must now struggle on as best it can with the worst of the three cows that once formed its stock. In some places the very bed itself became the perquisite of him who had knelt in prayer beside it, and spoken to the dying sinner of a Shepherd who gave His life for His sheep.[1] Contrasts of this kind appear to the poor in far more glaring colours than any words can paint; and, in spite of the fact that the parson, such as he was, might be the only approach to a friend whom they knew—in spite of the admirable self-sacrifice shown by many clergymen in that age, as in all ages and in all countries—we need hardly wonder that bishops based their constitutions, and popes their bulls, on the notorious fact that "the laity are bitterly hostile to the clergy". Before we can realize what actually happened at the Reformation, the story of the *Ancien Régime* must first be faced with unsparing frankness. Archbishop Winchelsey did indeed warn his clergy to "keep the fear of God before their eyes" in pressing these radically uncharitable claims; but, human nature being what it is, we need not wonder that Langham, half a century later, complains of the "too frequent quarrels" between clergy

---

[1] All the statements made here without further references may be verified on pp. 19–22 of Lyndwood. The clergy would deny the last rites of the Church to a sick man who ventured to alienate any possession of importance, since such alienations might materially affect their perquisites on his death. In Mr Fisher's admirable *History of England from 1405 to 1543*, p. 293, the significance of this fact is obscured by a slip. What St Germain says is not that curates *compelled* sick men to sell, but that they *prohibited* them. See his *Treatise*, fol. 24 *b*, and cf. Quivil's constitution in Wilkins, II, 158.

and people on this head, which he attempts to obviate only
by a more emphatic and detailed repetition of Winchelsey's
injunctions. These quarrels smouldered on, with frequent
bursts of flame, until the Reformation, as we may see by
the complaints of Church councils. In 1518 Cardinal
Wolsey revived an ancient constitution of the York province, enacting that, as the miserable earnings of many day
labourers scarcely enabled them to keep body and soul
together, therefore all who received no higher wages than
6s. 8d. a year should be held indeed to their Easter offerings
and similar payments, but excused from payment of tithes.
To put this in terms of modern money, a labourer at
13s. 6d. a week would be excused; but one whose wages
were 15s. would have to pay a yearly tithe of 16s., or more
than a week's wages, to his rector.[1] That this was felt as
a real burden by the poor can be proved from one of the
fragmentary Yorkshire visitations published by Canon
Raine. The parishioners of Masham are found enquiring
of the visitors in 1510 "also we desire to know what a
servant should pay to tithe for his hire, for as much as
draws ten shillings, for poor servants that hath but a small
wage to find them, it is sore for them to take so mickle".
The neighbouring parish of Kirby Malsherd put a similar
question in a briefer and more grammatical form: "We
desire to know what a servant should pay to tithe for ten
shillings wage".[2]

In 1529, again, on the eve of the Reformation, Parliament dealt by statute with the burning question of "corpse
presents". It was enacted (1) that mortuaries should be

[1] In addition to the 6s. 8d. money wage, which was tithable, the
labourer in question would receive board and lodging equivalent to
1s. a week. Money was then ten or twelve times more valuable than at
present; so if we take the extreme figure, and multiply these sums by 12,
we find that a labourer at 6s. 8d. a year wages, plus board and lodging,
would receive the modern equivalent of 13s. 6d. a week, and one
whose wages were 13s. 4d. a year would receive the equivalent of 15s. a
week. This latter would have to pay on his 13s. 4d. a tithe of 1s. 4d.,
which in terms of modern money would be 16s. See Thorold Rogers,
Six Centuries of Work and Wages, pp. 354 and 539.

[2] *York Fabric Rolls* (Surtees Society), p. 263.

commuted for a tax amounting at the most to $1\frac{1}{3}$ per cent., and in some cases to only a third of that amount; (2) that nothing at all should be paid for any man whose personal property amounted to less than ten marks (or about £80 modern currency); (3) that the inveterate abuses of exacting mortuaries in duplicate for certain cases, or for wives and children who had no legal property, should be altogether abolished. So radical was the change effected by this statute, in theory at least, that the orthodox lawyer St Germain, writing two years later, speaks of it as a total abolition of the old mortuary system. The statute, he says, had been rendered necessary by the patent injustice with which corpse-presents had been claimed, and the "variances" and "grudges" which this had caused between clergy and people. A tax which, in its origin, claimed to be no more than just compensation for tithes withheld from the Church, had gradually grown to be claimed not only for the death of a wife, who owned no property and could owe no tithes, but even for "servants and children, as well infants as others....And the mortuaries must be delivered forthwith, or else the body should not be buried....And under that manner mortuaries increased daily in many places, and of likelihood would have gone further if they had not been stopped in time. And they were in many places taken in such manner as made men to think that the curates loved their mortuaries better than their lives". Nor was even this parliamentary prohibition of immediate avail, for St Germain complains that "many curates, not regarding the King's statute in that behalf, persuade their parishioners when they be sick to believe that they cannot be saved, but they restore them as much as the old mortuary would have amounted to". Or, again, "if the executor at the first request pay not the money that is appointed by the statute, they will anon have a citation against him [in the Bishop's court]; and there shall he be so handled that, as is said, it had been most commonly much better to him to have paid his old mortuary than the costs and

expenses that he shall pay there ".[1] St Germain's assertions
are corroborated partly by the statute of 1529 itself, partly
by the famous cases of William Tracy and Richard Hunne.[2]
It was commonly believed by the London citizens that
Hunne, a well-to-do burgess, had been first accused of
heresy and then murdered in prison, merely because he
had withstood his parish priest who claimed the shroud
of his dead child as a corpse-present; and if, as seems just
possible, Hunne did in fact commit suicide in prison to
avoid the stake, the suspicions of the citizens are none the
less significant, as pointing to a widespread conviction
even among respectable men that the clergy were capable
of going to any extreme in defence of these ancient abuses.

Besides tithes and mortuaries, there were also "oblations" or offerings at Mass on certain feast-days. It was
admitted that these (like mortuaries) had at first been purely
voluntary; but already in the thirteenth century the clergy
insisted on them as a right, resting on the canonical
principle that long custom, if laudable in itself, acquires
the binding force of law—and what custom could be more
laudable than that a layman should offer to God for the
remission of his sins? These offerings were practically
treated in most cases as personal perquisites of the clergy,
and they were often extorted with the most cynical disregard of religious proprieties. From at least 1217 onwards,
different Church councils attempted to check priests who
began their examination in the confessional with enquiries
as to non-payment of tithes, and who refused to administer
the Holy Sacrament to parishioners in arrear with their
Easter offerings (Wilkins, I, 549). Towards the end of the
same century, this prohibition had to be renewed in stronger
language, "lest by this taking of money with one hand
while Christ's body is offered with the other, the mystery
of our Redemption be bought and sold". But the acts of
succeeding councils show the same continual struggle

---

[1] *Treatise concerning the Division, etc.*, ix.
[2] See Tyndale, III, 269 (Parker Soc.), and Fisher, *loc. cit.*

against trading in holy things, especially against injunctions of pecuniary fines in the confessional, whether nakedly or under the thin disguise of Masses to be said in the parish church, and therefore to the profit of the priest who imposed them. Wycliffe's complaints on this head are borne out by unexceptionable documents; and, more than ten years after Luther had raised the standard of revolt, such refusals to administer the communion to defaulting parishioners were perhaps more frequent in England than they had ever been before (see St Germain, *loc. cit.*). They ceased only with the abolition of the system which had given them birth; but, if we may believe Father Crowley and Mr Michael McCarthy, whose evidence has (I believe) never been fairly met, similar systematic extortions by means of Church sacraments are still among the chief emoluments of the Roman Catholic clergy of America and Ireland.[1]

A plentiful source of income to the clergy, and of scandal to the thinking laity, was the abuse of Indulgences. All our cathedrals, and many of our great churches, owe much of their magnificence to these Indulgences, which were frequently collected by absolutely unscrupulous rascals, as we know not only from such satirical pictures as Chaucer's *Pardoner*, but from equally plain complaints on the part of Popes and Church councils during the three centuries preceding the Reformation. About 1250, the great mission-preacher Berthold of Regensburg stigmatised such "penny-preachers" as "murderers of souls", who do indeed succeed in adding church to church and prelacy to prelacy, but meanwhile betray many thousands of men and cast them into the nethermost pit of hell (*Pred.* i, 393 and *passim*). The council of Mainz, in 1261, complained that they destroyed real Church discipline, and that much of what they wheedled out of the faithful was spent in drunkenness, gambling, and lechery. In 1390 Pope Boniface IX complained that some of these pardoners went

---

[1] *The Parochial School*, pp. 255–9, 312 (the latter contains a quotation from a bishop); *Priests and People in Ireland*, pp. 313, 316.

about "falsely pretending to absolve even the impenitent
for the most trifling sums of money". "Our soul shudders,
and is justly indignant at the recollection of such things,"
adds the Pope; but it never occurred to him to abolish
the system itself, and the abuses which he deplored did
but grow as years went on. Those who care to see how
many Church councils repeated similar complaints between
this date and the Reformation may consult Dr Lea's
learned treatise on *Indulgences*, pp. 287, 288. But Dr Lea
has not noticed the strongest evidence for England. In
1450, Chancellor Gascoigne complained of these abuses
in words similar to, but even stronger than, those which
were used by the fathers of the Church at the contemporary
council of Salzburg (1456). He wrote:

Sinners say nowadays, "I care not what or how many evils
I do before God, for I can get at once, without the least difficulty, plenary remission of any guilt or sin whatsoever through
an Indulgence granted me by the Pope, whose written grant I
have bought for fourpence, or for the stake of a game of ball";
for, indeed, these granters of letters of Indulgence run about
from place to place and sometimes give a letter for twopence,
sometimes for a good drink of wine or beer, sometimes to pay
their losses at a game of ball, sometimes for the hire of a
prostitute, sometimes for fleshly love. And Pietro da Monte,
who, about the year 1440, collected much money for Indulgences granted by Pope Eugenius, when he went on board his
ship to leave England, said to Dr Vincent Clement, "By God,"
he said, "Pope Eugenius shall never have a single penny of
these sacks filled with money, unless he first send me letters of
promise for the Archbishopric of Milan".[1]

---

[1] *Lib. Ver.* p. 123. In the face of this and several almost equally
bitter complaints from so distinguished and orthodox a churchman
as Gascoigne, it is difficult to understand how Abbot Gasquet can
write "There is no evidence that [an indulgence] was in any way
interpreted as a remission of sin, still less that any one was foolish
enough to regard it as a permission to commit this or that offence against
God....It is clear that abuses of the system were, so far as England
at least is concerned, neither widespread nor obvious" (*Eve of the
Reformation*, pp. 437, 439). It was in very natural reliance on these
statements of his fellow-Benedictine that Bishop Hedley attempted
to defend the system by arguments which are historically quite un-
tenable (*Nineteenth Century*, Jan. 1901).

Pietro did, in fact, obtain only the bishopric of Brescia;
but these embezzlements were, for centuries before the
Reformation, equally notorious and scandalous to the laity.
St Germain (fol. 27 *b*) names among the chief causes of
estrangement between clergy and laity in England "the
granting of Pardons for money", and the disgust of the
nation at finding that so few of its contributions have been
spent on the pious purposes for which they have been given:
"and thereupon some have fallen into a manner despising
of Pardons". It is true that we owe to the Indulgence
system a great deal of our most beautiful architecture;
but we owe to it also much of that widespread disgust
of religious greed which led to the violent destruction
of many equally beautiful buildings, by enlisting so much
sympathy on the side of the iconoclasts. The office of
"pardoner" was not even theoretically abolished until the
Council of Trent (1546); and we find, as late as 1563, an
orthodox Roman Catholic complaining that men were
forced to buy Indulgences not only by the exhortations of
the preachers, but by the fear of not being reckoned good
Christians (Lea, p. 414). Indeed, the most shameless
methods were frequently employed to change what should
have been absolutely free-will offerings into compulsory
taxes. Gascoigne refers several times to the extortions of
Archbishop Kempe. He writes: "Woe, woe to the greed
of the Church! since, nowadays, about the year 1440, by
command of the rulers of York Cathedral, every parish
priest in the diocese is bidden to teach and enjoin in
confession, to every parishioner, before he receives absolution, such yearly payment to the cathedral fabric as the
priest imposes on him". These parishes (he says) were often
farmed out to the clergy, who collected far greater sums
than they ever paid into the fabric fund, and who would
extort forty pence in confession from a poor man who
could not really afford four (*Lib. Ver.* pp. 1, 121, 123).

It would be impossible in an article like this to give
even in the shortest compass a full list of the different

methods by which money was raised for Church purposes
in the Middle Ages; but I must add one last word about
what was perhaps the most profitable of all—the supervision and probate of wills. Apart from the very small
minority who were rich enough to make written wills,
every man was obliged to dispose of his property on his
death-bed by word of mouth, in the presence of his parish
priest. Let us put ourselves for a moment in the dying
man's place. Whatever else the poor wretch may believe
or disbelieve, of hell and purgatory he has never been
allowed to doubt. Whenever he entered his parish church,
there stood the great ghastly picture of the Last Judgment
staring down on him from the walls—blood and fire and
devils in such pitiless realism that, when they come to light
nowadays, even sympathetic restorers are often fain to
cover them again under decent whitewash. A picture of that
kind, seen once or twice a week for fifty years, is indelibly
branded into the soul of the dying man; and, however little
he may have allowed these things to influence the conduct
of his life, however deliberately he may have over-reached
and cheated and robbed in his generation to scrape this
little hoard together, here on his death-bed he has at least
the faith of a devil—he believes and trembles. He knows
that gifts to the Church are universally held to be one of the
surest preservatives against the pains of purgatory; he has
perhaps even seen men burned at the stake for denying a truth
so essential to the Roman Catholic creed. What wonder,
then, if death-bed legacies to the clergy and to the churches
became so customary that the absence of such pious gifts
was taken for proof presumptive of heresy! and that in
some districts the dying man was compelled as a matter
of course to leave a third of his goods to the Church![1]
Moreover, this laudable custom, when once established,
would exercise a practically binding force over the written
wills, which themselves also were invalid until they had

---

[1] *E.g.* Synods of Cashel (1172) and Dublin (1348). Wilkins, I, 473 and
II, 746: cf. I, 675. These may, however, refer to mortuaries.

been duly "proved" in the Church courts. In spite of attempts by successive archbishops to cut down probate fees to reasonable dimensions, it was possible for Sir Henry Guildford to complain before Parliament, in the above-quoted year 1529, that he had been forced to pay 1000 marks (or £7000 in modern money) for the probate of a single will! A recent apologist, turning his eyes deliberately away from facts that stare us in the face even from the pages of Church councils, has declared that it "must always remain a mystery" how such vast sums were raised in the Middle Ages for church buildings and endowments. This was no mystery at all to our forefathers, who knew only too well how the money was raised, and only desired (as even the modern Irish layman now at last desires) to know a little more how it was spent. There was, indeed, far more lay control over the parish finances in later medieval England than in modern Ireland; but we find frequent records of clerical embezzlements, as might be expected at a time when the laity had so little power of enforcing their claims at law, and when Popes had been accustomed for centuries to collect, on the pretext of some future crusade, vast sums which they spent according to their own fancy. Gower describes how the priest sometimes lets his church fall into ruins, while his concubine flaunts her finery about the parish; and how the various death-dues wrung from the poor might well be spent in lechery and drunkenness by a pastor who neglected even the Masses due to the dead man's soul. This, however, takes us rather into another chapter of medieval parish life; for the present, it is important to emphasize the purely commercial causes which contributed to the Reformation in England, as afterwards to the Revolution in France. To quote St Germain again, one of the main reasons which made the sixteenth-century clergy so unpopular with their flocks was

the extreme and covetous demeanour of some curates with their parishes...and though many spiritual men be not fellows with them in the extremities, yet none of them that have been best and most indifferent have not done anything to reform them that use such extremities, nor to make them think that any default is in them in that doing, but rather as it were with a deaf ear have dissembled it and suffered it to pass over, and have endeavoured themselves more to oppress all the lay people that would speak against it, than reform them that do it (*loc. cit.* fol. 25 *b*).

I hope to sketch, in a concluding article, the social and moral relations between the pre-Reformation priest and his flock.

§ II

HAVING already dealt in this *Review* with the financial side of English parish life, I will turn now to the social and moral side. For it is impossible to understand how bitterly the Church dues of the Middle Ages were often resented, until we have realized to some extent the average parson—the Person of the parish *par excellence*, who by God's eternal laws possessed the right of taking tithes of all that grew, and the power of binding or loosing souls on earth and in heaven. If—as some argue in defiance of the obvious context—Chaucer's Poor Parson was no mere exception, but the typical parish priest of the Middle Ages, then the Reformation must remain for ever as mysterious and inexplicable as recent apologists have attempted to make it. If, however, the medieval clergy, while containing a fair proportion of such saintly and devoted characters as have seldom been lacking among any class of God's ministers, had yet drifted into a thoroughly false position; if the parish priests, less by their personal failings than through the influence of a worldly system, were too frequently idle, careless and ignorant; if, moreover, their ranks contained a far greater proportion of notorious black sheep than can be found in any modern denomination; and if, to crown it all, even the better clergy showed themselves more anxious to cloke the failings of their

brethren than to insist at all costs upon a radical reform—
then we have at once a sufficient clue, a moral and religious
clue, to the great revolution. Selfish and material causes
played too great a part in this change, as in all similar
upheavals; but to ascribe the Reformation to such causes
alone is to imitate Gibbon's cynicism without Gibbon's
extenuating circumstances. It is as easy to find personal
defects in the Reformers as to sneer at the gross falsehoods
and unedifying truths with which the early Christian
traditions are alloyed; but, when arguments of this kind
are unduly pressed, the simplest and truest reply is such
a *tu quoque* as Newman constantly used, as the Fathers used,
and as Christ used Himself. The Reformers, it is true,
were only men; but what manner of persons were those
from whom the Reformation delivered us? For centuries
the Church had attempted vainly, and not always even
sincerely, to reform herself. It is generally held, even by
her apologists, that she was in 1530 less pure than in 1230;
and though future students may very likely condemn this
as a somewhat superficial judgment, still it is agreed on all
hands that the 300 years preceding the Reformation had
brought no material change for the better. Yet now, 350
years after the Reformation, the difference is so enormous
that men are often tempted to reject the most definite
medieval evidence on no other ground than that it shocks
their present ideas of right and wrong! The very success
of the Reformation has become, after this lapse of time,
one of the chief bars to its full appreciation; and Protestants
may reflect with pride on the fact that so many modern
Englishmen can scarcely believe, even on the most unimpeachable documentary evidence, evils which our
Roman Catholic forefathers were tempted to accept as
ingrained and irremediable. From St Bernard to the
blessed Thomas More, the best churchmen saw clearly
that the Church was fatally weakened by the evil lives of
many clergy, and only despaired of getting better substitutes
even if the worse priests could be turned out. What man-

ner of men those worse priests were, and how numerous, must be told quite frankly sooner or later, if we are ever to have anything like a final verdict on the most vexed period of European history. After all, the writers who cry loudest for mercy towards their own dead can seldom resist the temptation of scalping a fallen foe; and some of them deliberately hoist the white flag at the muzzle of a loaded rifle. In common justice to men who are now scorned as knaves or fools for having shed their blood in that ancient religious revolt, it is necessary to ascertain the plain truth about the old order from which they broke away.

Among the most distinguished English ecclesiastics in 1450 was Gascoigne, Chancellor of Oxford University, who in his *Liber Veritatum* repeats almost to weariness that the clergy are ruining the Church. "Alas," he writes, "the man who nowadays undertakes the cure of souls either is very evil, or is good and perfect to no purpose: for if he do according to the works of many of his fellows he will be very wicked; and if he do not according to their works he will be reviled by many and despised by still more." He shows us how hard it was even for a determined bishop like Praty of Chichester to eject a notorious black sheep from his living, and how little most prelates were inclined to undertake such invidious duties: for by one bishop the love of sin has of late been fostered, since the parishioners of one rectory have said, "Now we believe adultery and fornication to be no sin; for if it were a sin our Bishop would have deprived our rector of his cure; for our Bishop knows that our rector has been publicly taken in adultery with his own parishioner, the wife of another man; yet the Bishop has not expelled him from his cure". Moreover, even at Oxford, where he had committed several rapes, this man was afterwards admitted to the degree of Doctor of Canon Law. (pp. 63, 32, 24.)

Some forty years later Dean Colet wrote:

O priests! O priesthood! O the detestable boldness of wicked men in this our generation! O the abominable impiety of those miserable priests, of whom this age of ours contains a great multitude, who fear not to rush from the bosom of some foul harlot into the temple of the Church, to the altar of Christ, to the mysteries of God! (*Life*, by Lupton, p. 71).

Again, only a few years before Luther's public appearance, the same cry of despair was raised by the great prelate who was so soon to suffer death for his loyalty to the Church: "And we take heed and call to mind", said Bishop Fisher, "how many vices reign nowadays in Christ's Church as well in the clergy as in the common people; how many also be unlike in their living unto such in times past, perchance we shall think that Almighty God slumbereth not only, but also that He hath slept soundly a great season" (*English Works*, E.E.T.S. p. 170). But it may be argued that we are in danger of interpreting too hastily, in their *prima facie* sense, these and the many similar medieval accusations against the clergy. This is, in fact, the approved line of apology nowadays, especially since the one historian who professes to have made an exhaustive study of the episcopal registers has assured the world that they and similar contemporary visitation records testify to clerical innocence. For this important assertion he steadily declines to give chapter and verse. I have already produced in my *Monastic Legend* and in this *Review* a small fraction of the counter-evidence in the case of the monastic clergy, and I will now do the same with regard to the parish priests.

There exist some, and probably many, reports of parochial visitations dealing with the spiritual offences of clergy and laity alike, ranging from inadequate attendance at church to murder and other felonies which, in a clergyman's case, could be punished only by the clerical courts. The visitor was usually a bishop or archdeacon, personally or by deputy; but in many cases a great church had its own separate jurisdiction over a considerable body of clergy and parishioners, and records of such jurisdiction at Ripon and York have been published by the Surtees Society— the latter, unfortunately, only in selections. A similar record has been published in Normandy, where in the Middle Ages, as now, the people and their customs resembled ours more closely, perhaps, than in any other part of the Continent. These are, so far as I know, the only documents of the kind accessible in print; but I have examined three other episcopal visitations of Norfolk parishes in manuscript, and will here give a brief summary of the total evidence.[1]

The most frequent offence noticed in these records is incontinence; and here the most remarkable fact is the altogether disproportionate number of clerical offenders. In editing the York records, Canon Raine has suppressed, as unedifying, nearly all "the cases of immorality with which every class was charged, especially the clergy in the Minster" (p. 242); but the Ripon Acts and the three manuscript visitations from Norwich diocese yield very plain statistics as to the "great multitude" of unchaste priests of whom Dean Colet complained. These four documents together record 276 presentations for immorality. Now, 276 grown-up people, with children to match, would make a population of at most 600 souls; and among 600 souls in the Middle Ages we should expect to find (following Abbot Gasquet's calculation) about six priests, or (according to Thorold Rogers) about twelve.[2] Therefore on the assumption that sacerdotal morals were neither better nor worse than those of the laity, we should

---

[1] Surtees Soc., vols. XXXV and LXIV; *Société des Antiquaires de Normandie*, 1880, pp. 270 ff.; Lambeth Library Reg. Morton, II, p. 75 ff.; Bodleian MS. Tanner, 100, pp. 56 ff.; and Bodleian Norfolk Rolls, No. 18.

[2] *Great Pestilence*, pp. 166, 205. In the case of Ripon we are not dependent upon such general calculations. The Chantry Survey of 1546 (Surtees Soc., vol. XCII, pp. 348 ff.) shows that there were twenty-eight priests (of whom five were non-resident) to 9000 people above the age of fourteen years. Yet the presentations of incontinent priests amount to twenty-four, while the lay cases are only 102. That is, the priests were presented *nearly eighty times more frequently*, in proportion to their numbers, than the laity. These figures are taken from records extending, with intervals, from 1452 to 1506, and I here adopt the editor's very moderate calculation in the Preface, although the clerical lapses are in fact more numerous than he notes.

expect to find among these 276 adult delinquents from six to twelve priests: while, if we prefer the more charitable supposition that priests were generally chaster than layfolk, we may hope to find only two or three clerical criminals among the 276—or even none at all, as might well happen in modern England. Yet the recorded fact is that *fifty-six* priests are to be found among these presented delinquents. The clergy, that is, formed perhaps only one-fiftieth, and at most one-twenty-fifth of the total adult population; yet they supplied one-fifth of the prosecutions for incontinence; or, in other words, they appear in these records as from five to ten times less respectable than their parishioners.[1]

Moreover, the matter-of-course way in which these delinquencies were treated is, if possible, more significant than mere arithmetical statistics. This can only be realized by specimens from the documents themselves, which I will give here as fully as my space will permit. I take them from Cardinal Morton's Norfolk Visitation of 1498 (foll. 76 ff.), and in the order in which the scribe has happened to record them.

Upwell, Sir Thomas Welbenen, chaplain of the parish, is noted of the crime of incontinence and incest[2] with Joan Brandhous, late of the same village, for that the said Joan, as it

---

[1] I here count the *presentments* only, without discussing the so-called "purgation" of many culprits. For reasons which will at once be suggested by Gascoigne's words quoted below, a greatly disproportionate number of clergy were able to "purge" themselves: but, even if we assume the innocence of all those who so purged themselves, the unquestionably guilty priests are still numerous out of all proportion to the laity—at Ripon, more than fifty times. It may no doubt be truly urged that the clergy lived under close scrutiny, and that mere statistics of this kind are apt to exaggerate the proportion of their actual guilt; but, whatever allowances we make, the indisputable fact remains that large numbers of priests were solemnly charged with immorality by their responsible parishioners—a fact which, without going further, would at once explain the moral force of the Reformation. I may add here that I shall be grateful to any other scholar who will take the trouble to verify my figures, and discuss them publicly if he thinks they need any correction.

[2] This only means that Joan was his spiritual daughter—*i.e.* his parishioner and his penitent at the confessional.

is reported, has thrice given birth to children in his house. He was cited and appeared personally at the accustomed place in Norwich Cathedral on the 6th July and confessed the aforesaid crime, wherefore the Bishop's commissary assigned and enjoined on him the penalty recorded below. The same Sir Thomas is noted of the crime of incest with Alice Bateman, blood-sister to the aforesaid Joan Brandhous, whom, as it is reported, he formerly kept as his concubine, carrying about with him at his [or her] will from place to place, committing with her the crime of incest, for which transgression she performed the public penance assigned her by Master Simon Dexter. On the 6th day of July he appeared before the Commissary in Norwich Cathedral and confessed the transgression. Whereupon the Bishop's Commissary then and there enjoined on him that on the Sunday next following he should walk before the cross in procession round the Cathedral of Norwich, in penitential guise, clad only in his shirt, with a lighted wax candle of the value of fourpence in his hand, and offer the same at the High Altar.

For the two Sundays next following, he was to make the same penitential procession in a short gown, bare-headed and bare-legged: on the fourth Sunday, in his shirt again in his own church of Upwell; and on some other feast-day the same penance was to be repeated in the parish church of Huntingdon, where no doubt one of the ladies was living.

This is one of the worst cases; and the punishment, however far short of the summary dismissal which would have been his lot nowadays, must still have had some real deterrent effect if it was really enforced. The next following is the least grave of the cases recorded (fol. 76 *a*): "*Bexwell.* Sir William Salter, Rector, keeps suspiciously a certain Joan who dwells suspiciously with him in his house". He appeared at Norwich and pleaded *not guilty*, whereupon he was put through the usual form of "compurgation", which could be claimed by any clerk accused of a transgression not too manifest to be disputed, and which simply consisted in bringing a certain number of witnesses to swear to their belief in the innocence of the accused. This primitive ordeal, though far from being a meaningless form in the hands of a really strict bishop, was yet in most cases equally far from a Solomonian procedure; and Chancellor Gascoigne, in the middle of the fifteenth century, entered a public and most emphatic protest against it as "an occasion of intolerable iniquities", which had "rendered many men indifferent to perjury" (*Munim. Acad.* R.S. pp. 536–7). To Gower, too, the whole thing seemed a sorry farce. The layman (he says) was pretty sure of losing money for his spiritual delinquencies, but the cleric escaped with the connivance of his brother-clerics; and indeed the visitations show, as we might have expected even *a priori*, that the cleric succeeded far more often than the layman in producing the necessary support. In the case of this particular Norfolk clergyman, the commissary required three clerical and three lay testimoniators, one of whom must be of gentle birth. He succeeded in collecting them, and was therefore acquitted. The third case on the list appears on fol. 76 c: "Sir John Richardson, Rector of Reymerston, is noted of suspicious intimacy with Agnes, wife of Thomas Evey". He pleaded not guilty, and was ordered to purge himself with the help of three priests and three layfolk of honest conversation. He failed in his purgation, could show no further cause why he should not be convicted, and swore on the Gospels to accept due penance—one instance out of dozens that could be quoted to show the difficulty of punishing these criminous clerks, for the law subjected them nominally to immediate and condign punishment, oath or no oath. The penance enjoined in this case was (1) to abstain from celebrating Mass for two months (by which the faithful were likely to suffer more than he); (2) to pay 13s. 4d. "for pious uses"; (3) to offer a candle of the value of fourpence before the altar of the Holy Trinity in Norwich Cathedral, and devoutly say then and there five paternosters, five aves, and five creeds.

These, the first three taken as they happen to come, are

thoroughly typical of the nine cases reported on this visitation. One other had "purged himself", but still lived under some suspicion; another succeeded in proving that the adultery had been committed before he was in priest's orders, and was only suspended from Mass for a month. One of the rest confessed; the remaining three tried to take their chance of compurgation, though each charge rested on the birth of children—in one case of several children—in their houses! These three naturally failed to purge themselves, and were condemned to penances similar to those above described, together with fines for the Cathedral fabric.

I have ventured above to hint a doubt whether the sentences of penance were strictly carried out. These Norwich visitations are too occasional to throw much light on the matter; but in the similar records of Ripon and Southwell[1] we find that the nominal penance was, in fact, constantly relaxed. At Ripon, for instance, the full sentence on erring priests is recorded in five cases; in only one was it actually performed. In one case the culprit redeemed it for a private penance and a fine of 3s.; in the other three, it was rendered for similar fines without even the private penance. For instance (p. 126, A.D. 1467), an incontinent chaplain is condemned

to stand or kneel in his surplice, with head and feet bare, reading in the Psalter at the church font, for three Sundays, from the beginning of his hour of penance until the advent of the procession to the church: then he shall rise and lead the procession to the choir door, kneeling and praying there over the said Psalter until the end of High Mass, with a wax candle of a pound's weight in his hand, and to beg and obtain pardon of the canons. Afterwards [proceeds the record quietly], he compounded with our office for his penance, redeeming it for a sum of 3s. 4d. to be applied to the Canon's alms.

In fact, the ordinary clerical tariff of "redemption" was evidently about 1s. per day; for, on p. 3, six similar

[1] Ed. A. F. Leach, Camden Soc., N.S.; see esp. Introduction, p. 85.

Sundays of shame are remitted for a fine of 6s. For the lower (and therefore poorer) orders of clergy, redemption was easier still; one of them (p. 36) escaped six "whippings in front of the Cross" at the easy rate of 2s. for the lot. One layman, on the other hand, had to pay £10 to escape six public whippings, unless we have here a clerical error (p. 123). But clerics and layfolk alike seem to have preferred the money fine, and this naturally suited the canons also, who loved not the blood of a fustigated sinner, but knew very well what to do with his fine. It is worth noting that this trade in sins was vainly discouraged by earlier Church councils; that the strictly orthodox Gower condemns it even more strongly than Chaucer,[1] and that it was one of the chief causes which frustrated all attempts at reformation, until the violent interference of the laity in the sixteenth century dealt the system a fatal blow.

The Norfolk records, as I have said, are not continuous, and the Ripon clergy were only quasi-parochial; so that it is difficult to gather from them the full effect on the parishes themselves of these very frequent clerical immoralities. To get a clear idea of this we must go to Normandy for the thirteenth-century visitations of Odo Rigaldi, and the fourteenth-century records of Cerisy. These last give us almost continuous statistics for four parishes during a period of thirty years (1314–46, with three omissions). In that narrow area eighteen public scandals are recorded, on the part of eight different priests. Perhaps the worst parish (though Deux Jumeaux is nearly or quite as bad) is Littry. Here, in 1332, the priest is reported as incontinent, and swears (like his Norfolk brother) to accept whatever fine the visitors may think fit. In 1341 he "keeps the same girl notoriously as a concubine" and has a child, is again ordered to pay a fine, and

---

[1] *Mirour de l'Omme*, v. 20,089 ff. In a passage of bitter indignation, too long to quote here, he says, "in all countries men may nowadays buy off their sins of the flesh...without repentance...thus our Dean covets sin rather than honesty: for he finds the prostitute more profitable than the nun".

swears to abjure his partner on pain of forty *livres*. Later
on in the same year he is again reported; again in 1342 and
1344, when he has two or more children. In 1346 the
same report is made; he is fined now ten *livres*, and she
five—the two together amounting to about £60 or £80
of modern money. Whether this was paid we shall never
know, for at this moment began the cruel ravage of
Normandy by Edward III, and the records fail almost
altogether for thirteen years. The contemporary visitation
of Norwich City (A.D. 1333) is not a whit more creditable;
one of the parish priests was charged with three different
women.[1] And these things were happening not only in
the lifetime of men who might have spoken with others
who had heard the living voice of St Francis, but also
before the Black Death. It is necessary to lay special
emphasis on this, in view of a spacious theory lately
started, and already popular even among well-read Anglicans. Now that the progress of historical research has
made it impossible even for apologists to ignore the
terrible corruptions of the later medieval Church, it is
contended that faith and discipline were still reeling, in
1518, under the blow dealt to Europe by the Great Pestilence of 170 years before—which, however, had been looked
upon at the time as the merciful interposition of a just
God, for the rekindling of a faith already decayed and for
the revival of purer discipline. This strictly Biblical view
of the great scourge was also, until recently, that of
orthodox Roman Catholicism: *mais on a changé tout cela;*
and sainted apologists of the past like Bonaventura, Fisher
and More would be startled to find how much has been
done of late years to make straight the crooked ways of

---

[1] The plea so often urged, that these connections were a sort of
morganatic marriages, will not bear examination: constantly the co-
respondents are married women, or several women, or common
prostitutes. By the end of the thirteenth century, all pretence of
legality had been stamped out of these connections in England, though
it apparently lingered longer in Germany, in Wales, and (tell it not
in Gath!) in Ireland.

Providence. As Abbot Gasquet assures us, "to the Church the scourge of 1349 must have been little less than disastrous"; "the immediate effect on the people was a religious paralysis"; "it is a well-ascertained fact, strange though it may seem, that men are not as a rule made better by great and unusual visitations of Divine Providence" (*Henry VIII*, 1, 6; *Great Pestilence*, pp. xvii, 216). This "well-ascertained fact" must indeed seem strange to all theists of every description; stranger, still, perhaps, to those who have heard that the Bombay plague has made the Hindoos more serious, even while it has shaken their faith in traditional Hinduism; and, indeed, the "fact" is simply one of those patent absurdities from which no subtlety of intellect can, in the long run, save the professional apologist. It would be instructive to dwell a little longer on this philosophy of history, and to imagine what it must feel like to live in a world in which the Almighty, with all His excellent intentions, is capable at times of perpetrating blunders too disastrous to be remedied even by an Infallible Church! But, in the case of Abbot Gasquet, it is always even more instructive to verify his documentary references. His theory is built on three main pillars: (1) that the clergy showed special devotion during the plague; (2) their ranks were consequently so thinned that it took generations to fill the dead men's places properly; and (3) that it is therefore only natural to find great abuses in the Church after the Great Scourge. Hence he draws the comforting conclusion that Luther gained a temporary success only because he struck at a Church still staggering under God's hand. I will attempt to confront these assertions, very briefly, with the documents on which they professedly rest. The third point is the only one on which the Abbot's references, though miserably scanty, are even approximately correct. He points out mildly and briefly some of the abuses of the later medieval Church, and leaves it to be charitably inferred that these were practically non-existent before the Black Death; which is as if a man should excuse his present intemperate habits by producing a list of police-court convictions "since my poor wife's death", without offering the least evidence to show what his life had been before that sad event. As a matter of fact, all the later abuses of any importance were rampant long before 1348; during the past century, at least, prominent ecclesiastics had been predicting that the vices of the clergy would prove the ruin of the Church; and it is equally difficult to understand how a medieval historian could be ignorant of this, or could find it in his conscience to ignore it.[1] On the first point, again (the supposed special devotion of the clergy), he makes out some sort of a case by suppressing the plain contradictory evidence of four of his own witnesses; by pleading in his own favour the mere *obiter dictum* of a modern antiquary who is far too careful and scholarly to claim that he speaks from a special and exhaustive study of the question, and by asserting "it is certain that the Bishops...remained at their posts", not only without offering any evidence, but again in contradiction to three of his own witnesses.[2]

With regard to the second point, we might very well ask, without troubling to verify references, "What sort

---

[1] This is the more inexplicable because many of the authorities whom he actually quotes lay stress on the general wickedness reigning *before* the plague, *e.g.* De Smet, *Collection de Chroniques*, II, 334, 347.

[2] The following are the four testimonies to priestly negligence which Abbot Gasquet has suppressed (figures in brackets refer to pages of his book): (26) Murat. XII, 926; (27) *ibid.* XIV (or XV), 123; (28) *ibid.* XII, 746; (34) Boehmer, *Fontes*, IV, 261. This last authority mentions the Pope's cowardly desertion of his flock: Dene and Ralph of Shrewsbury's register, both quoted by the Abbot, record how two English Bishops shirked their duties. In addition to these specific condemnations of the clergy, many other chroniclers record in general terms that the plague-stricken sick were deserted by *everybody*. Even when Abbot Gasquet does not altogether suppress such unfavourable evidence, he perverts it sometimes by changes or omissions: cf. (27) Murat. XVI, 286, and again his long quotation on p. 47. To estimate the full value of these suppressions, the reader must remember (1) that the Abbot is professedly engaged in enquiring how far the clergy rose to the occasion, and (2) that he quotes from the context of the suppressed portions.

of a testimonial is it to the Church to plead that its efficiency was so disastrously impaired for 170 years by a plague which carried off 50 per cent. of clergy and laity alike?" For there is no contention that the Church was under-manned: after, as before the plague, there was one priest at least for every 100 souls; and even Sir Thomas More, in his apology for the clergy, admitted that they were far too numerous. Abbot Gasquet's contention is that the plague crowded the benefices with more or less inexperienced men, not only for a short time, but for nearly six generations. In support of this he brings the evidence of Knighton, which is quite unfit to bear the stress laid upon it, and a tiny table of figures from the manuscript registers of Winchester. These are no doubt accurate in themselves, coming as they do from Mr F. J. Baigent; but the inference drawn from them is extraordinarily false to plain facts. They cover the institutions in the single city of Winchester during eleven years, and are designed to prove that the plague thrust into the benefices an enormously increased proportion of clerks in lower orders. But if, instead of confining himself to this ridiculously narrow area, he had taken the figures of a whole diocese, town and country alike, the Abbot would have found that the statistics from which he argues are wrong (incredible as it may seem) by *about one thousand six hundred per cent.*, a fact which makes this reference to manuscript episcopal registers as misleading as others which I have already exposed, and others again which I am ready to point out if necessary. Throughout his *Great Pestilence*, he has persistently falsified the actual evidence on the main questions. Of chroniclers who touch the point at all, the large majority assure us that the clergy in general did *not* show special self-sacrifice during the plague. Again, such statistics as we possess tend to show that they died in the same proportion as the laity, neither more nor less. Thirdly, instead of inaugurating a new era of youthful and ignorant incumbents, the plague accomplished what popes and councils had vainly attempted—it broke down the bad old system of putting ignorant boys into the best livings, while curates at starvation wages did the actual work. Let me give a typical instance from before the Plague. In Exeter diocese, between 1308 and 1324, 376 livings in lay patronage were filled up, and only 135 of these—scarcely more than one-third—were given to men in priest's orders! In many cases the presentees were not in holy orders at all, but mere tonsured clerks in their teens, to whom the bishop at once gave leave of absence for study at the university! These boys could of course do no parish work; that was done by cheap curates who had only the smallest and most distant prospect of a benefice. Into this state of things came the Black Death: half the clergy perished with half their flocks; 4000 livings went suddenly begging, and now the despised curates commanded the market. Like the agricultural labourers, they gained at this moment an advantage which no legislation was able entirely to wrest back from them; and though, on the eve of the Re-formation, it was again complained that very many parishes were served by incompetent hirelings in the absence of their incumbents, yet no later list of institutions that I have been able to find shows anything approaching to the scandalous proportion of boy-incumbents which stares us in the face from the pre-pestilence records of Worcester, Bath and Wells, Winchester and Exeter alike.[1] The Black Death did indeed deal a terrible blow to the *Ancien Régime*; it did indeed hasten the Reformation; but, like all other

[1] I have no space here to give the full figures; but I speak from an analysis of more than 1200 institutions, extending (with intervals) over nearly two centuries, and covering four dioceses. I omit the livings under clerical patronage, since a clergyman's own interests generally compelled him to present a priest. It is probable that no two workers would bring out the figures exactly the same: there might be legitimate variations of opinion even to the extent of 10 or 20 per cent.; but I dare boldly assert that no scholar, whatever may be his prepossessions, will arrive at a result even remotely resembling Abbot Gasquet's, or will refuse to endorse my conclusion that the Plague greatly diminished, instead of greatly increasing, the proportion of lower clerks instituted to livings. Cf. my *Black Death* in Benn's 6d. Series.

visitations of God, it left the world, on the whole, better, more serious, and more truly religious. That however is in itself an important chapter of Church history; and I have already exceeded the ordinary limit of space.

§ III[1]

ABBOT GASQUET'S recent book on this subject is assured of a wide circulation by the general excellence of the series in which it appears, the author's own reputation as an apologist of the Middle Ages, and the indiscriminate praise lavished on it, even by such journals as the *Guardian* and the *Athenæum*. The *Church Times* alone, as far as I know, has seen through its weakness, even on points of mere antiquarian detail; but nobody as yet has taken the course—always far the most instructive in Abbot Gasquet's case—of verifying his references. Critics might, indeed, plead the difficulty of the task, since there is only one unhappy footnote in all the 273 octavo pages, while chapter and verse references are frequently denied, even where the reader needs them most and they would have given no extra trouble to the printer; indeed, I have counted fifteen cases in which the Abbot withholds the very title of the book from which he is professedly quoting!* The list of mis-statements and misquotations on vital points which I am here about to give is therefore necessarily incomplete: it represents only the main cases in which my previous knowledge of the documents has enabled me to run him to earth without too great waste of time. Space forbids my referring to many others less important; and even these I am obliged to treat as briefly as possible, though I hope to add fuller quotations in reprinting this article, with two others on Medieval Parish Life, in about six months' time.

One of the chief sources of Church revenue before the Reformation was the Church Ale—a convivial meal held

---

[1] Reprinted from *The Churchman*, April, 1907.
* The notes on this section will be found at the end of the essay.

either in the church-house or in the sacred building itself, and therefore obnoxious to the Reformers.[2] Abbot Gasquet, of course, sets himself to whitewash this institution. He quotes all that is pleasant and picturesque from Peacock's paper in vol. XL of the *Archæological Journal*, which he further cites as his authority for the statement that "the drink itself was apparently a sweet beverage made with hops or bitter herbs. It was not the same as the more modern beer, but *was less heavy, and hardly an intoxicant*". It will surprise only those who have not been in the habit of verifying the author's references to learn that the crucial statement which I have here italicized is not only not to be found in Peacock, but is definitely and repeatedly contradicted by him. Church Ales (says Peacock) were "the direct descendants of those drinking-bouts of our unchristened Saxon and Scandinavian ancestors", who loved "something strong, heady, and heart-inspiring" at their feasts (p. 3). "They were originally solemn rites in honour of the gods or of dead ancestors; and so, when these feastings became Christianized, the objects of Christian worship—the Holy Trinity and the saints—were in like manner pledged" (p. 5). "We must not be too severe on our forefathers because they enjoyed coarse revelry and what we might perhaps think low society" (p. 10). Quoting the Puritan Stubbes's description of the participants in these Church Ales as "swillying and gullying, night and daie, till they be as dronke as rattes and as blockish as beastes", he adds: "There is no reason for regarding it as very much over-drawn" (pp. 11, 12). Lastly, he thinks he may safely identify a certain fragment of stained glass and a certain piece of sculpture as representations of Church Ales, because the figures therein are "in various stages of intoxication," and "hopelessly drunk" (pp. 14, 15). Moreover, Peacock remarks: "What will seem to not a few of us one of the most strange things connected with these festivals is the fact that, evil as their influence must have been, they seem to have drawn forth

hardly any remonstrance until the rise of Puritanism".
Of all this, which forms the very pith and essence of
Peacock's article, nobody would conceive the least suspicion from Abbot Gasquet's professed summary of it.
Out of the strong, under his deft touch, comes forth sweet-
ness; and this reckless misuse of authorities runs through
his whole book from beginning to end. There are, perhaps,
no contrasts quite so startling as this just quoted—indeed,
there scarcely could be. But of all his historically important statements—of all that profess to describe the real
inner life of the parishioners, and not merely the outward
pomp and bumbledom of the parish—there is scarcely
one which is not contradicted by irreproachable medieval
authorities, and frequently by the very documents which
he parades in favour of his assertions, however loosely
he may omit to lay them upon the table before our eyes.

He deals, for instance, with the custom of the Boy
Bishop just as he deals with the Church Ales.[3] An institution which, however it might be tolerated here and there
even by great churchmen, scandalized a man so little
scandalizable as the good friar Salimbene, and was actually
suppressed for its indecorum by the Council of Bâle,
wears an actual halo of sanctity in these pages (pp. 165
et seq.). The Sarum statutes are cited, but their complaint
of the "manifold disorders" and the "grievous damage
to the Church" is suppressed; nor is there a word of the
close connection with that Feast of Fools which Grosseteste and Gerson branded as "blasphemous" and "de-
vilish", or with those wild dances and profane songs in
sacred places which good prelates strove so vainly to
suppress, especially in nuns' convents.

Again, in his attempt to minimize the irreverent treatment of medieval churchyards, Abbot Gasquet speaks of
the customs as only "growing" in the latter part of the
fourteenth century, and as first mentioned in a Constitution
of 1367 (p. 159). This statement would, of course, fit in
admirably with his contention that all went pretty well

in the Roman communion until the great pestilence of 1349, which for a while disorganized society altogether; and that the Church is therefore rather to be pitied than blamed for the undeniable abuses of the later Middle Ages. But, unfortunately, the alleged fact is in direct contradiction with the documents on which it professes to be based—the Constitutions of different Bishops from the thirteenth to the sixteenth century. Archbishop Thoresby's Constitution of 1367 against holding markets on Sundays in churchyards *or in churches* (the italics mark another of his suppressions) is, in fact, not the first (as the Abbot asserts), but nearly the last of its kind. Between 1229 and 1367 there are eleven such episcopal injunctions recorded; while from that date to 1539—*i.e.* to the Reformation— there seems to be only one. Bishop after Bishop thundered in vain against those who " turned the house of prayer into a den of thieves "; and if such anathemas grow rarer in the century before the Reformation, it is probably only because a large number of prelates were then non-resident, and the bonds of discipline were notoriously relaxed.

Let me trace a third of Abbot Gasquet's most important contentions through the justificatory documents which he himself offers. "It is very generally stated," he writes (p. 15), "that [the impropriation of parochial tithes to monasteries, etc.] was one of the great abuses of the medieval Church redressed at the Reformation"; and he proceeds to combat this idea. Such impropriations were never made, he says, but "upon condition that the vicar should receive amply sufficient for his support and for the purpose of his parochial work." This statement, I may remark in passing, is flatly contradicted by a former argument of his own, at a time when the exigencies of his thesis required that he should exaggerate rather than minimize the poverty of the medieval clergy;[4] but I am rather concerned here to point out how little it accords with the evidence of a more trustworthy witness. The Oxford Chancellor, Gascoigne, writing in 1450, finds no words too strong to condemn what he calls the "robbery" of parish endowments by the monks under this title of impropriations. "The cure of souls," he says, "is ruined in England nowadays by the appropriation of churches"; and again, "The appropriation of parish revenues brings about the eternal damnation of many and even countless souls" (pp. 3, 106; cf. 195, and *passim*). Moreover, the whole University of Oxford had already made an equally strong complaint in their prayer for reform addressed to Henry V in 1414. Cathedrals and monasteries (the University asserted) swallowed up many parishes, "whence arises grievous desolation of the parishioners, the hospitable entertainment of the poor is withdrawn, and (what is worse still) the cure of souls is neglected" (Wilkins, III, 363). It is strange to pass on from these words to Abbot Gasquet's bland assurance: "The grievance of which so much has been made is an academic rather than a real one, and one of modern invention rather than one existing in the Middle Ages" (p. 17).

Again, he makes an equally false use of the evidence as to the hospitality exercised by incumbents. To begin with, he offers practically no evidence beyond the mere *theory* of Canon Law, which is just as legitimate as it would be to quote the rubrics of the Prayer Book in proof that all Anglican clergymen read the service publicly twice a day, and adhere to a fairly uniform and moderate ceremonial in church. Secondly, he cannot even thus make out his case without thrice misquoting the great Canonist Lyndwood almost as grossly as he misquotes Peacock (pp. 8, 84, 85; Lyndwood, ed. Oxon, pp. 132–4).[5] Moreover, even if Lyndwood's theory were in fact what the Abbot states it to be, yet we have the most definite evidence that it was constantly neglected in practice. For if Abbot Gasquet had been incautious enough to quote the *ipsissima verba* of the Constitutions on which Lyndwood comments, he would at once have cut the ground from under his own feet. After all the emphasis with which Archbishop

Stephen Langton had decreed in 1222, and Archbishop Peckham in 1279, that the poor parishioners should not be defrauded of their share of the tithes, it was still necessary for Archbishop Stratford to repeat their decrees even more emphatically in 1342. In spite (he complains) of theories to the contrary, "yet monks and nuns of our province, procuring appropriations of churches, strive so greedily to apply to their own uses the fruits, revenues, and profits of the same, that...they neglect to exercise any works of charity whatsoever among the parishioners. Wherefore, by this their exceeding avarice, they not only provoke to indevotion those (parishioners) who owe them tithes and ecclesiastical dues, but also teach them sometimes to become perverse trespassers on, and consumers of, the said tithes, and abominable disturbers of the peace, to the grievous peril of both monks' and parishioners' souls, and to the scandal of very many" (Wilkins, II, 697). Moreover, the Abbot writes equally patent falsehoods about the cheerfulness with which tithes were generally paid, and the popularity of the parish clergy—falsehoods which can be exposed from the very synodical decrees which he is constantly citing in his own favour! (pp. 14,20). We have it on the authority not only of the Bull *Clericis Laicos*, which Abbot Gasquet must surely have read, but also of many Church synods, that the laity were constantly at feud with the clergy. Again, probably the most frequent complaint of all, in Church councils and synods, is that of trespasses committed by the laity on Church privileges or incomes. Next to that, as I reckon roughly, come complaints of tithe quarrels: there are thirty-seven of these latter in the councils quoted by Wilkins between 1195 and 1540.

I can only deal in the most summary fashion with two other cases out of many in which the Abbot's contentions would be wrecked by the production in full of his own chosen authorities. His tenth chapter ("The Parish Pulpit") is in the main a réchauffé of Abbot Gasquet's own Catholic Truth Society pamphlet, and is written exactly on the lines thus indicated. While expressly recognizing the extreme controversial importance of the subject, he again deals with it mainly on the absurd assumption that medieval theories were always realized in fact, and studiously ignores the contrary assertions even of such well-known writers as Chancellor Gascoigne and Dean Colet.[6] Moreover, even his own evidence is shamelessly garbled before he produces it to the public. He himself, in another place, where the exigencies of his thesis required the argument, pleads that the practical futility of any particular legislation is always sufficiently proved by the two facts of (a) its frequent re-enactment, and (b) complaints of non-compliance.[7] Now, this double damnatory evidence is exactly supplied, in the case of medieval religious education, by Abbot Gasquet's own chosen witnesses, the Church synods! He therefore (1) disguises the fact of their frequent re-enactment (except once on p. 215, in a sentence so misleading as exactly to reverse the significance of the fact), and (2) altogether suppresses from his quotations and allusions the fact that the eighteen re-enactments during the period he chooses were accompanied in *eleven* cases with complaints of non-compliance![8] Convocation declared in 1413, for instance, that England was like a blighted tree for lack of the sap of wholesome doctrine; and the protest of the University of Oxford in 1414 complains of clerical unworthiness and incapacity with an emphasis which Wycliffe himself scarcely surpassed.

If, in this generation of easy publicity, such manipulation of evidence seems scarcely possible on the part of any man with a reputation to lose, let doubting students read carefully through the whole of Bishop Quivil's Constitutions (the historical value of which the Abbot expressly acknowledges, and from which he quotes fifteen times in his own favour), and then compare them with the extracts given in this book. I can here only briefly summarize the passages which, if he had honestly acknowledged them, would have destroyed his painfully woven apologetic cobwebs. In

one of his direct quotations he omits, without the least
warning sign, a complaint of the "grave scandal in the
churches and frequent hindrances to Divine service"
generated by the scrambling of parishioners for seats
during Mass. Three of his other citations, without equally
dishonest omissions from the text, blink no less awkward
facts in their immediate context—viz. (1) the "unhonest
games...stage plays and buffooneries [in churchyards],
whereby the honour of the churches is defiled"; (2) the
practice of paying private fines out of Church moneys;
and (3) the gross superstitions which, in Exeter as in other
dioceses, caused ignorant parishioners to "abhor" the
Sacrament of extreme unction (pp. 66, 197, 201). On
p. 207 he mistranslates the Constitution about marriage
to an extent which not only shows startling ignorance of a
very elementary principle of medieval Canon Law, but
also obliterates the fact that no medieval Englishman—
indeed, no English boy or girl—needed to drive to Gretna
Green, since they might at any time, and in any place,
bind themselves by a clandestine but perfectly valid
marriage without help of priest or Church.[9] Beyond these
grave misrepresentations, where the very facts lay under
his eyes, he omits all mention of the following other
matters dealt with by the Constitutions: (1) The dese-
cration of churches by farmers who, indignant at the
manner in which the clergy tried to enforce the tithes of
milk, would come and pour it out on the floor before the
altar "as an insult to God and to His Church"; (2) the
evidences of clerical ignorance and incapacity; (3) the
increase of crime; (4) the clergy who frustrated the archidiaconal visitations by carrying furniture furtively from
church to church; (5) the quarrels between clergy and
people about the offerings; (6) the prevalence of clerical
concubinage and consequent embezzlement of Church
property; (7) the clergy who haunted nuns' convents
"without honest and legitimate cause"; (8) the cleric who,
wishing to shirk daily service, suborns his clerk to deceive

the parishioners with a lying, "You're come too late to-day; the parson has just gone away"; (9) the layfolk who brought their dogs into church, or "made a tumult" during service; (10) the "damnable presumption" of the sompnours; (11) the confusions introduced into the Mass by the monks' habits of supplying appropriated churches with incorrect or worn-out books, in which the parson cannot find his place, and "the laity, at the sight of his ignorance, however innocent, begin to mock at him as a fool"; (12) the growing unpopularity of the parish clergy; (13) the difficulty of controlling pardoners with their fictitious indulgences and immoral lives; (14) the danger of venerating false relics; (15) the law that (in ninety-nine cases out of a hundred) the layman must make his will by word of mouth to a clergyman on his death-bed; and (16) the death-dues which the Church claimed out of his estate.

The foregoing heavy list is, as I have said above, far from specifying all the points on which he leaves his readers under very mistaken ideas of the actual evidence. I may add, in conclusion, that even on the purely anti-quarian side the book is very far from accurate. A poem is attributed to the author of *Piers Plowman* which all students of English literature for the last fifty years have known to be spurious; and, indeed, this quotation with its context is one of the passages (pp. 73, 76) which the writer has conveyed without acknowledgment from Cutts, whose book—though decidedly superior on the whole to that under review—is not even mentioned in the long list of authorities. Another quotation from *Piers Plowman* is so inaccurate as to make nonsense (p. 184). There is a bad blunder in the quotation from *Sir Gawayne* (p. 146), and even the Latin is far from blameless. But these are small matters in comparison with the systematic mis-statements by which he attempts to belittle our own "sordid age" (as he has called it) in comparison with the Middle Ages. This book will be read by hundreds of Churchfolk who are laudably anxious to know something of our past, but who would have no chance of checking the author's statements, even if he himself had supplied proper references. It is therefore important to enter a prompt *caveat* against his implications on all points of conflict between medieval and modern ideals.

NOTES AND ADDITIONS TO
SECTION III

1. The Abbot's neglect of these obvious guarantees for literary good faith is very inadequately explained by the General Editor's advice "to avoid multitudinous footnotes and references". Over and over again he mocks his readers with such meaningless phrases as "a writer says..."—"in the Episcopal Registers it may be seen that..."—"one sixteenth century authority states ..."—"in a sermon..."—"a chance story..."—"a writer in a late number of the *National Review*..." (pp. 17, 162, 172, 175, 203, 273; cf. pp. 2, 45, 94, 111, 140, 166, 175, 215, 220). The last of these quotations, which he twice adduces to prove the religious superiority of the Middle Ages to our own century, so stimulated my curiosity that I made up my mind to run it to earth. It then appeared that the words were from an interesting article by an Anglican clergyman who recently took a third class in the history school, who makes no pretence of writing here as an historian, and who must certainly smile to find himself quoted twice as a serious authority by one who enjoys such a reputation for special learning as Abbot Gasquet.

2. We probably have a local or rudimentary form of Church Ale in the long-established custom which so stirred the wrath of Archbishop Reynolds in 1325 (Wilkins, II, 528). "Certain sons of gluttony and drunkenness, whose god is their belly, hastily swallow the Lord's body at Easter, and then sit down in the Church itself to eat and drink as if they were in a tavern": whence come "manifold damnable errors", and "certain simpler folk...lose all distinction between the bodily food and the food of the soul, the very Body of Christ". A comparison of the numerous references to "scotales" and "compotations" in the episcopal injunctions of the thirteenth and early fourteenth centuries would seem to show that this practice, like some others, was violently combated during the Franciscan and Dominican Revival, but held its ground and was finally adopted in a somewhat more civilized form by the Church herself. (Cf. Wilkins, I,

474, 475, 530, 574, 600, 607, 624, 635, 642, 662, 672, 707, 718; Grosseteste, *Epist.*, pp. 73, 162, 317, 318.)

An attempt was made to put an end to the custom at the Reformation: cf. Archbishop Grindal's injunctions of 1571, that there be no "feasts, dinners, or common drinking kept in the Church" (*Works* (Parker Society), p. 135). In the seventeenth century, as Bishop Hobhouse points out in an appendix to his Churchwardens' Accounts (Somerset Record Society), Bishop Piers defended the custom against the attacks of the Puritans.

3. The first local council which attempted altogether to suppress this custom was that of Cognac in 1260. The decree of the Council of Bâle abolishes "that foul abuse practised in certain churches, whereby at certain festivals of the year some are blessed as bishops with mitre, crosier and pontifical vestments, others are clothed as kings and dukes, which in some parts is called the Feast of Fools, or of Innocents, or of Boys" (Labbe-Mansi, XXIX, p. 108).

4. *Great Pestilence*, p. 206, note.

5. Abbot Gasquet writes (p. 8): "Every rector and vicar throughout England not only regarded himself in theory as a steward of the *Panis Dominicus* (the Lord's Bread), under which name was meant charity to all that came to claim support; but if the laws of the English Church and Lyndwood's authoritative gloss mean anything whatever, this sacred duty was carried out in practice...."

So far is "Lyndwood's authoritative gloss" from bearing out this assertion, that it plainly denies the incumbent's duty of hospitality to *all* comers, and limits that obligation to poor parishioners in their extreme necessity, and to such travelling preachers as can prove their authority. A few lines lower down, again, the Abbot quotes Lyndwood as saying that "the clergy of the churches in England are well endowed, especially where the calls upon them for this hospitality are great"; and he repeats this with more emphasis on p. 84. What Lyndwood, in fact, says, is "ulterius [*uberius?*] dotari debent"—"they *ought to be* better endowed" than in other places; and his pious aspiration is thus made to do duty as a statement of fact. Thirdly, the Abbot writes (p. 85): "It seems to us, indeed, almost strange in these days to see what was the teaching of the medieval Church about the claims of the poor, and to remember that this was not the doctrine of some rhetorical and irresponsible preacher, but of such a man of law and order as was the great canonist Lyndwood ...the English canonists and legal professors, who glossed these provisions of the Church Law, gravely discussed the ways in which the poor of a parish could vindicate their right—*right*, they call it,—to a share in the ecclesiastical revenues of their Church". Here, again, after much painful search which even the roughest chapter-and-verse references would have spared, I can find nothing that bears out his main assertion. Lyndwood does indeed point out (pp. 133 ff.) that the bishop was bound, in theory, to compel the niggardly incumbent to give a fair proportion of alms—though even here he doubts how far this power holds good against the vested interests of monks and nuns. But how if the bishop neglects to appraise this sum to be given in alms? Then it is for the archbishop to compel him, answers Lyndwood gravely, though he knows quite well that it is quite beyond the archbishop's practical power to enforce upon his suffragans even so obvious and clamorous a duty as that of residence in their own dioceses![1] "Thirdly, I ask" (he pursues), "if the bishop has appraised this sum, have the poor any right of action [at law, to enforce it]? *It would seem not*: for, since the persons of these poor folk are uncertain, it cannot be determined to which of them the obligation [of receiving charity] applies"; and, though he continues discussing the question with a mass of other technical details, he comes back to the same point, that only the bishop or the archbishop can enforce the poor man's right in the courts.

6. I have already exposed this part of his argument in my *Medieval Studies*, No. 7.

7. *Great Pestilence*, p. 197.

8. The synods to which these refer may be found in Wilkins, II, 52, 54, 143, 176, 300, 416; III, 10, 59, 314, 315, 352, 361, 599, 620, 662, 712, 718, 829, 843, 844.

The constitution on this subject which was most frequently quoted by later councils was that of Archbishop Peckham in 1281. Abbot Gasquet does indeed base his argument on a reference to this constitution, but he takes care to soften down its most significant features. Peckham complains "we learn, by daily scandals, that the Lord's priests are many in number, yet few are his in truth (*merito*)": and he counts first among "their damnable negligences" the irreverence with which they consecrate, or reserve, the Lord's body. He then proceeds: "The ignorance of the priests hurls the people into the ditch of error; and the

---

[1] Lyndwood was a contemporary of Gascoigne's, who enumerates the unworthiness and non-residence of the bishops among the principal causes of Church corruption in his time, and complains that ecclesiastical discipline has become almost an empty form (pp. 34, 55, 63).

folly or ignorance of the clergy, who are commanded to teach the Catholic faith to the faithful, sometimes makes more for error than for sound learning". He therefore enjoins that all parish priests should, four times a year, expound in English to their congregations the Apostles' Creed, the Ten Commandments, the Duty to God and to one's neighbour, the Seven Works of Mercy, the Seven Deadly Sins, with their offshoots, the Seven Chief Virtues and the Seven Sacraments. "And, lest any should excuse himself on the plea of ignorance (though all ministers of the Church are bound to know these things), we here give a brief and hasty summary thereof." This summary occupies only two folio pages, and shows how elementary was the minimum which the Archbishop tried so hard but so vainly to enforce. For already again in 1287 Bishop Quivil, of Exeter, complained that ignorance was the mother of all error, and warned his archdeacons to enquire frequently whether the clergy themselves knew, and regularly expounded to their flocks, such elements of Christian teaching as Peckham had propounded. Soon again (1308) Bishop Woodloke, of Winchester, issued similar injunctions, with a preamble implying that they were sorely needed: "Since many ignorant and unlettered men, to the peril of their own souls, usurp the pastoral office, we enjoin our own official, together with the archdeacons and their officials, by the sprinkling of the blood of Jesus Christ, to enquire frequently, personally and carefully whether any other rectors and vicars are grievously unlettered". Four years later the Bishop of Durham held a synod to reform clerical morals and "remove the vice of ignorance". He complained of the transitory nature of previous reforms, and enjoined again, "lest our connivance should seem to give consent, and lest the blood of our subjects be required at our hands", that the clergy should, not only in theory, but in fact, teach as they were bound by canon law. And so on, to the very eve of the Reformation, for in 1518 we find Wolsey attempting again to enforce Peckham's Constitution, and explaining that he did so on account of its imperfect observance; while in 1529 Convocation resolved that bishops should take care in future to admit none to holy orders who could not construe the Gospels and Epistles in their mass-books. Most emphatic of all, perhaps, are the ordinances of Longland of Lincoln, in 1537 (Wilkins, II, 51, 143, 300, 416; III, 662, 718, 829).

9. Bishop Quivil does not say, and could not have said, that "no espousal or marriage was to be held valid" without the consent of a parish priest. "No one doubts what, at all events from the middle years of the thirteenth century until the Council of Trent, was the law of the Catholic Church: for the formation

of a valid marriage no religious ceremony, no presence of a priest or 'ordained clergyman' is necessary" (Pollock and Maitland, *History of English Law*, 2nd edn, II, 372). Indeed, Quivil expressly states, in the very passage which our apologist misquotes, that the present contract by mere word of mouth was valid, and must not be violated: only the parties must accept ecclesiastical penance for their clandestine marriage (Wilkins, II, 135). Indeed, Church councils not infrequently denounce the practice of getting married at inns, among scenes of riot. The reader should study the whole chapter of marriage in Pollock and Maitland in order to realize how justly the authors censure the "recklessness of mundane consequences shown by the Church in this matter", and "the incalculable harm done by a marriage law which was a maze of flighty fancies and misapplied logic".

To expose in detail all the mis-statements which Abbot Gasquet has crowded into this volume would need almost as much space as the book itself. Indeed, it would be difficult to find a better measure of the true moral causes at the root of the Reformation revolt than these desperate shifts of the ablest and most learned among modern English apologists of Roman Catholicism—for Abbot Gasquet, with all his shortcomings, may claim that title. He has spent a lifetime in collecting evidence of a certain sort—grievously one-sided, at the best, since he studiously looks away not only from the testimony of able heretics like Wycliffe, but from the equally damning witness of such great and orthodox Roman Catholics as St Bonaventura, Cardinal Jacques de Vitry, Gower, Chancellor Gascoigne and Dean Colet. But its one-sidedness is not the worst fault of his advocacy. Even after carefully packing his jury, he cannot afford to let the actual verdict leak out; only by constant suppressions or distortions of ancient writers can he make out even a superficial case for his own contentions. His writings do indeed serve their turn in the present age; but the next generation of Roman Catholics will suppress them as carefully as men already suppress dozens of equally able past apologists, whose methods move even their co-religionists to healthy, though somewhat tardy, shame.

IX

THE FAILURE OF THE FRIARS[1]

IN preparing an edition for English readers of that strange autobiography which Brother Salimbene of Parma wrote for the edification of his niece (1221–88),[2] I have often been embarrassed by the very wealth of my material. Those portions of the friar's story which are most significant for the study of thirteenth-century society are naturally just those which need, for the general reader, most explanation and illustration from other documents of the age. In many places, such full illustrations would have taken me too far afield, and I have been obliged to deal with them in separate essays. One of the most important of these subjects is the rapid decay of the Franciscan ideal—a subject often slurred over altogether, and never, so far as I am aware, thoroughly explained.[3] The friars, however they may once have been misunderstood in an age of bitter strife, are now recognized on all hands as the greatest of all Church reformers during the first fifteen centuries. But, far beyond this just recognition, there is a growing tendency to make party capital by whitewashing the friars,

[1] Reprinted by permission from the *Hibbert Journal* of January, 1907.

[2] See the *Nineteenth Century and After* of June 1905 for a brief account by the present writer of this too little-known chronicle.

[3] Karl Müller's *Anfänge des Minoritenordens* is confessedly a fragment. Lempp's *Frère Élie* deals with only one corner of the subject; Father Ehrle's articles in the *Archiv für Litt. und Kirchengeschichte*, however learned and illuminating, are often tantalizing in their avoidance of debatable questions. Professor Herkless, in his *Francis and Dominic*, has no space to do anything like full justice to the early Spirituals, whom he seems, moreover, to confound with their less defensible followers. Miss Macdonell gives some pleasant portraits from the earlier Spiritual circle in her interesting *Sons of Francis*; but her comparative unfamiliarity with other sides of thirteenth-century history often prevents her from grasping the real significance of the party. [Since this, an admirable essay has been published by E. Jordan in the memorial volume *St François d'Assise*, edited by Lemaître and Masseron, Paris, 1926.]

in contrast to correspondingly blackened pictures of the sixteenth-century reformers. The former, it is argued, were the real saviours of the Church: the latter were mere bungling marplots. This theory, however, impinges on one serious difficulty, for, in spite of Francis and Dominic, the Church was at least as corrupt in 1500 as she had been in A.D. 1200. To meet this difficulty the "Great Pestilence" theory has been devised; and we are assured that Luther found the Church still reeling helplessly under the effects of the Plague of 1349. But this again, even though supported by far more scientific evidence than has yet been adduced, would still fail to meet the facts of the case. Long before the Great Pestilence, good men despaired as deeply of the Church as their pre-Franciscan grandfathers had despaired. It would be difficult, I believe, to find a single writer between 1250 and 1350 expressing a real conviction that his own world was permanently better than the world of 1200. On the other hand, it is startling to find how many among the greatest Churchmen in this period—and especially among the friars—were haunted by an even exaggerated sense of the world's almost hopeless decay. Yet this striking fact is entirely ignored by the most popular Church historians; and the average reader, even though he be specially interested in Franciscan history, is seldom aware how rapidly the friars degenerated, or how directly the Roman hierarchy was responsible for their failure. The heroes of the *Fioretti*, of Eccleston, and of other noble Franciscan records, are indeed admirable to all time. But how many readers of the *Fioretti* realize that, within a century after the Saint's death, the very existence of such friars as Giles and Masseo and Conrad of Offida had become illegal? So far from condemning the sixteenth-century Reformation, the early friars are, in fact, among our strongest witnesses in its favour.

The story of Franciscan decay may be found written in the plainest characters within a few dozen pages of St Bonaventura's works: other documents (and they are many) do but corroborate the Saint's assertions, and illustrate his protest that only the bitterest necessity compelled him to speak. From his two *Epistles* to the Provincials of the Order, and his *Quaestiones circa Regulam*, we see how near the friar of the second generation stood already to the sturdy religious vagrant of Chaucer and Erasmus. He speaks of the idleness and viciousness of many, and the commercial spirit of the Order as a whole. Their importunate begging and legacy-hunting, the extravagance of their buildings and private expenses, their familiarities with women, are rapidly making them "wearisome and contemptible in divers parts of the world". The charity of the laity is naturally grown cold; the wayfarer fears to meet a friar as he would fear a robber. What is worse, these abuses are already so chronic and so widespread that many accept them as quite necessary and irremediable. So writes St Bonaventura; and other equally trustworthy contemporaries give us the same picture. The friar, whom you can no more keep out of your private affairs than you can keep a fly out of your plate, is often so unpopular already that the country-folk attribute the failures of their crops to the malign influence of these sons of Francis and Dominic. "St Francis cries aloud for reform, and the blood of Christ that was shed for us", pleaded St Bonaventura in 1257. Yet nine years afterwards we find him reiterating the same complaints; and a younger contemporary records the Saint's cry of despair: "I would willingly be ground to powder, if so the brethren might come to the purity of St Francis and his companions, and to that which he prescribed for his Order".

Paradoxical as it may seem, it was the Rule itself which made the keeping of the Rule impossible. In framing this code of precepts and restrictions, St Francis had deviated from that evangelical freedom and simplicity in which lay the real strength of his first teaching. By allowing his brethren to be formed into an Order under a formal Rule he assured the outward success and the essential failure

of his movement. At a very early stage, many of the most
enthusiastic friars had either perished under their im-
moderate mortifications, or only dragged on a broken
existence in the infirmary, where, in their own despite,
they set a dangerous example to the rest.[1] Among "the
multitude of those who entered in", few were proof against
the temptation of beginning on that lower plane on which
their worn-out predecessors were now forced to end. The
small luxuries which had become a sad necessity to the
seniors were claimed as of right by the juniors; and that
earlier prophecy was fulfilled: "Self-indulgence will grow
in the Order as insensibly as hairs grow in a man's beard"
(Eccleston, R.S. p. 69). St Bonaventura describes all this
in detail, complaining that the new generation of officers
in the Order, themselves relaxed in discipline, are fast
teaching the novices to be no better than themselves, "so
that the early brethren, so far from being looked up to
as examples, are now treated as laughing-stocks. Nay, by
so much less the men of this new generation know the
virtues of perfect brethren, by so much the more do they
imagine themselves to be better than their forerunners;
and, seeing that they keep certain examples of outward
discipline in divine service, or in processional entrances,
and in suchlike matters, therefore they dare to assert that
the Order was never in so good a state as now" (*Quaest.
XIX. circa Regulam*). His contemporary, David of Augsburg, speaks even more strongly: the most spiritual friars
"are thought lunatics and called heretics by other Religious"; "virtue is proscribed, and condemned as vice".

It was just this double movement in the Order which
made reform so impossible: this increase of pharisaical
formalism and observances and self-satisfaction, in proportion as the true spirit of Franciscanism decayed. This
alone can explain the headlong ruin of the strict Franciscan

[1] Cf. Étienne de Bourbon, p. 422, for the extent to which even St
Bernard, after ruining his own health, was obliged to set a dangerous
example to the rest.

ideal. Roger Bacon, writing about the time of St Bonaventura's death, mourns that both Franciscans and Dominicans are "already horribly fallen from their former worth"
(R.S. p. 399). Less than half a century later, Ubertino
da Casale complained to the Pope: "So high has the flood
of idleness and gluttony and continued familiarities with
women risen, that I rather wonder at those who stand
than at those who fall" (*Archiv*, iv, 80, cf. p. 187). Chaucer,
Gower, and the author of *Piers Plowman*, however much
they may differ on other points, agree in representing the
friar as a real danger to the purity of family life. Chaucer's
friar, tramping the roads with a sturdy fellow to bear his
bag, selling imaginary spiritual favours, and privately
erasing the names of those for whom he was publicly
pledged to pray, can be exactly paralleled from prosaic
and irrefragable documents (cf. *Archiv*, iii, 70, 104, and
Eubel Oberd. Minoritenprovinz, p. 239). But the very worst
of these abuses is already logically implied in St Bonaventura's complaint, only a generation after the Master's
death, that the few stricter friars were already a laugh-
ing-stock to the superficially correct, and self-satisfied
majority. The tide set more and more strongly against these
"Spirituals", who soon became not only laughing-stocks,
but martyrs in grim earnest. Angelo Clareno's *History of
the Seven Tribulations*—a book of passionate pleading
indeed, but one which only gains by comparison with
official or unfriendly records—shows what a terrible price
was often paid by those brethren who clung doggedly to
the plain letter of the Rule.

> Under a pot he schal be put, in a privie chambre,
> That he schal lyven ne last but litell while after!

writes the fourteenth-century satirist of the unlucky friar
whom his brethren find no longer useful to them as a
beggar; but this was a merciful process of extinction compared with the nameless horrors inflicted in convent
dungeons upon such as refused to beg for unlawful corn

and wine. It was worse still when the Pope interfered with a decree which startled even the medieval conscience. The constitution *Quorundam*, published by John XXII in 1317, made it heresy for a friar to disobey his immediate superior by wearing the short garments which he believed St Francis to have commanded, or by refusing to beg fresh stores to fill those barns and cellars which the founder had most explicitly forbidden. In other words, it became flat heresy for a friar to adhere strictly to that solemn vow from which, according to St Thomas Aquinas, not even a pope had power to absolve him! In accordance with this new move, four Spirituals were publicly burned as heretics at Marseilles (1318) for asserting that the Rule of St Francis was identical with Christ's Gospel, and that even the Pope could not dispense Franciscans from their solemn vow of poverty. These four were only the residuum from a body of sixty more who had gradually been induced to recant by a process of intimidation, and probably torture, lasting over six months; and no single episode is better calculated than this to explain the startling contrasts which we find between the ideal friar of the *Fioretti* and the real friar even of the first century.[1] The stricter friars pleaded for leave to form a separate congregation of their own, in which they might live unmolested after the tenor of their early vows: but even this reasonable request was refused; and Angelo Clareno, the leader of the Italian Spirituals, though beatified by the Church after his death, breathed his last in hiding and in apparent failure eleven years after Dante. The persecution in England seems to have been even more bloody, though more silent, than in France or Italy. The Chronicle of Meaux (R.S. II, 323) informs us quite

[1] The whole story is fully told at the beginning of the third volume of Lea's *Inquisition*: yet even Dr Lea scarcely brings out with sufficient clearness the cynical frankness with which loyalty to the first traditions of the Order was proclaimed to be heresy. This can only be fully realized by studying the official declaration of the thirteen Doctors upon the case, and by noting how distinctly they proclaim *that each one of the condemned propositions is separately heretical* (Baluze-Mansi, *Misc.* II, 271).

casually that twenty-five men and eight women of the
Spiritual Franciscans were burned "in England, in a certain
forest", about the year 1330. Facts like these are often
partly passed over in silence, partly falsified, by modern
historians. Thomas of Eccleston records how the General
Albert of Pisa praised the special zeal of the English
Franciscans, whom he found "ready to go with him to
prison or into exile for the sake of *the* reform *of the Order*".
Father Cuthbert, the recent Romanist translator of the
book, has suppressed the words italicized, thus concealing
the fact that the reform of the Franciscan Order was
already a pressing and dangerous duty, even in Eccleston's
days.

It is extremely significant that a man like Salimbene,
who was on intimate terms with so many of the leading
early Spirituals, should show such an utter want of sympathy with the party as a whole, and go on recording without remark a state of things so glaringly at variance with
the first Franciscan ideal. He shows us incidentally, over
and over again, that many of the main precepts of the
Rule were obsolete before the generation of those who had
known the living Francis was extinct. The Order, as a
whole, no longer even wished to be what it once had been.
A certain Spiritual friar prayed long and earnestly to see
St Francis in heaven: at last his prayer was granted. The
Saint, whom he had hoped to see in dazzling glory, was
discovered in an obscure corner, tending a leper covered
with sores from head to foot; and the disillusioned vision-
ary fell at his feet in bitter tears. "This leper", explained
St Francis, "is my Order, which I tend at Christ's bidding,
and for which I plead unceasingly before God".

It was partly the tragedy of all great movements—too
great, in many ways, for their age. But partly also we see
here the inevitable result of the Saint's own doubts and
inconsistencies. He had wavered to the very end of his
career between love of solitude and love of his fellow-men.
He himself lived each life so truly and so whole-heartedly

that in him we scarcely see the conflict of the two ideals; but it came out fatally in his Rule. The friars must teach others, and yet remain too poor to study themselves: they must evangelize the whole world, and yet bind themselves by the lifelong vow which cut them off from all natural intercourse with half of the human race. St Francis himself was both hermit and apostle, and a few followed him with steps not too unequal: of the rest, the best were those who forgot only one side of the Saint's example. Some became the most ascetic of hermits; others, the most adventurous of missioners; but vast numbers, who had no deep or enduring vocation for either sacrifice, drifted quietly amid the general uncertainty, and doubtless without realizing clearly how far they were drifting, into a fairly easy routine of life, safe for both worlds. Indeed, medieval conditions were eminently favourable to such rapid degeneration. Nothing contributed more inevitably to the inward decay of the Order than the desperate resolve to preserve an outward show of discipline and unity. In the modern world, men agree with more or less good grace to differ on even the most vital questions; thus ideals apparently irreconcilable, flourishing side by side, gradually forget much of their differences, and have leisure to realize the likeness of their general aim. The honest men of either party in the Franciscan Order had much to learn from each other: a common-sense division would have made them most valuable competitors in the long run. The minority might have continued, as they wished, to keep the Rule in all its first severity: the majority might have formed a separate Order, frankly avowing the necessity, to all but one man in a thousand, of certain relaxations. The questions at issue between the two parties were not deeper or more complicated than those which have been left open for three centuries in the Anglican Church under the so-called "Elizabethan Settlement". No doubt it is in itself regrettable that two or more religious bodies should cling with equal obstinacy to mutually exclusive doctrines, and pray with equal fervour for each other's corporate, if not personal, extinction. Yet this has also its good side; for each party thus remains a standing witness to one side of the truth, and each, in the face of its rivals, must needs practise to some real extent the doctrines which it professes; otherwise, it will surely die out in a world which has no use for stale unrealities. In the Middle Ages, this agreement to differ was impossible; and St Francis himself was too much a child of the Middle Ages even to dream of modern freedom. He, the freest of men in his own soul, inflicted on his brethren the bondage of a Rule which, as the medieval hierarchy was certain to enforce it, must needs become intolerable to one party or the other within the Order. Since the Spirituals were only a small minority,[1] the large majority got their own way. Strong in the medieval ideas of religious discipline and in the general sympathy of the ruling powers, the "Conventuals" buried their too stubborn opponents in filthy dungeons, or burned them publicly as heretics. If the Popes had allowed the Spirituals to form a separate "Order of Literal Observance", this would have kept the rest comparatively pure by the continued protest of its mere existence. As things were, relaxation and hypocrisy were positively officialized. The strict Rule was still retained in name, but its strict adherents were treated as heretics. The novice still vowed himself to lifelong obedience: the minister who admitted him solemnly promised eternal life as a reward for this obedience. But meanwhile the Vicar of Christ sent him to the stake in this world, and to hell in the next, for presuming to obey too literally those precepts of which the Saint himself had protested, on his deathbed, "By God's grace, they are plain and simple enough to need no explanation". Nothing but the most refined Jesuitry could reconcile this plain Rule, which all swore to keep, with the elaborate papal comments

[1] Father Cuthbert's contention (p. 67) that the relaxed friars were always in the minority is not only contrary to all contemporary evidence, but would also fail to explain how they became strong enough to immolate recalcitrant Spirituals.

which practically forbade the keeping of it; and St Bonaventura's writings show us how deeply this Jesuitry had
penetrated into the Order within thirty years of the Saint's
death. Meanwhile, by a common vice of human nature,
the less men wrought the works of St Francis, the more
glibly they took his name in vain. Salimbene, knowing
very well in his heart that he breaks the Rule every day of
his life, vaunts quite complacently the Saint's promise of
certain salvation to all who should truly keep that Rule.
He would have made an admirable example for Butler's
famous sermon on Balaam: "Let me die the death of the
righteous, and let my last end be like his". The fetishism
of the Franciscan frock—the superstitious investiture of
dying laymen with so effective a passport to Paradise—
began at a time when only a few condemned heretics still
clung to the strict form of life which that gray frock
implied.

This was the price paid by St Francis and the Franciscans
for having obediently conformed to the ruling hierarchy
instead of going their own way like the Wesleyans. It is
true that, in the thirteenth century, the nonconformist had
to face the probabilities of helpless martyrdom or bloody
rebellion. But St Francis's divine Master had long ago
shown the world that obstinate nonconformity, even in an
age of bitter intolerance, is quite compatible with the most
lamblike innocence and the most perfect charity. Even
while we praise St Francis as the most Christ-like figure
in later Christian history, the very comparison does but
serve to show how far he stands, in every respect, below
his great Exemplar. The spiritual iniquities of his time
were almost beyond modern belief;[1] but he himself lacked
the sterner fibre of a thorough reformer. His charity and

[1] I have dealt briefly with this subject in the *Independent Review* for
June, 1905. Even the third chapter of M. Sabatier's *Vie de St François*
gives, if anything, a too favourable idea of the early thirteenth-century
Church; and his readers are left to infer that the Franciscans and
Dominicans worked a far more thorough and lasting reform than was
actually the case.

humility, his intense respect for all who sat in Moses' seat, kept him always far above vulgar sectarianism; but he pushed this deference and self-effacement to an extreme at which it became a serious weakness. In the eternal fight against evil, obedience to an evil-doer in authority may prove the worst of treasons to the cause. When, therefore, we hear the Saint extolled so unreservedly for his conformity to a system already deeply corrupted—when we are told how the Papacy succeeded where Anglicanism failed, in keeping its Methodists within the pale—then we may well ask: "What was the ultimate consequence of this conformity?" In an independent rivalry for purity of doctrine and of works, the Franciscans would have shamed the hierarchy out of its worst abuses, as the Wesleyans unquestionably did much to rouse the Anglican Church from its torpor. Instead of that, we find the hierarchy deliberately corrupting the Rule in order to bring the new movement into line with current traditions; and soon the typical friar is no longer the reformer, but the willing tool of a worldly papacy—the Jesuit of the Middle Ages. The early friars had spoken out manfully against the growing abuse of indulgences; their later brethren became the busiest of pardon-mongers. Brother Berthold of Ratisbon, St Bonaventura's contemporary, speaks quite as bitterly against the "penny-preachers" as Luther himself. The penny-preacher is the "devil's huntsman", who "hath murdered true penitence".[1] Yet, three centuries later, Bishop Gardiner complained that "the devil used friars for his ministers" in the matter of false indulgences, "wherein heaven was sold for little money".

The early history of the Franciscan movement—the murderous violence with which the Papacy encouraged the suppression of all too inconvenient reforming energies within the Order—seems to give a very clear contradiction to Bishop Creighton's theory that a wiser statesmanship might have brought about the Reformation of the sixteenth

[1] *Predigten*, I, 208, 394; cf. pp. 132, 148, 154, and II, 12, 219.

century without any schism in the Church. Until long
after that century was out, men's minds were far too
exclusively haunted by the false conception of religious
unity as an outward conformity, and of faith as an assent
to a special form of words, to render possible such a yoking
together of divergent views as might be attempted in the
present century. All unnecessary differences are deplorable; and yet they have their uses in God's providence.
Nothing has done more to make Christians seek a deeper
unity and a deeper faith within their own hearts than the
competition of many separate, yet undeniably Christian,
bodies during the last three hundred years—bodies too
strong and well organized for violent extermination by
their enemies—outwardly conflicting, yet essentially (as
even the least tolerant cannot fail to see more and more
clearly) marching towards a common goal. "When the
half-gods go, the gods arrive." The violent rending of the
veil has brought mankind one step nearer to the Holy of
Holies: our eyes may ache still to pierce the darkness; but
every day more clearly the modern world sees God where
the Middle Ages only shuddered at a black and hopeless
void. Saints of all ages and of all creeds have taught us
to look for deeper spiritual truths in apparent spiritual
failure. "Where wast Thou, Lord?" cried St Catherine
of Siena in her passionate welcome of Christ's restored
presence after a long period of spiritual bereavement:
"Where wast Thou hidden, Lord, these many days that
I have sought Thee sorrowing?" "Daughter," replied the
Voice, "I was all the while in thine own heart".

It has always been the worldly strength and the spiritual
weakness of the Papacy to idolize outward unity and to
sacrifice everything to that idol. For this end the hierarchy
shrank from no bloodshed, and for this end they deliberately clipped the wings of the Franciscan reform. But, if it
is difficult to speak too strongly of the papal policy which
domesticated the Franciscan body by organizing hypocrisy
within the Order, on the other hand it would be very unjust

to apply so odious a word off-hand to individual friars. They stood in the position of the common soldier, who must indeed think to some extent for himself, but whose first duty is to obey his immediate superior. If modern freedom of conscience tempts us so often to cloak our self-will under the name of God's will, it was still more difficult in the Middle Ages to avoid the opposite error of mistaking a man's command for God's. No doubt very many friars were too earnest and simple-minded to take much harm from a system which solemnly promised them salvation for keeping strictly certain prescriptions which it forbade them strictly to keep; but the average friar was very much like the average convert in any great religious revival, and on him the official hypocrisy was certain soon to have a disastrous effect. The *fact* of the Order's rapid decay is undeniable: it stares us in the face from official documents as plainly as from the complaints of outsiders. The *causes* may not be so easy to analyse; but assuredly one of the most fatal was that false notion of authority and unity which enabled the majority, while swearing obedience to the Rule, and boasting themselves of the strictness of the Rule, to torture or slay those few who really followed the Rule.

The foregoing article was attacked in the next number of the *Hibbert Journal* by two Franciscan friars, Fathers Cuthbert and Stanislaus. While accusing me of ignorant or wilful falsification of the records, these two critics made little pretence of producing documentary proof for their assertions, finding it easier (as Thomas of Eccleston records of his fellow-Franciscans in the thirteenth century) to shout me down with cries of "Thou liest!" Nor have they since shown less unwillingness to face the actual evidence. I at once wrote for their leave to reprint their criticisms with my article and rejoinder, offering them also (what the *Hibbert Journal* cannot offer) the advantage of the last word in the controversy: thus, if I had indeed falsified the evidence, they had ample opportunity of pillorying me at my own expense. To this request, twice repeated, Father Stanislaus

opposed a refusal; while his fellow-friar returned no answer
to my second and registered letter. This is all the more inexplicable because their refusal cannot be ascribed altogether
to a dislike of controversy in itself (though I believe this has
weighed to some extent with Father Stanislaus): Father Cuthbert plainly hints, and his friend says straight out, that they
mean to pursue this subject in the columns of magazines in
which I, as a heretic, shall have presumably no right of reply.
Moreover, Father Stanislaus had himself gone out of his way
to taunt me in the *Hibbert* (heaven only knows on what presumed evidence!) with an habitual unwillingness to face
criticism. Yet I have put out a standing offer to his fellow-
Romanists to print at my own expense their criticisms of my
writings: I had repeated that challenge on the very page of my
From St Francis to Dante from which Father Stanislaus quoted;
and I can as little understand how he can have allowed himself
this ludicrously false insinuation as I can explain, on any
theory entirely creditable to them, the present reluctance of
these two friars to take the responsibility of their public
accusations. It is true that in this they follow the example of
the only other Romanist priests who have publicly attacked
me: it is true also that a bankrupt controversialist does gain
by refusing to permit a reprint, since the candid reader will
scarcely infer, even from the severest criticisms, how futile his
arguments really were; but one would have thought that, for
the sake of their own dignity and their authority in the eyes of
the Roman Catholic laity, men in such a position would be
ashamed to play this street-urchin's trick of a runaway
knock.

On one point made by my critics, and one only, I was indeed
at fault. I had quoted as an afterthought, and entirely contrary
to my usual principles, a passage of the Meaux Chronicle which
I had not personally verified, from Arnold's introduction to the
Clarendon Press edition of Wiclif (1, 10). The original passage,
as Father Cuthbert points out, does *not* give the precise number
of Franciscans burned in England; and I was therefore wrong
in stating that the persecution had been more bloody here than
in other countries. But, on the other hand, it entirely bears out
my main statement as to this persecution of friars by their
fellow-friars, and it puts the total number of victims far higher
than I had put them: for it asserts that, between 1318 and 1330,
113 Franciscans of both sexes were burned in France, Italy,

England, and the borders of Germany. Moreover, in attempting to set aside the authority of the Meaux Chronicle, Father Cuthbert himself commits an egregious blunder, arguing, "I do not know any English Chronicle which bears out this statement". This kind of argument from "I do not know" is dangerous even at the best; but it has no value whatever from the pen of a writer who also does not know that, in spite of its French-sounding name, the Chronicle was written by English monks at the Yorkshire monastery of Meaux. What is more (apart from the passage in Eccleston which Father Cuthbert has distorted as I show on p. 172), the poem of *Piers Plowman* distinctly corroborates this persecution of strict friars in England by their relaxed brethren (c. xxiii, 58 ff.).

As Father Cuthbert seldom vouchsafes documentary evidences for his contentions, I must say a little here about the work which constitutes his only pretence to speak on this subject— his translation of Thomas of Eccleston. The "Introductory Essay" to this work is simply an unintelligent compilation, with imperfect acknowledgment, from Professor Brewer's preface to the *Monumenta Franciscana*, and Dr Jessopp's *Coming of the Friars*; and the translation itself is neither scholarly nor even straightforward. I have already exposed a little of this in my *From St Francis to Dante*: I must here give more detail, in order to enable the reader to estimate this man who claims authority for his unsupported assertions. Most educated people of any kind know that the medieval Religious were bled periodically for health's sake. The ordinary Latin word for such bleeding is *minutio*: twice our translator comes across this common technical word; twice he mistranslates it ridiculously—the second, with such violence to grammar that one wonders how far he can understand the Latin of his own service-books (pp. 210 and 214). Other blunders in translation may be found by the curious reader on page 175 (omission of *in suis locis*, which seems to have puzzled him); 182, *ampliatus*; 207, *adinvenerant*; 210, *siquidem* and *clam*; 219, *omne bonum* (though he had the Quaracchi text to show him the way); 237, *penderem*; 241, note 1; 221, *quod*. Other mistranslations seem purposely designed to soften Eccleston's too plain-spoken text: *e.g.* pp. 156 and 157, where he omits the words *nimis* and *temptabant*; 166, where by altering the tenses of the original (*dicerent—essent*) he disguises a definite implication of indevotion against the friars; 213, where he leaves out the crucial

word *ordinis*;[1] 227, where he softens *Papa quicunque*, "*all*
Popes*", into "*a* Pope". Anyone who verifies these references
will understand why I do not trouble to reply in cases where
Father Cuthbert simply pledges his unsupported word against
my renderings of Latin documents.

Father Stanislaus, again, shows very great inaccuracy. On
p. 667 of his criticism, he bases attacks on my argument on the
assumption that "the two *Epistles*...were written in 1257":
whereas the second was written in 1266, as he might have seen
on reference to any standard authority, or even from the notes
to the page from which he quotes! Again, he assumes that in
1257 the Order was still fresh from the baleful influence of the
"relaxed" Elias: yet Elias only held the Generalate from 1233
to 1239; and the eighteen years between this date and 1257
were far more favourable to the "strict" party than any succeeding period.

Such, then, are the two friars who now accuse me of falsifying
St Bonaventura's words; though one makes no pretence, and the
other very little, of confronting me fully with the original
However, fortunately for me, they both pitch upon a passage
which is not too long for me to reproduce in full: I will therefore
give a bald and literal translation here, and the original Latin
at the end of the pamphlet. It is from the first *Epistle* of
St Bonaventura, who writes (after a preamble setting forth the
necessity of plain speech): "But now, because of the urgent
perils of the times and wounds of consciences, and likewise
scandals of worldly folk, to whom the Order, whereas it ought
to be a mirror of all holiness, is being turned to weariness and
contempt in divers parts of the world; [therefore], neither
altogether keeping silence, nor altogether expressing [what I
think]; neither making new laws nor inflicting bonds [on the
Brethren] nor binding and laying grievous burdens upon others,
—but as an announcer of truth, I briefly explain (seeing that

---

[1] It is quite impossible to accept Father Cuthbert's excuse (p. 664)
that this omission of a crucial word is not calculated to mislead. As
his mistranslation stands, the reader is left to infer that the English
friars were ready to suffer persecution for the reform of *other people*;
whereas the whole point of Eccleston's words is that the reform *of the
Franciscan Order* was already a duty exposing the reformer to persecution. It is impossible not to connect this omission with the fact
that Father Cuthbert contends in his preface (in the teeth of all contemporary evidence) that the strict friars formed the majority of the
Order.

they ought by no means to be left unsaid) the things which seem to me, after consultation with the Representatives of the Order, to need correction. In truth, when I seek out the causes why the splendour of our Order is in a manner eclipsed, the Order is tainted without, and within the clearness of consciences is befouled, there occurs to me (1) the multiplicity of [worldly] businesses, wherein money (the enemy above all things to the poverty of our Order) is greedily sought for, incautiously received, and more incautiously touched.[1] (2) There occurs the idleness of some Brethren, which is a cesspool of all vices, wherein very many being sunken, choosing some monstrous state between contemplative and active life, not so much carnally as cruelly eat the blood of [men's] souls. (3) There occurs the wandering abroad of very many, who, for the solace of their own bodies, burdening those through whom they pass, leave behind them not examples of life but rather scandals of souls. (4) There occurs importunate begging, whereby all who pass through the lands so abhor meeting the friars that they fear to fall in with them as [to fall in] with robbers. (5) There occurs the sumptuous and curious construction of buildings, which troubles the peace of the Brethren, burdens their friends, and exposes us in manifold ways to the perverse judgments of men. (6) There occurs the multiplication of familiarities, which our Rule prohibits, whereby arise very many suspicions, evil reports and scandals." Then come complaints Nos. 7, 8, 9, and 10, which would have strengthened my case, but for which I had no room; and then a sentence which (according to Father Stanislaus) I dishonestly refrained from quoting, but of which he himself quotes only a fragment, breaking off at a comma which I mark here by italics: "For though there are very many to be found who are not guilty in any of the aforesaid points, yet this curse involves all, unless those who do the things are resisted by those who do them not, *since it is clearer than daylight that all the aforesaid tend to the very great and in no wise to be concealed detriment of our Order: although to the lukewarm, to the indevout, to the worldly-wise—who consider the custom [which has grown up] and allege the multitude [of those who do these things]— they appear easy and excusable, nay, even as irremediable".*

My brief summary of this passage, which the two friars call

---

[1] Apparently the Jesuitical evasion had already begun by which a friar would put a glove on before accepting money, or would take a stick to count it with, so as to avoid the actual touch.

a falsification, ran as follows: "[St Bonaventura] speaks of the idleness and viciousness of many, and the commercial spirit of the Order as a whole. Their importunate begging and legacy-hunting, the extravagance of their buildings and private expenses, their familiarities with women, are rapidly making them 'wearisome and contemptible in divers parts of the world'". The reader can therefore now judge for himself; and he will probably guess not only why these two critics refrained from proving my guilt by confronting me with St Bonaventura's words in full, but also why one of them, when supplying what he calls a dishonest omission in my extremely brief summary, breaks off himself at a comma, where the Saint's sentence begins to tell far more against his argument than the former half had seemed to tell in its favour. My critics generally try to supply this lack of documentary evidence by mere vehemence of assertion; but once or twice they do venture just within arm's length. Father Stanislaus, alluding to the ten complaints quoted above, writes: "True, the Saint does speak [but always in qualified terms, which are conveniently omitted in Mr C.'s précis] of all these things; but he does *not* say that these faults are rapidly making the friars wearisome and contemptible in divers parts of the world. As a matter of fact, Mr C. has in this passage pieced together two wholly different contexts, and thus, consciously or unconsciously, heightened the effect of the whole" (p. 668). Father Cuthbert makes the same complaint in even stronger language: my summary is (he says), "as though one would take the letters of the alphabet and toss them up". Yet, as the reader may now see, the Saint does most distinctly assert what these two friars so confidently deny; and the only possible explanation is that here, as elsewhere, they have been unable to construe the somewhat crabbed Latin.[1] The same excuse must be made for Father Stanislaus's assertion that on these points the Saint *always* speaks in qualified terms: on the contrary, the reader may see that his vehemence on several points quite outdoes my brief summary.

---

[1] As Mr M'Cabe says, speaking from his own experience as a teacher among the modern Franciscans, "A large number of priests, secular and regular, lose all but the very rudiments of the language in which all their prayers are couched" (*Life in a Modern Monastery*, p. 179). Even Abbot Gasquet, who has certainly far more scholarship than these friars, makes a ridiculous blunder over a word which occurs seven times in the Vulgate Bible (*Great Pestilence*, p. 20, when he translates *non preco*—i.e. *non praeco*—"no prayer was said").

But (continue both critics) the Saint does not speak of "the idleness and viciousness of many"; and Father Stanislaus prints here one sentence of the original Latin, italicizing the *some* in one line, but quite neglecting the *very many* in the next. Yet the most elementary logic might suggest that, though *some* is in itself a colourless word, it takes its colour from the context. If the Saint speaks of "the idleness of *some* Brethren, which is a cesspool of all vices, wherein *very many* being sunken, etc., etc.", he does, in fact, speak of "the idleness and viciousness of many", nor do I see how else his words could be faithfully summarized. A passage from the writings of St Bonaventura's contemporary and fellow-Franciscan, David of Augsburg (whose book was in the Middle Ages generally ascribed to the Saint himself), exactly illustrates his meaning here: "To acquire and foster and maintain chastity avails (among other things)...the avoidance of idleness, which is as it were the gate of all vices, especially fleshly vices" (*De VII. Processibus*, VI, 40).

Next, in my précis I speak of "familiarities *with women*": and, according to Father Cuthbert, my insertion of these two words constitutes a serious falsification. "If", he writes, "Mr C.'s acquaintance with Franciscan literature were wider than perhaps it is, he would know that the word *familiarities* signifies too much concern with the worldly affairs of secular men. So it is used in the Constitutions of the Order." This assertion, made as usual without a shred of actual quotation or definite reference to back it up, is as false as it is absurd. I have taken the trouble to institute a search through all the Constitutions as published by Father Ehrle, S.J., until eighteen years after St Bonaventura's death; and I believe I am right in saying that the word *familiarities* occurs only once, where it refers primarily to women and secondarily to similarly suspicious intercourse with boys (*Archiv*, VI, 115; cf. Bonav. *Reg. Novit.* c. x, and *Epistola de xxv. mem.* 14). Moreover, the Saint's own reference to "suspicions, evil reports, and scandals" (which Father Cuthbert suppresses) would be quite incomprehensible on his theory. Thirdly, he makes a more serious suppression still—St Bonaventura's direct reference to the prohibition of such "familiarities" in the Rule. It is not possible to believe that Father Cuthbert is so unfamiliar with his own Rule as not to know that the only prohibition of any familiarities therein contained is in c. xi: "I strictly enjoin upon all the Brethren that they have no suspicious intercourse (*consortia*) or counsels with women"; and I must confess myself utterly unable to understand how he can reconcile his conscience either to what he says on this point, or to what he carefully leaves unsaid. My other critic, with these facts staring him in the face, admits freely that the Saint's reference *is* here to women, but contends that I have "misinterpreted" the phrase (though my only "interpretation" was to quote the corroborative words of other distinguished friars); and that, in taking these *familiarities* as something serious, I showed ignorance of the Saint's other writings. Here again he gives no reference, but simply flings the random accusation, on the chance that it may stick: I must therefore refer briefly to other words of the Saint. Section XI of his *Rule for Novices*, though headed simply *Of Worldly Familiarities*, deals for the greater part with women: "Flee from them as from serpents, nor even speak with any save under stress of urgent necessity, nor ever look hard (*respicias*) in a woman's face:... St Augustine saith: Your speech with women should be rough, brief, and stiff. Nor are they less to be shunned because they are holy women: for the holier they be, the more do they entice, and under pretext of sweet speech creeps in the slime of most impious lust. Believe me (saith he), I am a bishop, I speak the truth in Christ, I lie not. I have known cedars of Lebanon and bell-wethers of the flock ruined under this pretext, whose fall I should no more have suspected than St Jerome's or St Ambrose's". Again, in his 19th *Question on the Rule*, the Saint complains of the dangers of "intercourse with secular folk, whereupon arises matter for many temptations of the flesh". In the 14th section of his *Epistola de xxv. memorabilibus* he writes: "Avoid all women and beardless youths but for cause of necessity or manifest [spiritual] profit"; and his language is equally plain in his *Sermon on the Rule* (§ 27) and *Exposition of the Rule* (c. xi). Again, the *Pharetra*, ascribed to the Saint, has a chapter headed simply *De Familiaritate*, and consisting solely of seventeen quotations from the Fathers as to the extreme perils of women to spiritual men, of the type of that already quoted from St Augustine. Moreover, the Saint's secretary, Bernard of Besse, is still more emphatic (*Spec. Discip.* I, xxx, 3): so also is David of Augsburg (*De VII. Process.* IV, 13, VI, 34, and *passim*): indeed, a whole volume might be filled with quotations to the same effect.

I have only one last criticism of the same type to deal with.

Father Stanislaus writes: "If Mr C. will read very carefully [cc. xviii–xx of the *Quaestiones circa Regulam*] he will see that St B. is not speaking of the *Friars Minor*, but of *Religious Orders in general*, so that the evidence he adduces therefrom is not *ad rem*". It is strange logic in any case to argue that, because the Saint describes the decay of *all* Religious Orders without exception, he therefore means to except his own, the Order with which the whole treatise is concerned from beginning to end, and from which it takes its name! But, in fact, Father Stanislaus's criticism only shows that he himself, as usual, does not know the contents of these three chapters which he accuses me of ignoring. "*You, you, you,*" says St Bonaventura's interlocutor, repeatedly; and "*We, we, we,*" answers the Saint in his detailed apologies. Moreover, some of the causes he adduces for the decay of the Orders (*e.g.* the "frequent change of superiors") can refer to the friars alone; and the Mainz editor plainly says that the treatise was concerned with "all Religious, and *especially the Friars Minor*" (italics mine). Once again, I must confess myself unable to understand this device of reviling an adversary for not having read a document which in fact he has read only too correctly. It is, of course, no crime for a friar to be totally ignorant of the history of his own Order. That he should undertake, being so ignorant, to write on the subject, is perhaps only a venial sin: certainly it is a fault readily pardoned in the Roman communion, provided only that the history so produced be thoroughly "edifying". But that, being ignorant of certain obvious documents, and knowing himself to be so, he should make this ignorance an excuse for baseless and unsupported accusations of bad faith against a fellow-student, shows a blindness of prejudice comparatively seldom met with outside so-called religious controversy.

The other criticisms of my adversaries are based simply on their misunderstanding of my plain words. Because I compare the friars in one point only to the Wesleyans, Father Stanislaus imagines I deny that they meant to be loyal sons of the Church; thus showing an ignorance of early Wesleyanism as great as his ignorance of logic. Again, he accuses me of arguing "that the majority of the friars were wastrels or scoundrels". I need hardly warn anyone who has really read the foregoing article that I neither said nor thought anything of the kind; but I hope I have sufficiently proved that, great as was the reforming work done by the friars in their first few years, they soon lost much of the virtue which had distinguished them, and that this rapid decline may be attributed mainly to their association with a papal court which was necessarily worldly in its methods. If anything is needed to give force to my indictment, it may perhaps be found in the baseless and futile accusations which it has provoked from the accredited champions of the other side, and in their flat refusal to continue this discussion on ground which would leave room for the production of full documentary evidence.

APPENDIX

Original Text of the Passage summarized from
St Bonaventura's Epistle of 1257.

Nunc autem quia pericula temporum urgent, et laesiones conscientiarum, necnon et scandala mundanorum, quibus cum Ordo deberet esse sanctitatis totius speculum, in diversis orbis partibus in taedium vertitur et contemptum; quae mihi de consilio Discretorum visa sunt corrigenda, nec penitus tacens, nec omnino exprimens, nec nova statuens, nec vincula super-inducens, nec onera gravia alligans aliis et imponens, sed tan-quam annuntiator veritatis breviter exprimo, videns illa nulla-tenus reticenda. Sane perquirenti mihi causas, cur splendor nostri Ordinis quodam modo obscuratur,[1] Ordo exterius inficitur, et nitor conscientiarum interius defoedatur, occurrit negotiorum multiplicitas, qua pecunia, nostri Ordinis pauper-tati super omnia inimica, avide petitur, incaute recipitur et incautius contrectatur. Occurrit quorundam Fratrum otiositas, quae sentina est omnium vitiorum, qua plurimi consopiti, monstruosum quendam statum inter contemplativam et activam eligentes, non tam carnaliter quam crudeliter sanguinem come-dunt animarum. Occurrit evagatio plurimorum, qui propter solatium suorum corporum, gravando eos per quos transeunt, non exempla post se relinquunt vitae, sed scandala potius animarum. Occurrit importuna petitio, propter quam omnes transeuntes per terras adeo abhorrent Fratrum occursum, ut eis timeant quasi praedonibus obviare. Occurrit aedificiorum

---

[1] So reads the Mainz edition of 1609, which I had used for my article (VII, 433); the Quaracchi edition reads *obfuscatur*, "is darkened" (VIII, 468).

constructio sumtuosa et curiosa, quae pacem Fratrum inquietat, amicos gravat et hominum perversis judiciis multipliciter nos exponit. Occurrit multiplicatio familiaritatum, quam Regula nostra prohibet, ex qua suspiciones, infamationes et scandala plurima oriuntur.... Licet autem plurimi reperiantur, qui non sunt culpabiles in aliquo praedictorum, tamen omnes involvit haec maledictio, nisi a non facientibus his qui faciunt resistatur; cum luce clarius omnia supradicta in maximum et nullo modo dissimulandum vergant nostri Ordinis detrimentum, licet tepidis et indevotis et secundum carnem sapientibus, considerantibus consuetudinem et allegantibus multitudinem, quasi facilia et excusabilia, etiam[1] irremediabilia videantur.

[1] *ac,* ed. Quaracchi.

THE PLAIN MAN'S RELIGION IN THE MIDDLE AGES[1]

SINCE all civilization is a matter of comparison, and since every criticism of the past is by implication a criticism of our own age also, it is most important to make up our minds as to the real place of the Middle Ages in human evolution. *A priori*, all believers in human progress would expect the period to be better than antiquity, and worse than our own time. But we may not write history like this; we must check *à priori* considerations at every point by recorded facts; and, while surviving records have led some men to conclude that the Middle Ages were actually inferior to antiquity, others again believe that they were, on the whole, superior even to modern times. Very few would care to go back to them, but many argue, either explicitly or implicitly, that an age in which religion dominated all society was necessarily a greater age than this of ours; and that, however much we may have gained in many ways, we have lost, and are still losing, the Pearl of Price. Newman was one of the few who have dared to put this boldly and uncompromisingly; but very many seem to reason implicitly from some such premises, and still more seem to halt between two opinions. For the study of medieval history, therefore, one of the first requisites is to face this question, and to decide it as far as possible for ourselves. Medieval Europe accepted one single creed and one set of religious forms; was it, so far, more developed or less developed than we?

[1] Originally reprinted by kind permission from the *Hibbert Journal* of April, 1916, and again here because the first edition is exhausted. Nos. 10–12 are still in print with Simpkin, Marshall and Co. (10) *Monastic Schools in the Middle Ages*; (11) *French Monasticism in* 1503; (12) *Medieval Graffiti*.

Now, if we are to be quite frank here, we must begin by being frank with ourselves. In religion, as in most other things, are not we ourselves far more influenced by current practice than by current theory? Do we not too often pay lip-homage to the ideal, and practical homage to the average standard of life around us? And which of us has not recognized his own human nature in those wild words of Adam Lindsay Gordon, who had been trained under the Calvinism still common fifty years ago, who had broken away from it, and who summed up his future hopes in a single line: "The chances are, I go where most men go". In most cases, it may be said that ninety-nine points of our religion are matters of heredity or environment, while only the hundredth point is conscious and characteristic. But it is precisely the conscious and the characteristic that is worth our study; for, as Professor William James has put it, though there may be very little difference between one man and another, it is just that little which is of paramount importance. And, though the actual amount of difference has often been very much exaggerated, there was something very characteristic about medieval religion, as compared with classical times on the one hand and the twentieth century on the other—about religion as conceived in the mind of the average medieval man.

We can mark it best, perhaps, by going back a long way first. Gibbon sneers at Tertullian's boast that a Christian mechanic could give an answer to problems which had puzzled the wisest heads of antiquity. But is not Gibbon's criticism a rather dangerous half-truth? From a wider point of view, must we not count it a real step forward in civilization that the artisan should seriously attempt to answer these questions at all? Christianity certainly brought in this new spirit; and the spirit is all-important. The belief in a crucified carpenter—the conviction that the highest triumph may be begotten of the completest earthly failure—did, as a matter of fact, take more men out of themselves, and took them further out of themselves,

than anything else since the dawn of history. We may
see this best by taking a really striking example of later
Pagan culture, like Marcus Aurelius. When Marcus
Aurelius quotes, "The Poet hath said, 'Dear city of
Cecrops'", and adds to himself, "but wilt not thou say
(rather), 'O dear City of God!'", we feel no surprise that
those words should have been written a century and a half
after Christ. They might have fallen in the most natural
way in the world from the mouth of Tertullian's artisan;
it is in a pagan book that they come upon us with such
startling force: so far, Tertullian's boast is justified. Lord
Chesterfield reminds us that the first and foremost requisite
for the art of pleasing is the wish to please. Similarly many
philosophers, from Socrates, through Roger Bacon and
Descartes down to Darwin, have taught us that the first
and foremost requisite for knowledge is the wish to know;
that (to put it into very modern terms) the mind is like a
photographic camera, and even the enormous variations
of power or delicacy between one instrument and another
are secondary to the question whether the instrument
is being turned in the actual direction of the object, and
is being steadily focused upon that object. What the
medieval mind did was to focus itself in a practical spirit
upon enquiries which, hitherto, had been mainly academic.
Multitudes were now convinced that they had souls to
save, and that salvation was the most practical aim of every
human being; even the driest treatises of scholastic philosophy are inspired by that final aim. Even those who
think that the Middle Ages went as far wrong here as they
went in alchemy and astrology, must still recognize this
historical fact in itself. And, one-sided as this mental
impulse was, it is difficult to imagine any other impulse
living through the barbarian invasions. The study of the
mechanical and physical sciences, which had attained to
such an almost modern development in Alexandria, proved
quite unable to survive. Salvation, then, was the one
practical study of the Middle Ages; and different minds

pursued it according to their several bents. At the top of the scale, from St Augustine down to St Bernard and Nicholas of Cusa, really great men strove to reconcile the intensest pursuit of personal salvation with the highest altruism and the widest human outlook. At the bottom of the scale, of course, the jostle for salvation was gross and frankly immoral. The vulgar caught inevitably at what was least defensible in the official religion—not only its relic-worship, which became as materialistic as any savage magic, but also the static idea of salvation, the theory held even by the most spiritual Christians, that the one thing of importance was the last moment before death—that this, for good or for evil, could outweigh a whole life which had gone before it. Hence the frequent fights of saints with devils on their very death-bed. In the Middle Ages, as in later Puritanism, we find both extremes; on the one hand, a man going through life with the serene conviction that he was earmarked by God's mercy for final salvation; on the other hand, an equally good or better man trembling for his fate as long as he had physical strength left to think at all. While the very best felt like this, the vulgar naturally fell into grosser materialism. I do not think that mere callous inhumanity can account for one of the strangest phenomena of the later Middle Ages—the systematic denial of the last Church rites to condemned criminals, against which great churchmen often fulminated in vain. In modern Sicily, among the poorest classes, an executed criminal is a saint. Pitré has noted that men pray "in the name of the holy gallows-birds". This is perfectly logical. The crowd has seen a man publicly executed after partaking of the holy wafer, which would not be given to him unless he had just confessed and been absolved. His soul is, at that moment, unquestionably on the right side of the balance; next moment he is launched into eternity. By all ecclesiastical logic you are more certain of that man's final salvation, after due purification in purgatory, than of the most saintly liver whose last moments had been less convincing; therefore the Sicilian vulgar pray for help to the souls of the holy gallows-birds. It is difficult not to read this backwards into the refusal of sacraments to the medieval gallows-bird. The thing is perfectly logical; nothing could have saved the population from it but faith—reasonable faith as distinguished from credulity.

There never has been an age of faith, in this sense, and there never will be. Reasonable faith implies the highest tension of the human faculties—the determination on the one hand neither to contradict nor to overlook anything that reason can decide for us; and, on the other hand, the full stretch of our imagination to anticipate reason, to find living significance amidst the mass of what would otherwise be mere detached observations. This will be exceptional in every age. The Middle Ages were not Ages of Faith in the sense of holding firmly to certain dogmas with *all* their faculties; in the sense of proving all things and holding fast only to that which was good. It is usual and convenient to call them the Ages of Faith; it would be more accurate to call them the Ages of Acquiescence.

This acquiescence was enormously facilitated, of course, by the thoroughness with which Roman Catholicism had adopted the idea and discipline of an imperial State religion. The hierarchy was so exactly modelled upon the imperial bureaucracy that an ecclesiastical map of France before 1789 is practically a political map of Roman Gaul. There was therefore an enormous concrete element in medieval religion, and naturally the ordinary mind clings to the concrete. A great many medieval religious ideas grew up from below, and were only adopted and defended by the theologians after the official Church, having attempted in vain to eradicate them, had determined to adopt them and make the best of them. The more abstract dogmas, inherited from the early ages of Christian discussion—the Greek ages, tinged with Greek philosophy—these more abstract dogmas never seem to have influenced the popular mind very much. We may say of them, as Dr Johnson

said of the free-will controversy: "All theory is against
freedom of the will, all experience for it". In the Middle
Ages, even more than now, the ordinary mind was influenced infinitely less by current theory than by current
practice; "the chances are I go where most men go".

But the acquiescence was unquestionably enormously
greater than now; and we can perhaps arrive at the
clearest idea by taking complete acquiescence as the general
rule, and noting the main exceptions, whether intellectual
or voluntary; whether because people misunderstood, or
because they knowingly rebelled.

At the lowest end of the scale come the coarse and glaring
exceptions; the men who were temperamentally irreligious,
and in whom the current beliefs were only just strong
enough to lend point to their blasphemy. The case of
William Rufus is well known; his refusal to amend his
ways after a serious illness, and his answer to the remon-
strances of Bishop Gundulf of Rochester: "By the Holy
Face of Lucca, God shall never have me good for all the
evil that He hath brought upon me!" Medieval preachers,
especially in Italy, bear frequent testimony to the subtle
and deliberate blasphemies which disappointed gamesters
would excogitate from the distinctive tenets of the Roman
Catholic faith; to their exquisite outrages heaped upon the
Virgin Mary; and to the fury with which they would
turn upon the statues of Christ or His saints, breaking off
a hand or a nose in revenge for their disappointment.

Infidelity proper, however, was a great deal more common in the Middle Ages than is generally supposed. We
find it just below the surface in the most unexpected places.
Of Perugino, whose pictures certainly are more refined and
spiritual than the average, Vasari tells us that he never could
get any belief in God into that hard head of his. We may
roughly divide medieval scepticism into three classes:
(1) Academic scepticism, the centre of which was at Paris.
(2) Political scepticism, the disbelief of men like the
Emperor Frederick II, whose policy was anti-papal and

anti-clerical, and who therefore were under every temptation to attack the foundations of current orthodoxy.
(3) There was also a great deal of scepticism, generally
more or less involuntary, among clergy and laity. In the
nature of the case, it would be impossible to prove this
exhaustively by documentary evidence; but frequently,
and in the most unexpected places, we come across
scattered hints whose wider significance is unmistakable.
One of the best-known instances is in Joinville (§ 46);
still more illuminating is an autobiographical fragment
from Johann Busch, a contemporary of Thomas à Kempis
and a member of the same religious Congregation. Busch,
who became a fairly learned man, and a monastic reformer
of remarkable tact and energy, thus describes his own
noviciate in the years 1418–19 (ed. K. Grube, p. 395). He
had come to the monastery from a model religious school
as a model scholar of seventeen; and he writes:

How many temptations I suffered in that noviciate, especially
concerning the Catholic faith, is known only to God, to whom
all things are open. For God was so great and glorious in my
heart, that I could not believe Him to have put on our flesh and
to have walked upon this earth in such poverty and lowliness.
When therefore the Gospels were read in Refectory, I thought
within myself, "the Evangelists do all they can to praise that
man", and then my heart would cry out within me, "Thou
knowest, it is not true that this Jesus is God". Yet then I
said in my heart, "I will die for the truth of Christ's divinity".
Then would my heart cry again, "Thou wilt die for it, yet
shalt thou see that it is a thing of naught". And seeing that
our father St Augustine and other doctors of the first four
centuries wrote and preached that this Jesus was God, then
I thought within myself, "how strange, that such wise men
should fall into such a folly as to dare to assert of this man,
whom they never saw, that He is God!" Yet, notwithstanding all these temptations, I was all the while a good and true
Catholic. But God Almighty suffered me thus to be tempted,
because my experience enabled me, in after times, to free many
others who were buffeted with the same temptations.

Busch's contemporary, St Bernardino of Siena, who had

perhaps heard more confessions than any man then living, gives the same report of his experience. He says, "There are very many who, though leading exemplary lives, are grievously troubled concerning many articles of the Faith" (*De. Ev. Aet.* Opp. ed. De La Haye, II, 37). Other slighter indications entirely bear out this testimony as to the wide diffusion of involuntary scepticism. Moreover, in proportion as we draw nearer to the sixteenth century we get increasing evidence of a more voluntary popular scepticism. The author of *Piers Plowman*, who had lived through the Black Death and the other terrible visitations of the later fourteenth century, complains of the frequency with which the dogmas of the Church were now criticized by the man in the street (c. xii, 35 ff. and 101 ff.):

> Now is the manner at meat, when the minstrels are still,
> The lewd against the learned of holy lore dispute.

He gives detailed instances, and adds:

> Such motives they move, these masters in their glory,
> And maken men to misbelieve that muse upon their words.

Moreover, the author is himself an example of the spirit whose excesses he deplores. He is one of several fourteenth-century writers who try to escape from the hard saying of the Church that all pagans and Jews, even the best of them, must be damned. This humanitarian (and, to that extent, anti-dogmatic) leaven had long been working; kindly minds among the common folk had long sought every possible outlet from this terrible Calvinism of medieval doctrine. More than a century earlier, the great Franciscan mission-preacher, Berthold of Regensburg, shows us the efforts of the popular mind in this direction. Some men insisted that souls would become clinkered by perpetual roasting, so that hell-fire would have no further hold upon them. Others argued that God, in pity for his own handiwork, would finally give the sinner a comfortable refuge even under Satan's nose (*Predigten*, ed. Pfeiffer, I, 386). Dante, again, shows traces of this revolt of human kindness, when he exalts Ripheus to heaven, and dares to put the excommunicated Manfred in purgatory, adding "the priestly curse doth not so utterly destroy, but that a green shoot of hope may spring up from the blasted trunk". And perhaps the most interesting of all is that old woman whom Joinville's friend Brother Yves met in the streets of Acre, bearing a chafing-dish of live charcoal in her right hand, and a flask of water in her left, and saying that she meant to burn up Paradise with the one, and quench hell-fire with the other, so that no man thenceforth might do right for the hope of heaven or for the fear of hell, but only for the pure love of God, who is so worthy and can do for us what is best (§ 445).

I need not further labour the point that much of medieval faith was simply passive acquiescence, and that the attempt to grasp at a living faith, to understand as well as to believe, was often unsettling alike to the simple and to the learned mind. We may find the reason for this general passivity in the overwhelming pressure of a highly organized hierarchy—the strongest organization in all medieval society. There was a tendency to forgive everything in the flock so long as it was acquiescent, and therefore the mass of the flock tended more and more to leave religion in the hands of the professionals, and to restrict its own share to the narrowest and most mechanical routine. The layfolk understood even less of the Mass than an ordinary village congregation does in modern France or Italy; they often failed to follow the service even in its vaguest outlines. The burgomasters of Strasbourg regularly heard lawsuits in their official pew in the cathedral during daily mass; and it was one of St Louis's titles to sanctity that he very seldom suffered a minister to come and talk with him at this time, "except occasionally after the Gospel had been said".[1] During the sermon, as Berthold of Regensburg and St Bernardino show us, there was a running fire of con-

---

[1] Dacheux, *Geiler de Kaysersberg*, p. 67; *Acta Sanct. Bolland*, Aug. v, *Vita II*, c. III, § 38.

versation, and even of definite interruptions. The ignorance of the Bible text, not only on the part of the laity, but also on that of the clergy, is difficult to exaggerate.[1]

And this dissociation of ceremony and spirit, this dualism, was to an enormous extent encouraged by the hierarchy itself. Those who wished to communicate too frequently were constantly discouraged by the clergy. Anything like weekly communion was very rare indeed among the laity; the few who desired it could very rarely obtain it. Again, it is significant that the word *conversion*, in the religious sense, is almost entirely confined to monks. It is very rare indeed to meet with it in Bunyan's or Baxter's sense. To enter a monastery was to be "converted"; this is the sense the word bears even in canon law. The more personal devotions of the later Middle Ages were intimately bound up with popular mysticism; they were to a large extent unsacerdotal, though not antisacerdotal; and here, as usually in the history of religion, we find mysticism stimulating free thought. Popular mysticism was one of the main currents in the stream which led to the Reformation.

I have emphasized the routine character of most medieval religion; but we must fairly remind ourselves how much of all civilization is routine. All progress seems to follow the same rough formula; first, conscious effort, successful or unsuccessful; then what seems most successful becomes habitual and subconscious; lastly, the subconscious becomes even instinctive. The formalism of medieval religion must not blind us to the fact (which seems to me almost indisputable) that these forms were in general healthy and beneficent. The most hypocritical sinner among the clergy testified by his hypocrisy to what all clergy were supposed to be, and very many really were. The laziest and most useless priest did still form one link in a vast network of activities, and mainly beneficent activities. The remotest parish or ecclesiastical district was more or less directly linked up with the Pope; and the

[1] I have dealt in some detail with this subject in the seventh of my *Medieval Studies*: "Religious Education before the Reformation."

Papacy was not only by far the longest succession of sovereigns, but also by far the most disinterested. With all their faults, the Popes bore witness to an ideal which was more altruistic, more universal, more modern, than that of the temporal rulers of the Middle Ages. Moreover, amid all their lapses and infidelities, the Popes did, on the whole, work for that ideal more consistently than kings and princes worked for theirs; there was more continuity of policy in the Papacy than in any other European state. We may look upon the gradual submergence of this system by modern civilization as a consummation not only inevitable, but much to be desired; yet still we ought not to forget that many peaks now submerged did, in the Middle Ages, stand high above the average level of human thought and conduct.

Moreover, it is very difficult to see how the world could have got on, after the break-up of the Roman Empire, without some such routine. We can scarcely exaggerate the cumulative effect of the unselfish thoughts and higher aspirations which cling round the very walls of a church. The common, uneducated man who says *Our Father* there regularly, even with only a small fragment of his mind, and without consciously counting up the myriads of the past with whom those words put him into direct communion— the man who regularly says those two words *Our Father* is, even by this routine, made more conscious of the brotherhood of man than by almost anything else in the very dull course of his life, except, no doubt, by the direct action of his family affections, if he has a family. Even the many gross minds of the Middle Ages to whom the Devil was almost a greater reality than God, had at least advanced a little step beyond the aboriginal savage who has little or no power of conceiving anything but the tangible and the visible.

A French scientist, not without malice, recently took home a little phial of holy water from the stoup of the nearest church, and found in it, under the microscope, an extraordinary number and variety of bacilli. But, after all, an idea is as great a reality as a bacillus; civilization has to count as seriously with the one as with the other; and both are almost equally invisible to the uneducated multitude. Is it an exaggeration to say that there are as many ideas hanging about a church as there are bacilli? that even the commonest man may thus pick up one or two ideas which he probably would never have picked up in any other way? and, if this is to some extent true even in our age of board-schools, is it not a hundred times truer of the Middle Ages?

However, with all that can be said for the value of routine, historical fact compels us to place the religion of the ordinary medieval man in just that intermediate position which in logic we should have anticipated. It was an enormous advance to take religion so seriously as the early Christians took it, and to organize it so democratically as it was organized at first. But the religious democracy, in self-defence, became more and more of a despotism; formulas stiffened until they lost a great part of their meaning; the new became old, and this old became the enemy of all other novelties; over against the thousand beneficent activities of the Church we must put the thousand cases in which she forcibly suppressed other beneficent activities: in short, the development of mankind since the Reformation has not only been necessary—it is not only a fact which we have to face—but it is part of a world-process to which we must do homage. And we shall best and most sympathetically study our ancestors of the Middle Ages in the light of these facts and of this world-process. We shall know them best if we regard them not as men who enjoyed higher privileges which they were unable to transmit to us, but as men who struggled hard to become what we (if only we will) may be—who struggled hard and pathetically, and were held back partly through fear of the Great Unknown, but still more by positive physical obstacles, which have since been swept away by printing and steam.

APPENDICES

APPENDIX I

THE main reason for this republication is that which prompted the second edition; many of these points are still hotly contested, and a lapse into silence would be interpreted by a good many people as a willingness to let my cause go by default.

The recent death of the scholar who had been the main supporter of these contrary views, though most regrettable from the personal point of view, rather emphasizes than weakens the necessity for republication. For he lived to a great age, in full possession of his faculties, and personally respected by those who most disagreed with his writings; moreover, in death as in life, he has a band of devoted followers, able and anxious to defend his tenets and his memory as far as the actual documents will permit. It is therefore as fair now as it was in 1915 to remind readers of the guarantees that I have tried to give, and of the extent to which those guarantees seem to have been effectual. One serious error, pointed out by Mr Beck, was at once corrected in full, with an apology to my readers. But, on the whole, my most determined adversaries seem to acknowledge, if only tacitly, the general accuracy of the facts which I produce.

And this is the more remarkable, since my own challenge for some explanation of what seemed very unaccountable lapses have been echoed, by reviewers unknown to me, in two of the most widely-read papers of their kind in Great Britain. *The Times Literary Supplement* (September 23, 1915) remarked: "The chief interest of the new edition lies in fifty-four pages of appendix devoted to 'A rough list of Misstatements and Blunders in Cardinal Gasquet's writings'—a list which certainly helps to justify the following striking comparison between the position of History and that of Natural Science in the world of learning." (The reviewer here quotes textually from my preface to ed. II, beginning: "If any zoologist of repute" and ending "are already inclined to relegate her".)

The *Church Times*, with which I have naturally had not infrequent public differences of opinion on some serious points, was perhaps even more emphatic in its notice of my fourteenth Study, *The Roman Catholic Church and the Bible*. In a leader of July 15, 1921, it printed:

"[Mr Coulton] has put out a little pamphlet of thirty-six pages, entitled *The Roman Catholic Church and the Bible*, which will, in the windows of the Cambridge booksellers, attract the attention of Cambridge's visitors. He re-opens an old controversy with Cardinal Gasquet in such terms that it is difficult to see how the Cardinal can avoid replying. He makes a grave accusation against the Cardinal's literary reputation and honour, charging him with repeating a falsehood when its falsity had quite plainly been pointed out. Mr Coulton prints again the details of the case, claiming that any reader who troubles to follow 'will realize how impossible it would be to match this in civilized modern society.' Certainly he seems to make out his case and to have proved that the Cardinal repeated an error in a new edition of *The Old English Bible* after his attention had been several times expressly called to it. It was not an unimportant error, for on it the argument of his essay depended. But one story is good till another is told. We find it almost incredible that Cardinal Gasquet should be guilty of deceiving his readers in such fashion. He must have an answer if he chooses to give it. And we submit that he should give it. His challenger is not an unimportant and irresponsible person; he is a scholar of real learning whose word on such a matter as this carries weight. Nor is the Cardinal a person without responsibility. He occupies a very distinguished position and, whether rightly or wrongly, if he is silent he will inevitably bring discredit upon the Church he serves. For these reasons we hope that the matter will be cleared up once for all at the coming Bible Congress. Silence seems no longer possible after Mr Coulton's repetition of the charge."

And it concludes:

"We welcome, then, the Cambridge Bible Congress. If Catholics and Protestants are united by a common love of the Bible and knowledge of it, the gulf between them will not be so deep. It will help to advance the cause of reunion. But let Cardinal Gasquet give Mr Coulton satisfaction."

Both these appeals remain unanswered.

APPENDIX II

A ROUGH LIST OF
MISSTATEMENTS AND BLUNDERS
IN CARDINAL GASQUET'S WRITINGS

See Preface to second edition. The following list makes no pretence to completeness in face of the Cardinal's frequent habit of quoting without the vaguest reference to chapter, page, or even title of the book to which he professedly appeals. But the text, however incomplete, is necessarily long and wearisome. For the convenience of most readers, who may have no wish to wade all through so monotonous a record, a classification has been made by means of typographical indications. The sign **D** refers to cases where the real documentary evidence has been suppressed or distorted. Where such misstatements have further been reprinted in cold blood by the Cardinal, after their public exposure by responsible critics whose strictures can hardly have escaped his notice, such a repetition of the original offence is marked by a **DD**. Blunders with regard to the text of the Latin Vulgate Bible, or other blunders in Latin which throw direct light on his qualifications as a Vulgate critic, are marked **V**; blunders in monastic history are marked **M**. For convenience of reference, the paragraphs are numbered consecutively. Italics are mine, unless otherwise stated.

THE *OLD ENGLISH BIBLE*

It will be best to begin with this book, since this was the first in which Cardinal Gasquet's methods were pilloried, not by the present writer, but by a well-known Anglican clergyman, in the *Church Quarterly* for October, 1900, and January, 1901. References in this place to the *Old English Bible* are to the first edition (1897), and to the second (1908).

DD 1. *Old English Bible*, p. 129 [new ed. p. 111].

"We shall look in vain, in the edition of Wycliffite scriptures published by Forshall and Madden, for any trace of these errors" [*i.e.* the thirteen erroneous articles condemned by Bishop Fitzjames of London, in 1514, and printed from his register by Foxe (ed. Townsend, IV, 186)].

The *Church Quarterly* points out that every one of those thirteen propositions occurs, almost textually, in Forshall and Madden's edition (January, 1901, p. 292). The first occurs as early as p. 3. The *Church Quarterly* printed the two side by side, showing that Cardinal Gasquet had made a blunder as gross and as inexplicable as if he had denied that his own name began with a G. The Cardinal's only answer to this has been to print the falsehood, unaltered, in his second edition, eight years after the exposure. There was, in fact, only one other alternative, possible to most scholars, but quite impossible for a Roman Catholic prelate. Upon this alleged absence of the thirteen propositions, he had founded his theory that "it is hardly possible to read the prologue referred to, without seeing that the author of this translation had a filial reverence for the teaching of the approved doctors of the Church, and was most scrupulous in his endeavour to translate the words exactly in accordance with the prevailing authoritative teaching". To have admitted that this prologue did really contain the thirteen officially condemned propositions, and was in fact the very prologue which convicted Richard Hunne of "gross and manifest heresy", would have been to knock the bottom out of his own case. The Cardinal had therefore to choose between (1) withdrawing altogether an integral portion of his theory, or (2) reprinting not only the theory itself, but the false assertion upon which it had been based. He chose the latter alternative.

DD 2. *O.E.B.* p. 118 [new ed. p. 101].

Cardinal Gasquet, having quoted a dozen lines from this same prologue, adds "it would seem tolerably certain, from the above extract, that the writer had no knowledge of any previous translation".

The *Church Quarterly* pointed out that, if the Cardinal had read only twenty-six lines further, he would have found a passage in which the writer *explicitly refers to the previous translation*, using the words: "the English Bible late translated". The Cardinal (it appears) had borrowed this blunder, without acknowledgment, from J. H. Blunt's inaccurate article in the old edition of the *Encyclopædia Britannica*. Here again, however, a whole theory had been based upon the falsehood, which is therefore reprinted without alteration in the second edition.

DD 3. *O.E.B.* p. 113 [new ed. p. 97].

The Cardinal lays stress on "the silence of Wyclif himself" as to English translations of the Bible. Mr F. D. Matthew, one of the most eminent living editors of Wyclif's texts, answered this in the *Engl. Hist. Rev.* for 1895, pp. 93–4. He pointed out that, if the Cardinal had merely taken the trouble to refer to the word *Bible* in the indices to Wyclif's published works, he would have found at least eight or nine passages contradicting this assertion. The Cardinal met this only by a furtive insinuation of discourtesy against Mr Matthew (who is in fact one of the most courteous of men), and has twice reprinted the falsehood without alteration.

DD 4. *O.E.B.* p. 129 [new ed. p. 112].

Cardinal Gasquet argues "from the absolute silence of all records, both ecclesiastical and lay, as to any Wycliffite version of the Bible". The *Church Quarterly* (pp. 286–7) pointed out that this again was false, since the episcopal registers contain much evidence of the kind here denied. The statement is reprinted without alteration.

DD 5. The Cardinal appeals to Sir E. M. Thompson as saying that the Old Testament translation, "it is tolerably certain, owes nothing to Wyclif's pen". The *Church Quarterly* (p. 266) points out that Sir E. M. Thompson says, on the contrary, "the remaining portion of the Old Testament may have been finished by Wyclif himself". (*O.E.B.* p. 112; cf. p. 113: new ed. p. 95.)

DD 6. The *Church Quarterly*, on the same page, pillories a similar attempt to make Messrs Forshall and Madden say the opposite of what in fact they say. (*O.E.B.* p. 113; new ed. p. 96.)

DD 7. Professor Shirley is misquoted as saying that Wyclif's "poor priests" were really "mere *lay* preachers". Though corrected by the *Church Quarterly* and by Mr Matthew (*E.H.R.* 1895, p. 97), Cardinal Gasquet deliberately reprints this misstatement, to which he has given the emphasis of italics. (*O.E.B.* p. 153; new ed. p. 132.)

DD 8. He misquotes Cranmer as saying that, in pre-Reformation times, the English Bible was "in daily use", and that such use was "a well-known custom of the Church". Cranmer, as the *Church Quarterly* points out (pp. 271–2), says in fact the opposite of this. (*O.E.B.* p. 177; new ed. p. 154.)

DD 9. A copy of this English Bible was given to Syon Nunnery by Lady Danvers in 1517. Therefore, argues the Cardinal, it cannot have been a Wycliffite translation, since "it must appear as nothing less than the height of absurdity to suppose that any lady would insult its inmates by offering for their acceptance an heretical version of the English Bible". The *Church Quarterly* points out that the still existing catalogue of Syon shows the nuns to have possessed, in fact, several of Wyclif's tracts (p. 276) (*O.E.B.* p. 145; new ed. p. 125.)

DD 10. Another belonged to Bishop Bonner: could "that *malleus haereticorum*" (implies the Cardinal) have possessed an heretical Bible? The *Church Quarterly* (p. 276) points out that *the same source which names Bonner as the possessor, specifies not only that this particular Bible was "translated out of Latyne in time of*

Heresye", but also that another copy was in the possession of the contemporary Bishop of Lichfield, who has made a note in the margin which shows that he took its Wycliffian origin for granted. (*O.E.B.* p. 143; new ed. p. 123.)

DD 11. One manuscript of the so-called Wycliffite version, still existing, belonged to the ultra-orthodox Henry VI, and was given by him to the monks of the Charterhouse. Here again the Cardinal insists upon the absurdity of supposing that this can really have been any other than "the perfectly orthodox translation of the English Church". The *Church Quarterly* points out that the Cardinal had not actually consulted this manuscript before urging his argument. The medieval copyist, by a slip, has betrayed himself, and has shown most unquestionably that he copied Henry VI's Bible from Wycliffite originals (p. 278). (*O.E.B.* p. 140; new ed. p. 121.)

DD 12. The Cardinal (arguing that Archbishop Arundel's prohibitory constitution concerns not the whole Bible, or whole books of the Bible, but simply detached "passages") refers to Lyndwood's *Provinciale* in proof of this assertion. The *Church Quarterly* (p. 281) points out that Lyndwood, in fact, says the exact opposite of this, explaining that the words in dispute refer to "a book containing *the whole Bible*". To the page of Lyndwood thus quoted, the reviewer might in fact have added another, where Lyndwood goes out of his way to remind the reader, by a marginal note, that Arundel's constitution rehearses the perils of "translating *the Bible* into another tongue" (ed. 1679, App. II, p. 66). The Cardinal, as usual, reprints his assertion unaltered. (*O.E.B.* p. 170; new ed. p. 148.)

V 13. One even more interesting point, however, the reviewer has failed to note. Cardinal Gasquet, apart from his appeal to Lyndwood, bases his argument upon a point of Latin scholarship. He asks us to take it, on his own authority, that "aliquis textus" can only mean "any passage", and cannot signify a complete volume. Yet, in the ecclesiastical language of the Middle Ages, *textus* was the consecrated word for the whole volume containing the four Gospels; it is so common in this sense that Maigne d'Arnis does not trouble to specify any separate authority, but characterizes it as used "passim". The sense of "detached passage", which the Cardinal asserts to be the only possible sense, is comparatively rare—except, of course, in the sense of *text* as opposed to *gloss*, which lies quite outside his argument.

14. With regard to this tedious list of republished falsehoods, and the still more tedious list to follow, it must be remarked that the Cardinal has not even the partial excuse of reprinting from

stereotyped plates, which might have been expensive to alter. Only the later editions of his *Henry VIII*, from 1899 onwards, are printed from such plates. In all other cases, the printers have been instructed, in cold blood, to set up the falsehoods a second time in type.

M 15. Moreover, this is emphasized by the rare cases in which the Cardinal has actually made alterations in a later edition: his exceptional repentances are almost as significant as his habitual impenitence. For instance, on p. 238 of his *English Monastic Life*, he made the extraordinary assertion that St Clare was St Francis's sister. Even the *Athenæum*, usually so indulgent to him, permitted itself a mild sarcasm on this point. This blunder stood by itself; it could be silently corrected without in any way affecting the rest of the book; it was therefore silently corrected in the second edition. I know of no case in which the Cardinal has corrected any misstatement, however gross, which involved the slightest reconstruction of his theories, or any retraction whatever of an opinion once emphatically expressed.

HENRY VIII AND THE ENGLISH MONASTERIES

I have already pointed out that this book constantly confuses two entirely separate issues, the question of Henry's guilt and the question of the real state of the monasteries. The second question is the only one which seriously interests the modern public, yet Cardinal Gasquet scarcely devotes a tenth of his book to its direct discussion; he constantly tries to smuggle in a verdict for monastic innocence, under cover of our condemnation for the frequent injustices committed at the Suppression. Yet there is no lack of materials: the mass of monastic chronicles and official records is simply overwhelming; our knowledge of life in court or in camp during the Middle Ages is vague and insignificant compared to what we may learn of monastic life by studying the printed records alone. He avoids in his book all serious consideration of fourteenth and fifteenth century records; he has since refused the most direct challenges to discuss those records; and the late Father Gerard, who came forward as his champion, refused with equal obstinacy to discuss them.[1] The following corrections, therefore, deal only with

---

[1] See my article in the *Contemporary Review* for December, 1905, on *Catholic Truth and Historical Truth*, and the resulting correspondence in the *Tablet* from December 9, 1905, to February 10, 1906. I published my own share of this in a pamphlet now out of print; Father Gerard refused to let me print his letters side by side with mine.

those small portions of Cardinal Gasquet's book which really concern me; of Henry's injustice I have already spoken sufficiently plainly. Quotations are from the third edition, 1888. From the latest edition (1898) passages have been omitted which described too correctly, from orthodox sources, the decay of Church life in the later Middle Ages: *e.g.* episcopal non-residence—Bellarmine's confession that "well-nigh there was no religion"—the insufficiency of preaching—and Colet's famous Convocation sermon of 1511, warning the clergy that nothing but reform could avert a catastrophe (pp. 18–31). All these omissions, of course, aggravate the one-sidedness of the evidence put before the reader in this latest edition. Moreover, even in the early editions, Cardinal Gasquet ignores the strong evidence which may be gathered against the monasteries from Colet's life. Erasmus states that Colet "had very little liking for the monasteries, of which many in these days are false to their name[1]...not that he disliked Religious Orders, but because the men did not act up to their profession": Erasmus goes on to say that Colet himself would gladly have retired to a monastery "if he could find anywhere a community really determined to live the evangelical life", and that he had some hopes of finding one such in Italy or in Germany. He did in fact take rooms later on among the Carthusians of Sheen, but not as a monk. (Erasmus, *Ep.* 435, ed. 1703, vol. III, col. 458–9, quoted in Lupton's *Life of Dean Colet*, p. 216.)

D 16. In his third chapter, Cardinal Gasquet attempts to depreciate the moral significance of Wolsey's monastic reforms, and to represent them mainly as a political job. For this purpose (I, 71) he suppresses a sentence from a letter in which the Bishop of Worcester, approving of Wolsey's reforms from the moralist's point of view, anticipates that "many faults would be found" when it came to the turn of the English nunneries to be visited.[2]

---

[1] [Quae nunc falso nomine pleraque sic vocantur.] In Italy and Germany, while the general average of monasticism was lower than in England, a certain number of houses had been very vigorously reformed since the Council of Bâle.

V [2] Brewer, to whose Calendar the Cardinal refers as his authority, renders "many *errors* will be found in them (the nunneries)." The context (which I give below) shows that *errores* is here used in its not uncommon sense of *faults*. It may be noted that, in the previous sentence, Brewer's text exactly reverses the sense of the word *morigera* (not *complaining*, but *obedient*); and that Cardinal Gasquet, while arranging Brewer's text in other ways to suit his thesis, copies this blunder. Did not Brewer really write *compliant*, and is not *complain*

D 16A. The same bias, and even greater inaccuracy, may be found a few pages earlier in his account of Fisher's similar measures for the suppression of Heigham nunnery. The Cardinal writes (p. 65): "At the time of Bishop Fisher's proceedings, which were very regular, the convent bore a bad character and *one at least of the nuns* had been accused of serious immorality ten years before. No charge of later date was apparently brought against any of the three nuns, and, *as is remarked in the 'Monasticon'*, it seems to be probable that the fewness of the numbers had as much to do with the dissolution as the life". These sentences which I have italicized falsify both (*a*) Fisher's report and (*b*) the *Monasticon* text.

(*a*) The bishop's commissary, after reporting that the numbers of nuns had fallen from sixteen to three because the convent "was much frequented by wanton persons, especially clergy, by reason of whom the nuns therein dwelling were grievously ill-famed of incontinence", proceeds as follows: "after that your Paternity...had raised the number of the nuns in this convent to five, not only were several (*plures*) of the aforesaid nuns debauched by a priest, and some of them gotten with child, whereof they were convicted in due form of law before your Paternity, but also, etc. etc."

(*b*) The comment attributed to the *Monasticon* is certainly not anywhere on the page cited by Cardinal Gasquet, and seems to be a pure figment; so at least I am forced to conclude, after ascertaining by a double search on my own account, and a third search undertaken by a friend, that no words even remotely resembling these can be found in the whole *Monasticon* article on Heigham. Moreover, it is difficult to understand how anyone, in the face of the actual evidence given to Bishop Fisher, could surmise that "the fewness of the numbers had as much to do with the dissolution as the life".

M 17. Vol. I, p. 256. I have already pointed out that the order for the strict claustration of monks and nuns, which is here made a sin against Cromwell, is really a prominent provision of the

a printer's error, which the Cardinal has unsuspectingly adopted? The text runs (British Museum, Vit. B. III, f. 282 *b*: old foliation 231 *b*): "Verum enimvero, quantum per multos annos, in quibus diversis vicibus istuc [animum] contuli, conspicere possum, magna mihi reformandi monasteria necessitas visa [es]t: quod nunc D. V. R^{mam} facturam haud vereor; quae res ipsi apud Deum [m]agno merito et ingenti penes istud inclytum regnum laudi certissime [fu]tura est. Meae diocesis eidem, quoad possum, commendo monasteria, [q]uae ut spero morigera reperientur. Monialium vero monasteriis magna [ad]hibenda est cura, in ipsis enim multi invenientur errores".

Benedictine Rule itself (p. 60). In order to prejudice Cromwell still further, Cardinal Gasquet quotes a letter from Ap Rice to the effect that the monks cannot be expected to keep this strict seclusion. But he carefully omits from Ap Rice's letter the further remark, that he considered it equally difficult, in the then condition of English monasticism, to enforce another still more essential clause of discipline which Cromwell had revived at the same time—that no women should be admitted within the monastery precincts. The full text of Ap Rice's letter shows that the monks of the sixteenth century had (as orthodox disciplinarians had long before complained) grown to consider indiscipline as their established right.

D 18. Vol. I, p. 266. Cardinal Gasquet quotes a story of the wickedness of Henry's visitors in 1535 on the authority of "Sanders, *almost a contemporary*". Sanders, a bitter partisan, was in fact five years old in 1535. To take a parallel instance, what decent modern historian would venture to blacken Queen Mary's character on similar hearsay evidence from a bitter Protestant, born only five years before the alleged occurrence, and recording it without further corroboration fifty-five years later?

The Cardinal then quotes a similar rumour on Thomas Fuller's authority. Fuller, who was born seventy-three years after the alleged occurrence, *warns the reader that he quotes it as a partisan rumour*. But the Cardinal attempts to weaken the force of this warning by adding "he [Fuller] then goes on to relate a story *which bears out what he has said*". Yet, on reference to this second story, we find that Fuller records it with an even more emphatic *caveat* than the first. After warning the reader that it comes, at second-hand, from "Sir William Stanley, Kt., afterwards employed in the Low Countries", Fuller adds: "All I will say to this story is this, that if this Sir William Stanley was he who, contrary to his solemn oath to the earl of Leicester and the United States, betrayed the strong city of Deventer to the Spaniards, and lived many years after in a neglected, forlorn condition, one so faithless in his deeds may be presumed false in his words, and the whole credit of the relation may justly at least be suspected" (Book VI, sect. III, p. 8). All this Cardinal Gasquet carefully suppresses; and, under cover of this suppression, he writes later on, "It is evident that the blood of the old Puritan [Fuller] was stirred within him, and he must have felt that the disgraceful relations made to him were only too true." (Vol. II, p. 225, n.)

DD 19. To the equally glaring suppression of the crucial points in Thorold Rogers's verdict, I called the Cardinal's attention in

1906, in a registered letter (see *Monastic Legend*, p. 11). The passage is reprinted without correction in the latest edition; Rogers is still represented as testifying to the exact opposite of his real convictions; in short, the only notice which the Cardinal takes of the correction is to abuse me in his preface. (Ed. 1906, pp. vii–ix).

20. Vol. I, p. 278. The Cardinal, in order to discredit the hostile evidence of a monk, quotes from Brewer's *Calendar* (vol. IX, no. 231–2), to stigmatize him as a lazy and self-indulgent member of the convent. Though there is nothing to warn us that this is not a verbal quotation, a reference to the actual *Calendar* will show that the Cardinal (1) has suppressed the fact that the monk had been excused Matins "*considering my infirmity*" (an indulgence very frequently granted in the most orthodox times), and (2) that, where the Cardinal represents him as writing "*I do not like*" the full burdens of monastic observance, he does in fact write: "*He* [*my Abbot*] knows that I cannot *endure* (*i.e. support*) them".

M 21. In the same letter, Cardinal Gasquet thus glosses the word *frayter*: "*i.e.* the community recreations". *Frayter* or *Frater* is a very common word in medieval monastic documents, and means exactly the opposite of this: viz. the *refectory* and its regular diet, which monks very commonly avoided by exchanging it for more generous meals outside the refectory; such meals being often called *recreations*.

D 22. Vol. I, p. 279. He deals equally unjustly with another witness, John Musard the monk of Worcester. The very authority on which he relies (*Calendar*, IX, no. 497) shows Musard claiming that "many of our convent" had formally accused the prior of incontinence before the visitors, a claim which Cardinal Gasquet conceals partly by calculated omissions and partly by actual distortions of fact. A fuller reference to Noake's *Monastery and Cathedral of Worcester* (pp. 198, 202) shows that Musard's other accusations against his superior receive considerable corroboration from official documents, and that the bishop himself, as early as 1522, had been compelled to subject this same prior to much the same disciplinary measures which Cardinal Gasquet abuses Cromwell for using.

Moreover, while dealing at length with this subject of complaints from different monks to Cromwell, the Cardinal omits all reference to the Bodmin and Pershore cases in the same collection, which would have been far more difficult to explain away (Wright's *Suppression*, pp. 130, 132). The Prior of Bodmin complains that his own flock "of long continuance have lived unthriftily and against the good order of religion, to the great slander of the same, as all the country can tell", and that the bishop's recent attempts to bring them back to the Rule has simply roused them to revolt. At Pershore, a monk complains of the nightly compotations of his fellows in words which are borne out by visitation records and other unexceptionable medieval sources.

M 23. Vol. I, p. 307. The Act of Suppression of 1536 is based upon the vices alleged to be common in monasteries *where the inmates number less than twelve*. To this Cardinal Gasquet objects "on the face of it, it is absurd....Such a limit...is made ridiculous, when it is set as the line of demarcation between virtue and vice". To this he adds in a note: "The number 12 was probably introduced *ad captandum*".

On the contrary, it had long been a commonplace among medieval monastic disciplinarians that houses of less than twelve were difficult to keep in moral health. Hugh of St Victor, four centuries before this, alludes to it as a fixed principle among the Benedictines. The Cistercians, Dominicans, and Franciscans, always tried to ensure that no community should fall below twelve. There was even a technical word, *conventualis*, sometimes applied to monasteries which came up to this necessary standard. It is true that disciplinarians constantly failed here, and that large numbers of convents fell below the "conventual" standard; but the failure was often deplored as disastrous. St Bernard wrote to a fellow-abbot "it is by God's inspiration...that thou art destroying the synagogues of Satan; that is, cells apart from the parent abbey, wherein dwell three or four monks with no order and with no discipline; that thou keepest women away from the monastery," etc., etc. A Benedictine reformer of 1503 lends his support to the same accusation, repeating St Bernard's words (Bernard, *Ep.* 254; Guido Juvenalis, *Reformationis Monastice Vindicie*, Paris, 1503, fol. 17 a). Cromwell, who fixed this number of twelve, is thus held up to the scorn of the modern reader, simply because he was familiar with an important monastic principle which the Abbot President of the English Benedictines happens never to have met with in his studies.

M 24. Vol. I, p. 333-4. Cardinal Gasquet's description of an ordinary monastic visitation, purporting to be taken from Nicke's Norwich visitations as a typical example, is grossly misleading all through, and in some cases flagrantly inaccurate. I have already pointed out the falsehood of the assertion that the bishop always meted out stern punishment to serious faults against good morals (*Monastic Legend*, p. 3; cf. p. 96, here below); and here is another assertion which can be met equally briefly. "The monk of generally anxious temperament" (writes the Cardinal in describing Nicke's reports) "eases his conscience by the declaration that in his opinion everything is going to the dogs (*omnia patiuntur ruinam*)". My notes on Nicke's visitations enable me to test, by comparison with actual fact, this attempt to put a jesting construction upon serious and responsible testimony. This actual phrase *occurs only once* in Nicke's visitations (Westacre, p. 104), where Richard Anger first testifies that "omnia edificia dicti prioratus patiuntur ruinam", and Richard Cobbe, following him, repeats "omnia patiuntur ruinam". On more than fifty other occasions monks apply the word *ruinam* to their monasteries: in every case the context shows the reference to be to actual dilapidation of buildings or possessions. To take the first two instances: "aedificia patiuntur ruinam magnam" (St Faith's, p. 19), and "propter ruinam et destructionem in domibus" (St Benet's, p. 63). In many cases the witnesses give further details, *e.g.* 75 (Norwich Cathedral) "monasterium in nonnullis locis (viz. ecclesia, dormitorio, domo capitulari) patitur ruinam in tectura plumbea". Nobody who had read these visitations with the least care could fail to see that the word *ruina* is there used literally, and that these records testify to widespread mismanagement and dilapidation in the monasteries, long before the Dissolution. It must be remembered that the preamble to Henry's Act of Suppression lays almost as much stress on this waste and dilapidation, as on the accusations of immorality brought against the monks.

V 25. Vol. I, p. 344. The Cardinal translates *fatentur* "they are reported", apparently taking it for some part of *fari*. If this blunder on the part of the President of the Vulgate Revision Commission seems intrinsically incredible, let it be compared with Nos. 34, 36, 60, 61, 64, 69, 71, 89, 90, 109, 110, 122, 163, here below. These, again, should be compared with similar ignorances of the Vulgate text (though not of the Latin language) which are quoted from a distinguished Jesuit professor in my "From St Francis to Dante", second edition, p. 356, n. 7. Few priests know their Vulgate so well as a capable Sunday-school teacher knows the English version; and these lapses on the part of distinguished Roman Catholics would cause far less surprise to their own colleagues than to the general public.

DD 26. Vol. I, p. 344. (Bury St Edmunds.) Cardinal Gasquet, professing as usual to quote literally from Dr Gairdner's *Calendar* (vol. X, no. 364), makes Cromwell's visitor write: "There is a grave suspicion that the abbot and convent had agreed together not to tell anything about themselves, for though *report* says the monks here live licentiously, still there never was less confessed to" [italics his]. The reader who verifies his reference will find that he has here garbled his extract; Dr Gairdner's words run: "though no monks *are more notorious for licentious living*, yet there was never less confessed". And Dr Gairdner is true to the original, which runs "nam, ut nusquam alias licentiosius aut insolentiosius vivunt monachi quam illic, *ex communi fama*, ita nusquam minus confessum quam ibi". Dr Gairdner (who, as a Scotchman, knew something of Roman law) was aware of the legal signification of *communis fama*, which is defined by medieval canonists as "the general testimony of credible people in the neighbourhood". The Cardinal (who, as will presently be seen, is sometimes extraordinarily ignorant of canon law) mistranslates this phrase *communis fama* into *report*, italicizes the word, and thus transforms the correct legal phrase of the visitor into the complaint of a baffled scoundrel. Yet it is a very common complaint among orthodox visitors of the Middle Ages that the monks conspired together to conceal the truth; ecclesiastical authorities legislated frequently against this, but with small success. A distinguished medieval abbot actually boasts in his chronicle how he and his fellows thus successfully shielded their grossly immoral superior against the bishop.[1] The most orthodox of visitors, in cases where the monks' silence was inconsistent with the *communis fama*, drew exactly the same inferences which Cardinal Gasquet abuses Cromwell's agents for drawing at Bury St Edmunds.

D 27. Vol. I, p. 369. A monk of Wigmore, John Lee, accused his abbot to Cromwell of various offences. Froude prints his letter in full, and (as is often the case) goes decidedly too far in the inferences he draws from it.

After correcting Froude's inaccuracies, Cardinal Gasquet undertakes to justify the Abbot, from the injunctions given by the bishop's commissary appointed to visit and enquire into the case. Of these injunctions, he gives his own version from the manuscript register at Hereford. Let me here translate five paragraphs from these injunctions (Reg. Fox, Heref., fol. 21 *a*), which Cardinal Gasquet manipulates to support his thesis. It must be premised that *he suppresses No. 2 altogether*: how he deals with the rest can only be understood by a comparison of the Cardinal's "summaries" on p. 369 of vol. I, with these following translations:

[1] This is the well-known *Evesham Chronicle* in the Rolls Series; I have given full references on this point in the *English Historical Review* for January, 1914, p. 37.

(*a*) "First, considering that the lives of prelates ought to provide a model of living to their subordinates (since a prelate cannot, with any free face, rebuke in others that which he approves in himself), we strictly enjoin and command thee, beloved brother and Suffragan,[1] in virtue of holy obedience, (that so thou mayest live as an example of good, religious and laudable life to thy brethren the canons), that thou be careful to avoid the companionship of any suspected women whatsoever, and of those in especial (if any there be) with whom thou art ill-famed [*notatus*] of incontinent intercourse, under the penalties lately proclaimed against incontinent [clerics]; and know that, if in this matter thou obey not our injunctions, thou wilt forthwith incur these said penalties, without further warning from us."

(*b*) "Item, we command thee not to dissipate, waste, or consume the lands, chattels, possessions or other goods of the monastery, but rather to employ them to the uses of the monastery; nor to farm out or alienate the same without the consent of the Chapter."

(*c*) "Item, that thou inform thy brethren whether thou hast redeemed the jewels pawned by thee in times past; and, if not, that thou redeem them now and restore them to thy monastery, under the penalty decreed against embezzlement." (Then follow what Cardinal Gasquet calls "the usual regulations for the yearly accounts and for the custody of the monastic deeds"; the fact being, that such regulations are found in medieval visitatorial injunctions only where suspicions of mismanagement or dishonesty have been excited by the visitation.)

(*d*) (Addressed to the Canons): "Item, seeing that it is most indecent that a man polluted with the stains of lechery should offer sacrifices (*hostias*) in the House of God, therefore We, wishing that chastity, as the gem of all other virtues, may shine in the Religious who dwell under Our care, do decree, command and enjoin upon you Canons aforesaid, all and severally, that ye keep your chastity in all things, and that each one of you do keep it, avoiding utterly the company of all women whatsoever, except in the cases permitted to men of Religion, under the penalty above rehearsed."

(*e*) "Item, since that part is base which agreeth not with the whole [whereof it is part], we solemnly command that Richard

[1] The Abbot was also a Bishop Suffragan; Bishop Fox is therefore bound to address him with all consideration. Cardinal Gasquet deduces from the phrase "if any there be", presently following, "that no case had been proved against him, appears tolerably certain." It is scarcely necessary to observe that this phrase is a piece of "common form", frequent in medieval documents, like the cautious "be they more or less", of our own lawyers.

Cubley[1] do bear himself religiously in morals, in monastic uses, in dress, in conversation, and in honesty; that he be present in choir at the day and night services together with the other brethren; moreover, that he abstain from hawking, hunting, quarrelling, fighting [*pugnis*], and all suchlike unlawful occupations."

Cardinal Gasquet, after giving a version of these injunctions so garbled as to rob them of all real significance, adds triumphantly: "Thus, after a careful examination, little appears against the character of Wigmore and its abbot, John Smarte. The visitation really discredits the charges and base insinuations of John Lee". It is only by carefully comparing his version with these actual translations (as I have said above), that the reader can realize his methods of dealing with unpublished evidence.

28. Vol. I, p. 470. Cardinal Gasquet ends this volume, and his review of the very doubtful characters whom Cromwell employed to report on the Monasteries in 1535, by asserting that "no other evidence is forthcoming" beyond the untrustworthy word of these men.

This is simply "the thing that is not". The orthodox Gascoigne, in 1450, had written of the monasteries in words quite consistent with Henry's accusations in the Suppression Bill. Pecock, set up specially to defend the monks among other clergy, could do so only half-heartedly: even Sir Thomas More's words would often seem half-hearted to a modern apologist; and More's friend, Colet, "had but very little liking for monasteries", because "those who took [religious orders] did not come up to their profession".

But let us accept the Cardinal's own limitation, and take official documents of the sixteenth century only. Nicke's visitation of 1514 reveals a state of things which no modern government would tolerate (*Monastic Legend*, p. 4). It will presently be seen that Archbishop Lee's York visitations, if the Cardinal had left them ungarbled, would have told much the same tale. Others of his omissions, as the reader has seen, are simply caused by his anxiety to conceal similar evidence. Lastly, the Cistercian abbot of Combe, somewhere about 1515, appealed to the General Chapter to reform the English houses. Let them decree, (he said) "under the strictest censures and pains, that, before the year be past, the entering and frequenting of women within the monasteries of our Order be shut off; for otherwise the honesty of Religion, and the monks' observance of their Rule will never be well thought-of, seeing that this thing

---

[1] The Abbot's chaplain, whose misdeeds Lee had accused the Abbot of abetting or overlooking.

causeth, and hath caused, the ruin of many; for, as we think, this abuse hath grown more inveterate among us than in any other nation".[1]

Cardinal Gasquet may reasonably excuse himself for never having met with this important letter; but he would find it difficult to justify his ignorance—or rather, his elimination—of the other evidence unfavourable to sixteenth century monasticism.

M 29. Vol. II, pp. 95-6, 221-4, 500. I deal with these almost incredible blunders about Monastic Schools in the tenth of my *Medieval Studies*, nn. 5, 9, 10, 11, 34.

D 30. Vol. II, p. 220. I have already pointed out how the Bishop of Worcester's letter was so garbled in vol. I, as to suppress his prophecy that, when the time came for visiting the nunneries, "many faults will be found in them". In the sixth chapter of vol. II, Cardinal Gasquet develops his case in favour of the nuns. In order, as he says, to give "an insight into the conventual life" of a typical convent just before the Suppression, he quotes the injunctions of Archbishop Lee to the nuns of Sinningthwaite in 1534. He prints four and a half pages of this document, from the manuscript register, implying again on p. 219 that this extract is typical, and fairly illustrative of convent life in general at that time. Now, these injunctions, together with the bishop's other visitations of that year, have since been very carefully printed by Mr W. Brown for the *Yorkshire Archaeological Journal* (1902, pp. 440 ff.). This publication now shows that (to take no notice of frequent small blunders in transcription and minor omissions, of which some, at least, seem to be dictated by "economy" of truth) the Cardinal has taken the following liberties with his documents:

(*a*) *Gasquet*. "The dormitory door is to be fastened 'until service time', and the key kept by the prioress."

Original. "That the prioress there, every night, provide that the door of the dorter be surely and fast locked, that none of the sisters may get out until service-time, nor yet any person get into the dorter to them, and that the key thereof be in the custody of the prioress." In the simultaneous and parallel injunctions for the convent of Esholt (to which the Cardinal himself refers in general terms on p. 219) this injunction is still more significant, for it is followed by the warning "that she suffer not any manner person, of what degree soever *he* be, secular or religious, to lie or be lodged in the cloister, or in any chamber opening into the cloister".

[1] The original may be found in *Eng. Hist. Review*, January, 1914, p. 39 (note).

(*b*) *Gasquet*. "From henceforth the prioress shall diligently provide that no secular or religious persons have any resort or recourse at any time to her or any of her said sisters, on any occasion, unless it be their fathers or mothers, or other near kinsfolk.". . . Here the Cardinal breaks off, but the

Original goes on: "in whom no suspicion of any ill can be thought. In like manner we command and enjoin the said prioress, under pain of privation, that she admits no person, secular nor religious, to her company suspectly, or be in familiar communication with her in her chamber or any other secret place".

(*c*) Shortly afterwards, without any mark of omission, Cardinal Gasquet suppresses the Archbishop's command "that all sisters sleep in the dorter, under pains and penalties due on this behalf".

(*d*) Again without warning, he suppresses the following paragraph: "item, we command and enjoin the said prioress and convent, that she nor they admit nor take any person, secular or religious, to be her or their ghostly father, to hear her or the nuns' confessions, without special licence obtained of us or our successors under our seal".

(*e*) *Gasquet*. "Also that no one shall be blamed or rebuked for any *injunction* made at visitation". The word I have italicized must be noted; it necessarily fixes the reader's thoughts upon the archbishop or his commissaries, who alone did or could make injunctions in this case.

Original. "Also we enjoin and command, under pain of the great curse, that the prioress shall not rebuke or worse intreat *her sisters* for anything said or done in this our visitation, or shall make any rehearsal thereof, but shall lovingly and charitably intreat them. And in like manner, under the same pain, we command the nuns, that none of them grudge or murmur at the prioress, nor any of their sisters, for anything said or done at the visitation, or make any rehearsal thereof to any sister's rebuke".

Here we have not a word about archiepiscopal injunctions, but, on the contrary, the very great risk (for which medieval authorities legislated with a desperate frequency which suggests their impotence), that witnesses who spoke plainly at a visitation might be persecuted afterwards by their superiors or fellows.

(*f*) After thus garbling the Sinningthwaite records, Cardinal Gasquet refers vaguely and generally to the contemporary visitations recorded in the same portion of Lee's register, and quotes four paragraphs from the Nunappleton injunctions, giving us to understand that all the evidence is of this same character.

Yet the fact is that the archbishop was able to visit only five nunneries on this occasion. *To two of the five, he gave injunctions*

identical with, or similar to, those which Cardinal Gasquet has
suppressed in the Sinningthwaite case, with all their significant
implications. At Esholt, moreover, he found that an ale-house
had been set up on the convent premises, and that one of the
nuns had lately borne a child. In two letters of the same date as
the Sinningthwaite visitation, the archbishop deals with a
prioress of Basedale, who had left her convent and lived "inde-
center et irreligiose" among secular folk, then had professed
repentance, but finally had returned "fragilitati antiquae". Why
does Cardinal Gasquet, while professing to deal so fully with the
subject, give no hint whatever of all this? Is it not because, even
on his own chosen ground, he cannot afford to put the full
evidence before his readers? Even if, under his guidance, we
turn our faces away from the whole mass of damning evidence
contained in official documents of the fourteenth and fifteenth
centuries—even if we arbitrarily confine all serious consideration
to the first few decades of the sixteenth—even so, he cannot allow
his readers to face the actual recorded facts.

31. Vol. II, p. 329. "The learned antiquary, Hearne", is
quoted as voucher for the educational activities of the Glaston-
bury monks. The words are not Hearne's at all, but those of a
well-intentioned and very ignorant Roman Catholic antiquary,
whose words are clearly distinguished from Hearne's in the book
referred to by Cardinal Gasquet, and who produces no evidence
whatever for his assertion.

M 32. Vol. II, p. 492. "It is remarkable", writes Cardinal
Gasquet, speaking of seventeenth century literature, "that the
evil repute of monks and nuns dates from this period". He
supports himself merely on a remark of Macaulay's, which will
not bear the stress he lays upon it. This has been dealt with in
Monastic Legend (p. 21); but, as readers might feel that this
simply leaves them to weigh the Cardinal's judgment against
mine, let me here quote the verdict of a modern scholar whose
orthodoxy is as unimpeachable as the Cardinal's, and who is
attempting to estimate the value of those accusations of vice
and mismanagement against the Templars which gave the excuse
for their suppression by the King of France and the Pope in
1311. "The literature of the Middle Ages", writes the Abbé
Mollat, "whether rightly or wrongly, censures monastic morals
crudely and indiscriminately".[1]

[1] *Les Papes d'Avignon*, Paris, Lecoffre, 1912, p. 234. I am not, of
course, quoting the author as agreeing with me about monastic
morality, but as simply bearing out my assertion of the notorious fact
that attacks on monastic morality are among the commonplaces of
pre-Reformation literature.

COLLECTANEA ANGLO-PREMONSTRATENSIA
(Royal Historical Society, 1904–6).

These foregoing corrections, confined to a small portion of his book, may show how little the Cardinal's statements can be trusted, even on points where his profession ought to give him most authority, or where he claims to rest upon most definite documents. This weakness comes out even more clearly in these three volumes of his *Collectanea Anglo-Premonstratensia*, because the necessity of editing and commenting a definite text gives him less opportunities of vague subterfuge, and enables the reader more definitely to check him at every point.

The text of this work is printed from two manuscripts: one at the Bodleian, original, and another, since lost, but transcribed by the antiquary Peck about 1750.

33. In dealing with Peck's transcript, the Cardinal corrects some obvious mistakes, but falls himself into others hardly less obvious. On pp. 11, 13, 14 of vol. 1, and in half a dozen other places, he corrects Peck for what he calls (Pref., p. 13) "the not inconsiderable error" of transcribing *testimonium* where the sense demands *witness*. This *testimonium*, therefore, Cardinal Gasquet everywhere alters to *testis*, in evident ignorance of the fact that medieval writers often used *testimonium* in that sense (as indeed the modern French word *témoin* might have sufficed to suggest).

V 34. Vol. 1, p. 17. He is puzzled by the phrase *in praesentiarum*, and hints at some mistake of Peck's. The phrase is quite common in medieval Latin, and occurs even in the first book of the Vulgate (Genesis l, 20).

35. Vol. 1, p. 129. He criticizes Peck for transcribing *capiciorum* instead of *caputiorum*; but the former spelling is very common in fifteenth century documents, and there is not the least reason to doubt that Peck found it exactly as he has written it.

V 36. Vol. 1, p. 183. He shares Peck's bewilderment at *efferbuit*, though it occurs, *e.g.*, in Job xx, 27 and Ezekiel xxiv, 5.

37. Vol. 1, p. 238. *Se.* This, though unclassical, is the normal medieval usage; and it is astounding that the Cardinal should here suggest a mistranscription of Peck's.

38. Vol. 1, 239. *Repentes errores* is perfectly comprehensible; it means "grovelling (or "furtive") heresies," as Horace speaks

of *sermones repentes*. The Cardinal, unable to construe this, is driven to suggest that Peck ought to have written *recentes*.

39. Vol. 1, p. 258. He alters Peck's *rubendo* to *loquendo*, where both paleography and sense should have suggested *ridendo*.

40. Nor is he much more fortunate with his own manuscript, the original register in the Bodleian. On 1, 78, he proposes to change *nostrum* into *vestrum*, where the next sentence shows clearly the correctness of the manuscript reading: *vestrum* would spoil the whole sense.

41. Next page, the manuscript has "ea que vestre *sedant* utilitati;" *i.e. cedant*, a common medieval licence of spelling and a common medieval phrase. The Cardinal would change this to *spectant*.

42. Vol. 1, p. 82. He alters *indebitater* to *indubitanter*, where *indebitate* gives the exact sense required.

43. Vol. 1, p. 83. He turns the passage from *donati sunt* to *opponat* into nonsense, by two false stops and the running of two words into one.

V 44. Vol. 1, p. 85. He amends *vobis* into *nobis*, which renders the sentence frankly ungrammatical; the obvious sense is obtained by reading *vos*.

V 45. Vol. 1, p. 121 (n. 3). He is unable to construe a perfectly clear sentence, and suggests adding a word which again does violence to the grammar.

46. Vol. 1, p. 136 (n. 3). He amends a sentence which reads quite correctly as it stands, in order to obtain a different sense which, in fact, would be at plain variance with Canon Law. How could a General Chapter in 1459 decree that no succeeding General Chapter should licence any Premonstratensian to serve in a parish church? A General Chapter can no more bind the decisions of future General Chapters, than a Parliament of future Parliaments. The decree was aimed at the *Commissaries of the General Chapter*, as its plain words declare.

47. Vol. 1, p. 143 (n. 1). He first mispunctuates, and then suggests a gratuitous emendation to correct the nonsense thus produced.

V 48. Vol. 1, p. 159. *Fueret* is altered to *fuerit*, which makes bad grammar; *foret* is the obvious correction.

49. Vol. 1, p. 221. The change of *absolutum* to *absolutos* shows that Cardinal Gasquet has never realized the not unusual medieval concord of a participle when *vos* refers to one person

only. Here, again, modern French might have suggested the facts to him.

M   50. Vol. II, p. 23. *Traditoris inde* makes sheer nonsense of the sentence: it is of course a blunder of the Cardinal's for *traditoris Jude*. In a later document this is correctly given: but the original error would have been quite impossible to any scholar really familiar with medieval visitation literature, in which this comparison of a "proprietary" monk to Judas is a stock formula.

51. Vol. II, p. 133 (n. 2). The alteration is quite unnecessary: the text construed well enough.

V   52. Vol. II, p. 149. *Innotescimus*, though here employed in a sense used by St Augustine, and of which Ducange says "utuntur passim scriptores", proves so incomprehensible to the Cardinal that he again makes a very unhappy emendation.

53. Vol. III, p. 3. *Et non solum, etc.* These three lines are so punctuated, apparently deliberately, as to make nonsense.

54. Vol. III, p. 4. The suggested emendation makes worse sense than the text. The Cardinal seems not to have realized that *hoc* may be a neuter ablative of comparison.

55. Vol. III, p. 65. *Utendo* is here in its common medieval sense of a present participle; there was not the least need to alter it; nor the *sub* of p. 98 to *ad*; nor again p. 105, n. 2.

56. Vol. III, p. 148. The manuscript reads *cera* (or, we may probably conjecture, *ceram*). Here again we have a common medieval licence of spelling for *seram*, which makes the sense required. Cardinal Gasquet alters this to *arcam*.

57. Vol. III, p. 206. *Infra festum Beate Marie*. This is a quite common and intelligible medieval phrase; but the Cardinal changes it to *ante* festum, etc.

58. On the other hand, while emending texts which are comprehensible enough, he leaves not a few obvious blunders uncorrected. In vol. II, p. 60, line 11, *exharando* should evidently be *exhonerando*. On the penultimate line of vol. II, p. 62, *brachi* makes nonsense; it seems plainly intended for *bracei*, "malt". On the twentieth line of the next page, a *non* is required before *nisi* to make sense. Vol. I, p. 200, line 17, *et equo* makes untranslatable nonsense, further aggravated by the Cardinal's punctuation; *et e contrario* is not only paleographically probable, but would, with a comma after *ecclesia*, give the required sense.

M   59. Again, vol. II, pp. 114, 123, 146, the Cardinal thrice prints *gravator* as the title of a monastic office; it would be interesting to know what sense he attaches to the word. It is an obvious blunder for *granator* (or, more probably *granatorius*, as it is correctly printed on p. 125); this and *granatarius* are quite common monastic terms.

V 60. Take, again, vol. II, p. 66, where a certain Robert Wolfet, "a nobis impetitus, premissorum [criminum] aliquid negare non valuit, sed misericordiam anxius imploravit, cui tamen pro rebellione prout infertur xl[ta] dierum gravioris culpe penitencia sibi injuncta, et emissione per triennium ad monasterium de Tore. Necnon eciam pro incontinencia sua injunximus xl[ta] dierum gravioris culpe et emissionem per triennium ad prefatum monasterium de Tore duximus subiturum", etc. It is difficult to understand how such a hash as this can be printed without any attempt at emendation, or how the Cardinal would propose to construe it, though of course its general sense is obvious enough.

V 61. Vol. III, p. 200. The text runs "eidem Ricardo *purgatione* criminis supradicti *manum* confratrum *nostrum induximus*". Here, again, it would be interesting to know how the Cardinal proposed to construe this. The obvious sense seems to require *purgationem*, *manu*, *nostrorum*, and *indiximus*.

62. Vol. III, p. 3. *In tantum* to *peractis* is so punctuated as to make nonsense: so again p. 56, line 25. Vol. III, p. 23, line 1, again makes nonsense; for *ultima et* read *ulterius*.

63. To turn now to minor errors: Vol. II, p. 68, line 6, *voce* should obviously be *vocem*; p. 74, line 4, *maxima ruina* should be *maximam ruinam*; p. 127, l. 26, for *verei* read *viridis*; p. 131, line 22, for *indignus* read *indignos*; p. 180, line 16, for *extinguetur* and *reticetur*, *extinguatur* and *reticeatur*. Vol. III, p. 139, line 4 from end, for *perdantur, perduntur*; p. 184, line 5 from end, for *providentia, improvidentia*; p. 54, line 2, for *sustinuit, sustinuerit*; other words needing correction may be found in vol. II, p. 122, line 15, and p. 127, line 8. No doubt the large majority of these are errors of the medieval scribe, to whose carelessness the Cardinal bears witness in his preface; but the editor might well have applied to these passages a little of the ingenuity which he wasted on amending what was already correct. Moreover, I am informed that in some cases the reading which makes nonsense is not even in the manuscript, *e.g.* vol. II, p. 76, *indie* is misread for *inde*; and p. 127, line 26, the manuscript has not *verei*, but *via*.

V 64. Most unhappy of all, however, is his effort to supply a list of the Biblical references in a letter of Peter of Blois which happens to be copied into the register (vol. I, pp. 256 ff.). In the first eight lines, he fails to recognize two Bible texts (*quos elegit, hos predestinavit*, and *novum indueris hominem*), and only succeeds with the third, I Cor. xiii, II. In the succeeding pages he fails to identify the following texts: "producat de thesauro suo nova et vetera" (Matt. xiii, 52)—"Deus non irridetur" (Gal. vi, 7)—"usque ad novissimum quadrantem" (Matt. v, 26)—"ut reddas populum acceptabilem Domino sectatorem bonorum operum" (Titus ii, 14) —"latere sub modio" (Matt. v, 15)—"oleo caput peccatoris impinguant[1]—non sumus meliores quam patres nostri" (2 Chron. xix, 4).

If it be pleaded that one or two of these are rather allusions than exact quotations, it must be replied that the Cardinal has, in some instances, identified even vaguer allusions than these; *e.g.* p. 258, n. 3, p. 260, n. 1, and p. 259, n. 5, where he ascribes the proverb "Vox populi, vox Dei" to Isaiah lxvi, 6.[2]

Let us now turn from mere blunders to questions of literary conscience. The Cardinal, when he edited this book, knew that he had been publicly accused of gross and palpable misstatements as to the proportion of inculpated Religious recorded by official visitors, and as to the regularity with which they were punished (*Monastic Legend*, pp. 4–10). He knew that this accusation had been supported by an array of documentary evidence which constituted, in the words of his own former supporter, Dr Gairdner, "a powerful indictment" (see above, p. 102). He was therefore, in this *Collectanea Anglo-Premonstratensia*, doubly on his honour (1) not again to minimize the proportion of inculpated Religious, and (2) not to exaggerate again the regularity or severity of their punishment. Yet in fact his assertions are here even farther than before, if possible, from the facts which actually stared him in the face while he was writing. For full proof of this, any reader specially interested in monastic evidence may refer to Appendix III, here below. For the present purpose, it is sufficient to summarize that evidence briefly here.

D 65. *Proportion of offenders.* The Cardinal only calculates this for vol. II (*i.e.* for the monasteries taken alphabetically from A to

---

[1] Psalm xxii, 5 Vulgate. So utterly is the Cardinal baffled by this quotation, that he prints *impingant*, which makes sheer nonsense.

[2] This verse of Isaiah runs: "Vox populi de civitate, vox de templo, vox Domini reddentis retributionem inimicis suis." A reference to the text of Peter of Blois will show that he is simply quoting the common proverb; it is his introductory phrase "scriptum est" which seems to have misled the Cardinal into the idea that this must be some Biblical text: he, therefore, looks up *vox* in the Concordance and gives the nearest text that he can find.

H), while implying that this arbitrary division is typical of the rest. As a matter of fact, these houses from A to H happen to present a distinctly better record than the houses from L to W, which are thus omitted from the calculation.

In his calculation itself, he counts each canon afresh at each separate visitation, thus bringing the total of canons to 1806, and the proportion accused of incontinence to 1 per cent. Yet there were in fact only about 470 canons visited in these houses; this brings the real proportion up to nearly 5 per cent., or considerably more than the percentage which, under Cromwell's visitation, the Cardinal dismisses as incredible.

Again, he speaks as if these figures which he quotes formed an exhaustive record of all that the visitors discovered "in the quarter of the century". Yet in another place, he is perfectly well aware that a large proportion of the visitation records of these twenty-five years are missing; and the documents printed in his first volume (of which he here takes no notice) prove that these lost visitations produced a heavy crop of discovered offences. Lastly, he takes no heed of the fifty-one apostates recorded, many of whom were pretty certainly leading far from model lives outside the convent walls. The real facts of these visitations, if the editor had honestly faced them, are amply sufficient to justify Dr Gairdner's significant palinode: "I fear that there is much to be said about the state of matters in a considerable number of monasteries, to show that they were no good schools of delicacy or chastity". (*Nineteenth Century and After*, July, 1909, p. 55.)

D 66. Coming to the question of punishment, the Cardinal writes: "Those found guilty were punished with exemplary severity...*generally* the culprit was actually sent *at once* to some other monastery". This statement is false even on the face of his documents; in the large majority of cases, the words recording this sentence are followed by a second formula, clearly recording that execution was *deferred*. Moreover, even where the sentence was pronounced unconditionally, a little patience would have enabled the Cardinal to see that it was often disobeyed. The documents themselves prove pretty conclusively that the punishment which the Abbot describes as *general* was actually inflicted in less than 25 per cent. of the cases. Moreover, there were numerous offences which passed quite or almost unpunished; *e.g.* a canon who "had lived in an abominable and disorderly fashion", yet escaped with a warning (vol. III, p. 196); another who had illegally pawned three of the conventual books, and was let off with the recitation of seven psalms, which he could have done in a quarter of an hour, even if his conscience had forced him to do it at all (vol. ii, p. 212). In short, there was as little strictness of punishment among these Praemonstratensians as (to quote one instance out of many) among the Ripon clergy whose doings are analysed in my eighth *Study* (p. 145). The cases given below in Appendix IV are far from exhaustive: to represent the real facts with any fulness, one would have to edit the whole book over again.

D 67. Again, the Cardinal insists that these sentences of banishment entailed a complete loss of rights as members of the community. Here, again, the contrary facts lie on the very surface of his own documents. The first two cases recorded are those of canons who, though sentenced to banishment for incontinence, were actually *promoted* to higher offices during the term of their sentence, and of whom one became abbot of the same house which had witnessed his sin.

D 68. These falsifications—for it is impossible to use a milder word—are often cloaked under a similar manipulation of facts in the English summaries which, as editor, the Cardinal prefixes to each visitation report printed. It is notorious that the large majority of readers—even of competent scholars—find no time to study the actual text of a book of this kind, but simply follow the preface and the summaries. In a large number of cases where the Cardinal writes that the culprit "is sent" away, the text itself shows that he was not sent; and many other similar misstatements, which can scarcely be accidental, are pointed out in Appendix iii.

RULE OF ST BENEDICT
(*King's Classics*, 1909.)

The Cardinal's preface explains that he has based his translation upon an older one of 1638, "although it must be confessed that I have found it necessary to take considerable liberties with the text of the seventeenth-century translators". The version thus revised is now styled among the faithful "Abbot Gasquet's translation". (Cf. the Abbot of Downside, in *Cambridge Medieval History*, i, 540, n.)

V 69. The Cardinal's worst treachery to St Benedict is in c. xi (p. 74). Here the saint's *infirmorum imbecillitatem* is translated "the weak state of the sick", thus suggesting that St Benedict allowed wine to his monks only in the infirmary. Even though Cardinal Gasquet has obviously failed to recognize the phrase as a quotation from Romans xv, 1, which would at once have set him straight, yet a reference to Martène's classical *Commentarius in Regulam* would have shown him that the medieval commentators understood the Saint's words not of bodily, but of spiritual weakness.

D 70. A few lines lower, the Cardinal takes the liberty of suppressing altogether the last two sentences of this chapter, in which St Benedict forbids the monks to murmur if they cannot get their daily pint of wine.

V 71. Another curious Biblical blunder occurs in c. ii (p. 14). Cardinal Gasquet, while slightly altering the seventeenth-century translator's earlier words, quotes St Matthew as writing: "Seek first the kingdom of God, and His justice, and *all things* shall be given unto you". Yet St Benedict himself writes quite correctly *haec omnia*; and it is very difficult to imagine an Anglican prelate printing such a misquotation from the Bible.

V 72. Again, in the last chapter (p. 122) the Cardinal fails to recognize that *zelus amaritudinis* is as directly taken from James iii, 14, as (for instance) other references to St Matthew and 1 Corinthians, which he identifies successfully in nn. 19 and 20.

V 73. Finally, he mistranslates St Benedict's prayer in the last sentence, rendering: "Christ, Who *can* bring us into eternal life". The Saint's words are: "Christo omnino nihil praeponant, qui nos pariter ad vitam aeternam perducat". Even without the *Amen*, which follows in many manuscripts and editions, the obvious grammatical sense of *perducat* in this passage is that of a prayer.

THE GREAT PESTILENCE

References to first edition, 1893. All these following blunders and mis-statements are, I believe, textually reproduced in the second edition (1908), though I had exposed many of the worst, a year before, in the *Contemporary Review* (since reprinted as No. 8 of *Medieval Studies*.

In this book his main thesis is twofold: (*a*) that the clergy in general clung faithfully to their posts throughout the plague, and (*b*) that the Pestilence struck the Church a blow from which she was still reeling when Luther attacked her; in other words, that medieval civilization and morals before 1348 were far purer and better than they were between 1348 and 1518. It will be well, therefore, to arrange the distortions of the evidence under these divisions.

A. FAITHFULNESS OF CLERGY.

The Cardinal, writing as a partisan, very naturally emphasizes cases which seem to lend themselves to his interpretation, while passing lightly over evidence to the contrary. But he also goes far beyond the limits of honest partisanship, by actually suppressing the most definite evidence against his contention, even while he quotes from its immediate context. The four following explicit assertions of chronicles, for instance, *are entirely suppressed* by him.

DD 74. *G.P.* p. 26 (*Chron. Padua*, p. 626). "Many were buried for money by vile persons, *without priests* and without candles."

DD 75. p. 27 (*Di Tura*, p. 123). All fled from the sick: at burial "*neither priest nor friar* went with them, nor was funeral service said".

DD 76. p. 28 (*Parma. Murat.*, XII, p. 746). "And the sick were abandoned by servants, doctors, notaries, *priests, and friars*, so that the plague-stricken wretches were neither tended nor healed, nor could they make their wills nor die confessed or absolved."

DD 77. p. 34 (Matt. Nuewenburgensis, p. 261). "Men died *without sacraments*."

In addition to these, there are several who declare, in general terms, that *all men*, or *almost all men*, avoided the sick, who were thus left helpless.

DD 78. p. 37. Again, quoting from Martin's *Histoire de France*, he omits the whole passage describing how, in many places, "*the* priests retired through fear, leaving the administration of the Sacraments to *a few* Religious who were more bold". And on p. 47, having to quote in full from the contemporary chronicler from whom Martin takes this passage, he omits the words I have italicized, puts a comma after Religious, and so distorts the whole sense.

D 79. p. 53. His two quotations from Gilles li Muisis are not only so translated as to exaggerate the chronicler's vague evidence for the numbers of clergy who died in doing their duty, but entirely omit the chronicler's remark that "*parsons and chaplains*, clerks and sextons, complained of not getting sufficient money" for their duties (lines 407 ff., p. 373).

DD 80. p. 84. The Cardinal, in a long passage designed to show the devotion of the clergy, quotes from the register of Bath and Wells, but omits the editor's note pointing out that the bishop *fled* to his manor during the plague.

D 81. p. 81. He does indeed let his readers see the bishop's complaint that "priests cannot be found...perchance for dread of infection or contagion": but, two pages later, he quotes this as proving that the clergy were dying too rapidly for the work to be performed. Now, there was probably one priest to about 145 souls in England before the Black Death; and statistics tend to prove that priests and people died in fairly equal proportions. There is therefore no apparent reason why the Sacraments should not have been administered, so long as the bulk of the priests stuck to their work. On this subject, the chroniclers, Birchington and Dene, bear most explicit testimony which the Cardinal has taken care not to give in full. "In this pestilence", says Dene, "many (*plures*) chaplains and curates would not serve without an excessive salary...*plures* beneficed clergy also, since their parishioners were so diminished by the plague that they could not live on such oblations as were left, deserted their benefices" [*deserverunt* prints Wharton ungrammatically: we must, of course, read *deseruerunt*]. Birchington writes "Then also priests were so dear and so few [*tanta caritas presbyterorum et paucitas erat*] that parish churches remained altogether unserved, and beneficed parsons had departed from the cure of their parishes for fear of death, not knowing where they might dwell". Let the reader compare this with Cardinal Gasquet's words on p. 105, where the evidence of the two chroniclers is not only given very incompletely, but also spoken of as exceptional: these are, "perhaps, the only cases in England". Yet his own documents might have shown him that the archbishop's encyclical letter was sent to all the dioceses of the Province of Canterbury, with its bitter complaint that the greed of the clergy, who "care not...for the cure of souls" unless they can get higher salaries "is giving an evil and pernicious example even to lay workmen" (*e.g.* Ralph of Shrewsbury's register, p. 639).

D 82. On p. 204, again, he writes "It is certain that [the bishops] did not shrink from their duty, but according to positive evidence remained at their posts". To this, let us oppose the actual evidence, supplied by the Cardinal's own documents. The Pope "shut himself up in his own chamber, with great fires continually lighted, and gave access to no man" (Matt. Nuewenburgensis, p. 261). The Bishop of Bath and Wells, as we have seen, fled to one of his manors. The Bishop of Rochester remained at two of his manors, never visiting his cathedral city. Finally, the Archbishop of Canterbury "after perfunctorily visiting the dioceses of Rochester and Chichester, then dwelt in his own manors, wearying his flock by numerous citations" (Birchington, in *Anglia Sacra*, 1, 43). From all these chroniclers the Cardinal *has quoted passages in the immediate context* of this unfavourable evidence which he so deliberately blinks in this place.

DD 83. p. 206. *G.* "It is interesting to note that in normal times very few were ordained after their appointment as incumbents." He supports this astounding mis-statement by an argument based upon only forty-four cases, taken from a single town: compare this with the statistics of about 1200 cases from four different dioceses, which I have given on pp. 150, 151, of my "Priests and People Before the Reformation" (*Medieval Studies*, No. 8). The wider generalization shows that the Cardinal's crude generalization from forty-four cases is wrong by some 1600 per cent. Indeed (considering that he confessedly quotes from manuscript records which his readers cannot verify), it seems extremely probable that he has blundered over his figures; if we reversed those figures, putting each under the opposite category to which he attributes it, this would give a fairly normal result.

B. Civilization shattered by Black Death.

D 84. p. 37. Cardinal Gasquet quotes from a chronicler who speaks of the deterioration after 1348; but he omits the passage in which this deterioration is described as only transitory.

D 85. p. 54. He paints social life before 1348 in glowing terms, professedly quoting all the while from Siméon Luce. It would be tedious to quote all his distortions of Luce's evidence; but here are two examples:

G. "The general population of France...was equal to what it is in the present century." This startling assertion omits Luce's all-important qualification "en exceptant les grandes agglomérations urbaines"—which, in Normandy alone (of which Luce is especially speaking), amount to nearly two millions and a half of people: *i.e.* about half the total population.

G. "*Numerous villages* were scattered over the face of the country, *every trace of which has now disappeared.*" *Luce,* "nous y voyons [avant 1348] des villages nombreux, plus nombreux même qu' actuellement *sur certains points*".

D 86. p. 106. The Cardinal attributes the poverty of two particular nunneries to the Black Death. His reference to his own chosen authority shows that this chronicler traces their poverty, on the contrary, to "longstanding mismanagement"— *malam diutinam custodiam.* (Dene, p. 377.)

D 87. p. 179. He quotes the poverty of Canterbury Cathedral as solely due to the Black Death. Yet the contemporary Dene of

Rochester, who is more than once cited in this book, attributes this mainly to Papal extortions, simony, and the mismanagement of the monks themselves. (Wharton, *Anglia Sacra*, I, 367.)

D 88. Again, there are many cases where the Cardinal's own authorities expressly attribute the plague to God's vengeance for the wickedness *already prevalent in the world before* 1348. The most briefly emphatic, perhaps, is the Rimini chronicler, p. 285 (*Gasquet*, p. 27): "Man's iniquity, and sins of every kind, had so multiplied upon earth, that their stench and the cry thereof came to the just ears of the Almighty". Abbot Gilles li Muisis of Tournay writes equally strongly, but far more diffusely, pp. 334–64. Other witnesses are Knighton (ed. Twysden, col. 2600); *Magnum Chronicon Belgicum*, p. 328; Boccaccio, *Decameron*, Giorn. I; De Mussi (Haeser, p. 54); Paduan Chronicler (*Murat*, XII, 626). To all this inconvenient evidence the Cardinal pays no attention, though he quotes from its immediate context.

C. MERE BLUNDERS, with no intention of bolstering up any thesis. (Italics as usual, are mine.)

V 89. p. 20. The Cardinal translates "no *prayer* was said, nor *solemn office* sung, nor bell tolled". The original runs, "non preco, non tuba, non campana". *Praeco* occurs seven times in the Vulgate, and is regularly spelt *preco*, of course, in medieval documents.

V 90. p. 120. *G.* "The world is placed in the midst of evils." He is here translating from a chronicler who, quoting from I John v, 19, writes correctly "mundum *totum* quasi in maligno positum". It becomes still more evident that Cardinal Gasquet has failed to recognize this Biblical quotation, if we compare his words with the Douay version: "the whole world is seated in wickedness".

91. p. 20. *G.* "The father or the wife would not touch the corpse of child or husband." The chronicler says the contrary, that *others* would not touch the corpse, so that parents and spouses were obliged to put it in the coffin themselves.

92. *Ibid. G.* "*Without* rite or ceremony." *Original*: "*brevi* ecclesiastico officio".

93. p. 26. *G.* "Appealed *in vain*." The original chronicle says the contrary, that, whether for love or for money, all *succeeded*.

94. *Ibid. G.* "*Hardly a third* of the population *was left*." *Original*: "forsan in comitatu tertia pars defecit" = "perhaps a third died".

95. p. 28. *G.* "By rote." *Original*: "pro consuetudine".

96. p. 46. *G.* "It *never* entered a city or town without carrying off *the greater part* of the inhabitants." *Original*: "*a paines* s'en partit sans emporter *toute* la ville".

97. p. 48. *G.* "*Villages.*" *Original*: "castris", *i.e.* towns.

98. p. 106. *G.* "As is thought, *from the present age* to the Day of Judgment they can never recover." *Original*: "quod, *durante isto seculo*, usque ad diem judicii creditur ea non posse reparari". *Seculum* is of course here in the common medieval sense of *world*: "so long as this world lasts".

99. p. 120. *G.* "I *add* parchment to continue [my chronicle]." His original has "*dimitto* pergamenam pro opere continuando, si forte", etc., *i.e.* "I leave some parchment blank".

RELIGIOUS INSTRUCTION IN ENGLAND DURING THE 14TH AND 15TH CENTURIES
(*Cath. Truth Society Pamphlet.*)

In this essay, one of Cardinal Gasquet's main arguments is that the people must have been well taught from the pulpit, *because the prelates, in their provincial or diocesan synods, repeatedly enjoined that the priests should thus regularly teach the people* (pp. 8 ff.). Yet it is a well-known canon of historical evidence that this wearisome reiteration on the part of lawgivers is usually an indication not of general obedience, but of general disobedience to the command so reiterated. As Cardinal Gasquet himself says in another book, where his argument requires it, "the constant repetition of the royal commands, addressed to all parts of the country, as well as the frequent complaints of non-compliance with the regulations are evidence, even if none other existed, of the futility of the legislation" (*Great Pestilence*, p. 197).

But, it may be said, in this particular matter we lack the second factor which would conclusively prove the futility of the legislation; we have indeed some "constant repetition", but no "frequent complaints of non-compliance". This is, indeed, the impression carefully conveyed by the Cardinal's treatise; but only because, *while quoting from the immediate context, he has deliberately and repeatedly suppressed the evidence of non-compliance.*

D 100. His first quotation, for instance, is from Archbishop Peckham's celebrated constitution of 1281. This runs: "The ignorance of priests casteth the people into the ditch of error; and the folly or unlearning of the clergy, who are bidden to instruct the faithful in the catholic faith, sometimes tendeth rather to error than to sound doctrine. For some blind ones search not always those places which are most known to need the light of truth, as the Prophet saith: 'The little ones have asked for bread, and there was none to break it unto them', and as another Prophet crieth: 'The needy and the poor seek for waters, and there are none; their tongue hath been dry with thirst' (Lam. iv, 4; Is. xli, 17). Wherefore, in remedy of these dangers, *we order that every priest having charge of a flock do, four times in each year,...instruct the people"*, etc., etc. Incredible as it may seem, Cardinal Gasquet begins his quotation only at the words here italicized, without the least warning of omission. He not only suppresses, but silently suppresses, the more important half of his own witness's testimony; the evidence which, by itself, would suffice to knock the bottom out of his whole argument. Nor can he plead that these despairing words of Peckham are isolated or peculiar. Other prelates had publicly said or implied the same thing before 1281, though Cardinal Gasquet takes no notice of their evidence. Stephen Langton's constitutions of 1222 imply that some of the parish clergy could not even read the Canon of the Mass, and that others were "dumb dogs" (Wilkins, 1, 586, 589). Cantilupe of Worcester, in 1240, published an injunction with implications almost as damaging (*ibid.* pp. 669 ff.); so did St Richard of Chichester in 1246 (*ibid.* p. 693) and Bishop Walter of Durham in 1255 (*ibid.* p. 704). In 1287, Bishop Quivil of Exeter, following out Peckham's policy in somewhat fuller detail, gave as his reason "lest *both pastor* and people fall into the ditch" (*ibid.* II, 144). Moreover, nearly all these wearily reiterated injunctions about pulpit-teaching, throughout the Middle Ages, repeat also (explicitly or implicitly) the famous accusation brought by Peckham against his clergy in 1281.

For this legislation of 1281 was that on which succeeding medieval injunctions were based; Cardinal Gasquet himself points out that "the constitutions of Peckham are referred to constantly in the fourteenth and fifteenth centuries as the foundation of the existing practices in the English Church". But he takes good care *not* to point out that Peckham's damning preamble, *Ignorantia Sacerdotum*, was echoed also down the centuries to the very Reformation period. Even in 1518, we find Cardinal Wolsey proclaiming in full synod to his Province of York "the ignorance of the priests casteth people into the ditch", etc., etc., down to the last word of Peckham's arraignment.

Wolsey, in short, takes care to emphasize all those facts which the Cardinal now so laboriously conceals from his readers; all those facts which would compel us to amend his phrase "existing *practices*" into "existing *theories*". For Wolsey, in his own individual preamble, specially excuses himself for now republishing so many time-worn constitutions, on the ground that *they had not been kept in the past* (Wilkins, III, 662). It is difficult to understand the mentality of an author who, carefully omitting this, can go on to write on p. 8: "But, was this law faithfully carried out by the clergy, and rigorously enforced by the Bishops in the succeeding centuries? *That is the real question. I think that there is ample evidence that it was*". It is only by the most systematic garbling of his own authorities, that he has managed to escape from his own canon of criticism laid down in the *Great Pestilence*. (1) He garbles the question of "constant repetition" by showing his readers only just enough to colour the contention that medieval prelates always kept religious instruction in view; while at the same time concealing the wearisome frequency with which they were compelled to reiterate their predecessors' injunctions. (2) "Frequent complaints of non-compliance", again, though conspicuously absent from the Cardinal's quotations, are conspicuously present in the documents upon which he professedly bases himself. Here, therefore, we have "evidence, if none other existed, of the futility of the legislation". The theory that priests should teach their flocks from the pulpit, at least four times a year, was as partially realized as most other medieval theories.

D 101. Nor are these the Cardinal's only falsifications in this brief treatise. On p. 9, still bent on proving how well the priests taught their flocks from the pulpit, he quotes from Archbishop Thoresby's little catechism drawn up for the Province of York in 1357. Here, again, he suppresses the principal and most direct evidence, *beginning for that purpose in the middle of a sentence, and garbling the opening words in order to disguise this liberty he has taken with the text*. The words he has omitted run thus. The Archbishop begins: "Seeing that some of those Christians over whom we are set, however unworthily, are not instructed (whereat we grieve) even in the rudimentary [*grossis*] and necessary points of Christian doctrine, which [defect] is said to be caused not only by our neglect (not to say ignorance) but also by the neglect or ignorance of rectors, vicars, and parish priests, who ought to instruct them according to that duty of the cure of souls which we have taken upon us; by reason whereof (though God forbid!) a way may easily be opened for errors and for grievous peril of souls: We therefore, willing (as is our bounden duty) to bring some healing remedy thereunto, through the counsel of our clergy,[1] have thought fit thus to ordain: That each rector, vicar, parish chaplain, or other curate, do openly", etc., etc.; the rest following pretty nearly as in Cardinal Gasquet's version.[2] After this suppression, the Cardinal has no difficulty in convincing unsuspecting readers "that this duty of giving plain instruction to the people was not neglected up to the era of the Reformation itself" (p. 11).

102. For the above-cited contention he then undertakes to produce "ample evidence", which amounts to no more than this, that in the later Middle Ages many manuals were drawn up to assist parish priests in their teaching work. He attempts no critical examination of these books; and some of those which he glibly quotes (*e.g.* the *Liber Festivalis*) would, in fact, give results by no means flattering to medieval religious education. The very unfavourable evidence as to preachers, which he has suppressed from his *Dives and Pauper* quotations, will be shown in the examination of his *Eve of the Reformation*.

THE EVE OF THE REFORMATION (1900)

In this, and in some later books, the Cardinal professes to quote a good deal from early printed books of very difficult access; and many of his *soi-disant* quotations show an appalling lack of literary conscience, which is emphasized by his habit of withholding adequate references. I have pointed out how, on the subject of "the Open Bible", the Cardinal makes Sir Thomas More say the opposite of what that great man says in fact (*Medieval Studies*, No. 7, p. 121). Again, in quoting from *Dives and Pauper*, a rare fifteenth-century printed book, *he never once gives any reference*; but leaves his readers to search through the whole folio volume. With kind help from a fellow-student, I have, however, run all his quotations to earth. Quite apart from his habit of modernizing whole words and phrases (including some perfectly familiar to all Bible readers), only one of these quotations (p. 300) is unmarred by omissions from the

[1] So writes the fourteenth-century paraphraser; the Latin original shows the Archbishop to have intended "with the approval of our Provincial Synod". There is no ground for Cardinal Gasquet's implication, perhaps unintentional, that the original suggestion came from the parish clergy themselves, and not from the Archbishop.

[2] The original is printed in *Lay Folks' Catechism*, E.E.T.S., 1901, pp. 3 ff. A comparison of this text with Cardinal Gasquet's reveals several obvious errors of transcription in the latter.

immediate context, or by actual (though unacknowledged) suppressions, some merely careless, but others with evident intention.

D 103. *G.* p. 284 (*D. and P.*, com. v, c. x). The Cardinal, who is striving to prove how well the duties of teaching and preaching were fulfilled by the pre-Reformation clergy, omits one of the opening sentences of this passage, which runs as follows, "also men of holy church slay men and women ghostly of God's word and of good teaching"—*i.e.* kill men's souls by withholding due religious instruction.

104. *G.* pp. 297 ff. What the Cardinal presents to us as a fairly continuous passage is in fact taken from different parts of the book. The first two fragments are from com. III, c. xix. Then comes a quotation of which the Cardinal only tells us that it occurs "later on, under the same heading". It comes in fact twenty-three pages lower down, under quite a different heading (com. IV, cc. xi–xii); and even within the passage actually quoted, the Cardinal makes two separate omissions, unacknowledged to the reader, though of no great importance in themselves.

D 105. p. 355. This brief quotation, professing to be single and homogeneous, is really an extraordinarily garbled version of fragments from two different chapters, not even put together in their proper order (com. VII, cc. xii and xiv). It would be impossible to represent the carelessness with which the thing has been done without reprinting too much of the original text for any reader's patience. Moreover, while seeking hither and thither in these two chapters for words which seem favourable to the Church as a charitable institution, the Cardinal carefully omits more than one passage in which the author speaks most bitterly of the riches and uncharitableness of many clergy. *Dives*, for instance, asks on the second page of c. xii "it seemeth by thy words that men of Holy Church which spend the goods of Holy Church in wicked use (as in pomp, pride, gluttony, lechery and in other vanities) be thieves". To which *Pauper* (who represents the official teacher in this dialogue) replies: ":That is sooth... Men of Religion, monks and canons and such other that use great riches of silver and gold...more pompously than lords, be strong thieves and do great sacrilege, so spending the goods of Holy Church in vanity and pride, in lust of the flesh, by which goods the poor folk should live. A lady of a thousand mark by year can pin her hood against the wind with a small pin of latten, seven for a penny. But a monk, that is bounden to poverty by his profession, will have an ouch or a brooch of gold and silver, in value of a noble or much more". With the help of this and similar omissions, the Cardinal succeeds in making his author testify quite favourably for the medieval Church.

D 106. Moreover, apart from this treatment of the context, even in the passage actually quoted, he makes the following unacknowledged alteration, which decidedly softens the author's accusations against neglectful clergy:

G. "Therefore they prefer to leave their own sins openly reproved generally, among other men's sins."

Original (in modern spelling). "And therefore *liever they have to lose the souls that Christ so dear bought,* than to hear their own sins openly reproved generally among other men's sins." This case may be a mere blunder, like his substitution of St Anselm for St Austen in the same passage, and his translation of "charged" (*i.e. valued*) as "discharged", which makes nonsense: but the Cardinal's similar omissions in other cases can scarcely be merely accidental.

D 107. He shows as little conscience with the *Sermo Exhortatorius* of W. de Melton, on which he lays great stress, but, as usual, without vouchsafing adequate references (pp. 149–53). This very rare little treatise, read as a whole, strongly corroborates Wolsey's and Colet's complaints as to the prevalent ignorance and carelessness of the early sixteenth-century clergy. Yet the Cardinal, by picking out the preacher's pious exhortations to his ordinands, and suppressing most of his implications that such exhortations were foreign to the majority of the actual clergy, completely misrepresents his testimony. Here, for instance, are some omitted passages. "Ye will not, I trust, come up promiscuously, according to the usual practice [*ut solet fieri*], or insolently or waywardly or wantonly, as claiming admission [to holy orders] from the examiners, by some unlawful law" (fol. 1 *b*). If you find yourself ploughed, "beware of [uttering] any insolent, opprobrious, or contumelious word" (fol. 2 *b*). Do not rely upon external pressure exercised upon the examiner, since such illegal pressure "is so pestilent that, unless it be altogether extinguished, the church will never be freed from its multitude of uncultured and foolish clergy" (*ibid.*). Later on, he speaks of ordination by bribery of examiners or their clerks, and by false representations as to age (fol. 5 *a*, *b*), remarking that this last at least was common (*saepe*). Finally, he exhorts the ordinands with great earnestness to avoid "that ravening and pernicious plague of covetousness, whereof *almost all* priests are *much* accused and noted among the people" (fol. 6 *b*). It is obvious how vital these points are to any true estimate of the pre-Reformation clergy.

D 108. Moreover, the Cardinal's crooked methods become even more obvious at the point where his summary becomes so full as almost to equal the original in bulk, *e.g.*:

Original (sig. A, iiij r⁰). "*Everywhere, throughout* towns and country places, rude and rustic priests *abound*; partly busying themselves with servile and sordid labours, partly giving themselves up to taverns, swilling [*ingurgitationibus*], and drunkenness; some cannot get on without women;[1] others *spend their whole day* playing at dice and hazard and suchlike pastimes; others spend their time in the vanities of hunting and hawking; and thus they spend a whole life of utter idleness and *irreligion* [*vitam irreligiosam*], even to extreme old age."

G. p. 151. "Both in towns and country places there are priests who occupy themselves, some in mean and servile work, some who give themselves up to tavern drinking; the former can hardly help mixing themselves up with women, the latter employ their time in games of dice, etc. Thus do they spend their whole lives to extreme old age in idleness and non-religious occupations."

We have here, of course, a virtual translation, complete in every particular except the one essential of fidelity to the original.

V 109. And the blunders are as remarkable as the infidelities, *e.g.*:

Original (fol. 3 *a*). "Qui, grammaticalium litterarum *expertes* et inopes", etc., etc.

G. p. 150. "Who, though *skilful* in grammar", etc., etc. *Expertes*, it may be noted, is here in the nominative, so there can be no excuse of confusion with *expertos*. Not only is *expers* a regular catch for fifth-form boys, but the word also occurs in an important verse of the Vulgate (Heb. v, 13). The translation of the whole passage is far from scholarly; but I confine myself in this record to the more conspicuous blunders.

V 110. *Original* (fol. 6 *b*). "Contra hunc indignum torporem et *fastidiosam desidiam*."

G. p. 152. "Against unworthy sloth and *foolish desires*." Though *desidia* does not occur in the Vulgate, *desiderium* occurs more than fifty times.

D 111. On p. 438, the Cardinal quotes from a rare little book by Bishop Gardiner. Here he does, indeed, vouchsafe a reference, but it is wrong; the actual words occur not on fol. 2 but on fol. 5 *a*. And, after the word *trumpery*, the Cardinal has taken his usual liberty of suppressing a dozen lines of the original

---

[1] "Hii mulierculis carere non possunt; isti", etc., etc. *Muliercula*, by this time, had at least as uncomplimentary a connotation as *wench*: nor will the words *hii* and *isti* bear the special limitations which the Cardinal tries to impose upon them.

without any mark of warning, and altering the next sentence in order to disguise his omission. The omitted lines would have revealed Gardiner's inconvenient assertion that the friars' traffic in indulgences had amounted "to thus buy and sell heaven", with the result that "both the merchandise is abhorred, and the ministers also; we cannot away with the friars, nor can abide the name [of friar?]". Under cover of this suppression, the Cardinal writes "In the literature of the period, it must be remembered, there is nothing to show that the true nature of a 'pardon' or indulgence was not fully and commonly understood. There is no evidence that it was in any way interpreted as a remission of sin, still less that any one was foolish enough to regard it as permission to commit this or that offence against God" (p. 437).

D 112. In order to write the foregoing sentences, the Cardinal is compelled not only thus to garble his own documents, but to turn his face altogether away from the Oxford Chancellor, Thomas Gascoigne, whose *Liber Veritatum* is one of the most important original authorities for *The Eve of the Reformation*. Gascoigne's evidence is quoted fully in the eighth of my *Studies*, p. 133; one sentence may suffice in this place. "Sinners say nowadays [*i.e.* about A.D. 1450] 'I care not what or how many evils I do before God; for I can get at once, without the least difficulty, plenary remission of any guilt or sin whatsoever through an Indulgence granted me by the Pope, whose written grant I have bought for fourpence'." Gascoigne, it must be noted, was as unimpeachably orthodox as Gardiner, and hated Wycliffe as bitterly as Gardiner hated Luther.

D 113. p. 145. Sir Thomas More is quoted as "categorically denying a charge made by Tyndale against the clergy in general, and against the Popes for permitting so deplorable a state of things in regard to clerical morals". In the passage from which the Cardinal proceeds to bring a very partial quotation, More does *not* categorically deny Tyndale's accusations against the clergy in general. He tacitly admits (what other orthodox medieval writers confess in so many words) that it was not uncommon for bishops and archdeacons to wink at clerical incontinence for the sake of the revenues which they themselves derived from the sin; this he tacitly admits, and only pleads that the *universality* of Tyndale's accusation "falsely belieth *many*" bishops and archdeacons, and that the "evil demeanour" of others must not be imputed to the law, but to the frailty of human nature (p. 619). In an earlier passage (pp. 224 ff.), his defence of clerical morals in general is even less "categorical". Not only does he write generally: "I wot well the whole world is so wretched that spiritual and temporal everywhere all be bad

enough; God make us all better!" but he also expressly admits
one of the heaviest counts in Tyndale's accusation, the prevalence
of clerical incontinence in Wales, saying: "but truth it is that
incontinence is there in some places little looked unto, whereof
much harm groweth in the country" (*English Works*, p. 231).
If the Cardinal had ventured to print More's words in full, the
admissions of that distinguished apologist would be found far
more destructive of the thesis maintained in *The Eve of the
Reformation*, than anything which can be quoted from him in
support of it.

Moreover, Tyndale's accusation of habitual incontinence
against the Welsh clergy is directly supported by Gascoigne, who
asserts that the contemporary Bishop of St David's positively
refused to countenance the reform of clerical morals in his
diocese, because the fines levied from erring priests brought him
a yearly sum which, in modern money, would amount to more
than two thousand pounds (*Liber Veritatum*, ed. Rogers, pp.
35–6).

D 114. p. 148. The Cardinal asserts, with Dr Brewer, that a
certain document published on p. 470 of vol. II of the *Letters and
State Papers of Henry VIII* constitutes a testimonial to London
morals in the year 1519. The reader who troubles to hunt this
reference down, not stopping at Brewer's interpretation but
reading the actual document for himself, will find that it shows
the Bishop of Winchester to be harbouring, in his "liberty of
Southwark", more prostitutes than were to be found in all the
rest of the city and the suburbs together.

D 115. p. 43. The Cardinal, in pursuance of his thesis that the
Religious Orders kept up their interest in learning to the last,
argues that "the Visitations of the Norwich Diocese (1492–1532),
edited by Dr Jessopp for the Camden Society, contain many
references to the monastic students at the university". He quotes
two instances which he leaves us to take as typical, but without
giving any page references; the student can check him only at
the expense of great waste of time. And the net result is this, that
Westacre, which the Cardinal represents as typical with its three
monks at the university in 1520, is (I believe) the only monastery
which is reported at any time to have so many: even the great
Cathedral priory at Norwich had sometimes none at all, although
it was bound by statute to maintain two (*e.g.* pp. 7, 266). Westacre
was bound to pay for one of its brethren at the university; but
this duty was not performed in 1514; and only one of the five
recorded visitations is free from the complaint that studies are
being neglected within the monastery itself (pp. 50, 104–5, 165,
251). The other case which the Cardinal quotes as an instance

of monastic love of learning is that of Butley. This house, in 1514, allowed one of its monks to go to the university at his own friends' expense; so far the Cardinal quotes correctly; but there he stops. A reference to the other visitations of Butley will show that, *on every other occasion*, it is complained of for its *neglect* of due monastic education. On four of these occasions it had neglected to send a single monk to the university; and on two it had not even a single person within its walls who was able or willing to instruct the younger brethren in Latin (pp. 54, 132, 178, 217, 289). The Cardinal's assertion, that, later on, the house itself paid for a scholar at the university, seems to be a pure figment, like some other assertions for which he gives no chapter or verse. Moreover, it may safely be said that, of all the references to the university throughout these Norwich visitations, at least two-thirds are cases in which the monasteries are recorded not as *fulfilling*, but as *neglecting*, even their statutory obligations to send one or two monks to study. I have pointed out how strong is the visitatorial evidence on this point, from many sources, in the tenth of my *Studies*, p. 32; the facts lie on the very surface of the documents. It is most significant that the Cardinal's inaccuracies are most flagrant where he is professedly quoting from rare books, or where, by withholding references, he has rendered the task of verification extremely laborious.

PARISH LIFE IN MEDIEVAL ENGLAND (1907)

116. Here, again, are many quotations from *Dives and Pauper*, but without a single indication to guide the student through the whole folio volume. Of the fourteen quotations, only three are free from blunders or infidelities. In more than a dozen places, the Cardinal prints *thing* instead of the *ymage* of his original, evidently mistaking the *y* for a *th*, and reading the rest carelessly. In another place, he prints *things* again for the *tithes* of his original. There are a few omissions which seem merely careless, but others which are evidently dictated by convenience; not understanding his original, he has simply left out the puzzling phrases without warning.

117. For example, "as they come to honde without chose" (*G.* 12; *Dives and Pauper*, com. VII, c. xiii), where *chose* = choice. On p. 161, *erynge* is quietly omitted twice, and *motynge* once, evidently for the same reason (*Dives and Pauper*, com. III, c. vii). On the same page, the *for heuenly mede* of the original becomes *for heaven made* in the Cardinal's transcript, and makes sheer nonsense. On p. 180, another silent omission is evidently due to the puzzling word *skyl* (*i.e. skill*, reason) (*Dives and Pauper*,

com. I, c. iv). Finally, he prints *spectacles* for the curious *steracles* of his text, though the next three lines make it plain that this is a misprint for *miracles* (*G.* 249; *Dives and Pauper*, com. III, c. xvii).

D 118. Other omissions, however, equally furtive and disguised, are evidently dictated by "economy" of truth. On p. 32, passages are omitted which show that a good deal of medieval church building and ornamentation was not only "perhaps" (as the Cardinal puts it) but *actually* done rather in a spirit of vain-glory and worldly rivalry than out of pure devotion. "For the people nowadays", writes the author of *Dives and Pauper*, "is full undevout to God and to Holy Church, and they love but little men of Holy Church, and they be loth to come in Holy Church when they be bound to come thither, and full loth to hear God's service. Late they come, and soon they go away. If they be there a little while, them thinketh full long. They have liever to go to the tavern than to Holy Church; liever to hear a song of Robin Hood or of some ribaldry than to hear mass or matins or any other of God's service or any word of God. And, sithen that the people hath so little devotion to God and to Holy Church, I cannot see that they do such cost in Holy Church for devotion nor for the love of God. For they despise God day and night with their evil and wicked living and their wicked thewys" (*i.e.* manners: com. I, c. li). What an "economy" lies in the omission of this passage, and the Cardinal's introduction of that delicate "perhaps" into his own summary from *Dives and Pauper*!

D 119. The same motive, apparently, has dictated certain omissions (partly unnoted) on p. 247. The original (com. IV, c. xi) asserts: "But now men say that there should no lewd folk enter-mit them of God's law [*i.e.* presume to busy themselves with the Bible], nor of the Gospel nor of Holy Writ, neither to con it nor to teach it". This would be very difficult to reconcile with the Cardinal's theory as to the free use of the vernacular Bible among the laity before the Reformation.

D 120. p. 249. Several lines are here omitted without warning and the text is garbled to disguise the omission. They show that the miracle plays, for which the Cardinal in his text has nothing but admiration, were sometimes in the judgment of his author, "medled with ribaldry or leasings" (com. III, c. xvii).

V 122. p. 179. *Dives and Pauper* quotes the well-known Passion Sunday hymn quite correctly as "O crux ave, spes unica". The Cardinal, with equal violence to his text and to Latin metre, prints it as "ave crux, spes unica" (com. I, c. iv).

In the appendix to the eighth of my *Medieval Studies* ("Priests and People before the Reformation") I have exposed a good many further mis-statements in Cardinal Gasquet's *Parish Life*; these need therefore only be mentioned briefly here.

D 123. p. 238. Peacock, a careful antiquary, is cited as authority for the absurd contention that the ale drunk at Church Ales was "hardly an intoxicant". In fact, he says precisely the contrary.

124. p. 159. Thoresby's constitution of 1367, far from being "the first order" of its kind, was one of the last: it had been preceded by eleven others (from 1229 onwards), and was succeeded by only one. This vitally affects the Cardinal's argument.

125. p. 17. Speaking of the appropriation of parish churches by monasteries, he writes: "The grievance of which so much has been made is an academic rather than a real one, and one of modern invention rather than one existing in the Middle Ages". The grievance is, in fact, exposed in language of extreme bitterness by Church councils of the Middle Ages, stares us in the face from the episcopal registers, and is described in 1450 by the Oxford Chancellor, Gascoigne, in language which few, if any, modern writers have equalled in vehemence.

D 126. p. 84. He describes the hospitality exercised by the clergy in words which are contradicted by the very documents on which he professedly relies. Moreover, where Lyndwood says "*ought to be* better endowed" the Cardinal translates this into the tense of fact, "*were* better endowed"; and on p. 85 he translates "*divitibus* et pauperibus" as "*sick* and poor" with equal advantage to his thesis.

D 127. p. 62. In quoting from Bishop Quivil's constitutions he omits, without warning, a sentence which throws a lurid light on the irreverent behaviour of medieval worshippers in church: "whereby grievous scandal is generated in the church, and divine service is often impeded".

D 128. p. 207. He quotes Quivil's synod of Exeter as "laying down the law of the Catholic Church on the point [of marriage]; no espousal or marriage was to be held valid unless the contract was made in the presence of the parish priest and three witnesses". This is not only directly contrary to the words of the document from which it is professedly taken, but also betrays an astounding ignorance of canon law, and even of so common a phenomenon as the Gretna Green marriages of comparatively recent times. A boy of fifteen and a girl of twelve might, in the

Middle Ages, contract a valid marriage wherever they liked, without help of church or priest or witnesses.

129. p. 20. "That on the whole [the duty of paying tithes] was cheerfully complied with in the Middle Ages, would appear to be certain." The contrary of this is the constant theme of medieval clergy on the one hand, and medieval satirists on the other. In Church synods of all centuries, the irregularities and unpopularity of tithe-paying are among the most frequent subjects of complaint.

Further mis-statements, for which I had no room in the above-cited *Study*, are as follows:

130. p. 7. "To 'Holy Mother Church' all were the same, and within God's house the tenant, the villain, and the serf stood side by side with the overlord and master." This is false. The squire or the "advocatus" had many rights within the church which others lacked; and pews were often hired for money, as in our own day.

131. p. 47. Nothing but extreme archaeological ignorance could attribute this picture of a church interior to the "fourteenth century". Didron's *Annales*, from which it is taken, date it correctly as sixteenth century.

132. p. 67. He derives *porch* "from the Latin porta". It is of course from *porticus*.

133. p. 68. A quotation from Myrc is limited to *children*. This is wrong: Myrc here speaks expressly of all the parishioners, which puts a very different face on the evidence.

134. p. 72. "In the diocesan registers, also, episcopal dispensations *de defectu natalium* are frequent, and show that a not inconsiderable number of the English clergy sprang from the class of 'natives' of the soil, or serfs, upon whom the lord of the manor had a claim." This assertion, though there is no acknowledgment, is evidently borrowed from E. L. Cutts, *Parish Priests and their People*, p. 130. Both fact and inference are false.

(*a*) The phrase *de defectu natalium* does not refer to serfs, but to illegitimates; not only is it thus glossed by Van Espen (*Jus. Eccles.*, index, s.v. *natales*) and regularly used in this sense in the episcopal registers, but two Papal Bulls to Bishop Grandisson, of Exeter, place the matter beyond a doubt. In 1349, Clement VI granted to Grandisson the right to dispense with fifty clerks or scholars *defectum natalium patientibus* and in 1353 Innocent VI gave the right of dispensing with twenty more (*Register*, ed. Hingeston-Randolph, pp. 147, 150). The Popes do not contemplate the possibility that any of these seventy persons will be of servile origin: the Bulls clearly explain that the dispensations are all for illegitimates, and the first Bull even divides them into categories; thirty are to be sons of unmarried folk, ten of married folk in adultery, and ten sons of priests; a most significant apportionment considering that the priests did not form anything like one-fifth of the total adult male population of the diocese—poll-tax returns show them about one in forty, at the most liberal computation.

(b) Moreover, the Cardinal's canon law is here altogether at fault; no ecclesiastical dispensation was needed to ordain a serf; it was simply a question between the serf and his master. If the man had not been manumitted, no ecclesiastic could ordain him without injustice to his master; if, on the other hand, he was already a freedman when he came up for ordination, then no further dispensation was needed; a freedman had as much right to seek ordination as a man born free; in other words, the ordination question with the serf was no question of *birth*, strictly speaking, but of *present status*: the law is put very clearly in the *Summa Angelica*, s.v. *Servitus*, sect. 3, 4. Episcopal registers do sometimes record the *manumission* of serfs (which misled Cutts): but these events are very rare in comparison with the others. For instance, Stapeldon's register (A.D. 1307–26) records only one such manumission (p. 163), while it records fifty-three dispensations for illegitimates, of whom eight were sons of priests. Stapeldon's successor, Grandisson, amid his very numerous dispensations for illegitimates, manumitted only six serfs in all his forty-two years (1327–69). Facts like this are all the more important, because the Cardinal owed much of his authority among scholars, until a few years ago, to his implicit claims of great familiarity with the episcopal registers.

D 135. p. 73. The Cardinal, while conveying two other passages from Cutts without acknowledgment (pp. 132–3; cf. p. 278) falls into the blunder of ascribing *Piers Plowman's Crede* to the author of the *Vision*, and takes the liberty of omitting some inconvenient lines from his quotation.

136. p. 76. This quotation again is conveyed without acknowledgment from Cutts (p. 133), reproducing its peculiarities of spelling and the blundering omission of two words.

137. p. 77. "The ordinary course [at the universities] was lengthy": on the next page Cardinal Gasquet computes it at eleven years. Dr Rashdall, on the contrary, points out that "large numbers of students—probably the majority—never proceeded even to the lowest degree"; *i.e.* to the Baccalaureate

which could be obtained in three years (*Univ. of Europe*, II, 595; cf. p. 584). Dr Rashdall, to whom I pointed out this and the following page of the Cardinal's book, has no hesitation in characterizing them as "very misleading". We may work out the proportion statistically from the episcopal registers. The Mastership of Arts required only seven years of study; yet in early registers M.A.'s were only a very small proportion to the rest of the parish clergy. To take the diocese of Exeter; Bishop Stapeldon's register (1307–26) records only 7 masters in 232 livings. Even a century later, Bishop Lacy (1420–55) records only 237 masters among the 2733 institutions to benefices; and 81 of these were deans or canons of great churches; the remaining 156 amount only to about 1 master for every 17 clergy. The Hereford diocese gives a far lower percentage: Trillek (1344–61) records only 38 masters among 7032 ordinations (or, to take the priests alone, 4 masters among 1741 ordained priests).

D 138. p. 78. "They would have to prove themselves to be sufficiently lettered and of good life before they would be accepted for ordination." We have seen that the *Sermo Exhortatorius* ascribed the "multitude of uncultured and foolish clergy" to the neglect of proper strictness in examination (No. 107 here above). Colet, in his famous sermon before Convocation, spoke even more plainly: "there is the well of evils, that, the broad gate of Holy Orders opened, everyman that offereth himself is all-where admitted without pulling back. Thereof springeth and cometh out the people that are in the church both of unlearned and evil priests" (Lupton's *Life of Colet*, p. 300: the word *people*, of course, means "multitude"). It is noteworthy that the Cardinal, who quotes from or alludes to Colet nine times in his *Eve of the Reformation*, completely ignores this famous sermon, which contradicts all his main contentions throughout the book.

139. pp. 77, 83. The implications that benefices were rarely given to clerks in lower orders, and that rectors were priested at least within a year of their presentation, are false to the plainest evidence from the episcopal registers. From an analysis of more than 700 institutions, in the thirteenth and fourteenth centuries, it transpires that more than 30 per cent. were presented to livings before they had even reached the subdiaconate.

D 140. p. 84. The Cardinal appeals to a manuscript visitation of Exeter diocese in 1340 as containing "many references to the hospitality kept by the clergy". This visitation has since been printed (*Eng. Hist. Review*, 1911, p. 108). It contains only *two* notices of hospitality among the ninety churches visited—*i.e.*

just those two cases which the Cardinal selects as "instances" of the "many" which might be cited—and, even in one of these two cases, the visitors report that the former hospitality has now ceased. There are two other minor blunders in the half-dozen lines which he devotes to this subject: the date is wrong, and *divitibus* is rendered *sick*.

141. p. 88. The *matrix ecclesia* of Wilkins's *Concilia* (II, 160) is translated *parish church*. It means, of course, *cathedral*.

142. p. 92. "The assistant priests, known as *Curates (curati)*." This is a patent anachronism; *curatus*, by itself, is equivalent not to the modern English *curate* but to the French *curé* (*i.e.* incumbent) in medieval Latin.

143. p. 112. "The office [of parish clerk] was often held by a married layman." No quotation or reference is vouchsafed, and it is extremely doubtful whether one could be given. The Cardinal is pretty evidently misled by the fact that the parish clerk, being only in minor orders, was sometimes a married man.

144. p. 146. The Cardinal has blundered over his quotation from *Sir Gawayne and the Green Knight*: he takes *ho* for a masculine pronoun, and so transfers line 1308 of that poem from the lady to the knight. The line really runs "Ho dos hit forth", etc. The Cardinal similarly makes nonsense of a line of *Piers Plowman*, on p. 153, by printing *mate* for *mete*, and much worse nonsense of another on p. 184 by repeated misspellings, transpositions, and omissions.

145. p. 167. His summary of the Sarum statute of 1319 omits the fact that the disorders at Boy Bishop processions had resulted in "grievous damage both to persons and to the church"; and on p. 180 his summary from Lyndwood disguises the fact that Lyndwood speaks of "tumultuous talking *in church* or outside". (Ed. 1679, p. 99.)

146. p. 198. "All, rich and poor, noble and simple, on coming to the Sacrament of Penance, were treated alike." On the contrary, Church synods constantly speak of the abuse of selling absolution in the sacrament of penance for money. Quivil's Exeter synod, from which the Cardinal has quoted half-a-dozen lines before, shows that the evil was serious enough to need vigorous repressive measures: and the almost contemporary Winchester synod bears the same testimony (Wilkins, II, 294). Again, in *Piers Plowman*, from which the Cardinal quotes almost as freely as from Quivil, there are constant references to the extortion of money for absolution; and Chaucer refers to it more than once.

147. p. 201. This professed verbal quotation from the synod of Exeter degenerates, in the fourth and sixth lines, into a paraphrase which shortens the original by something like two lines, and which disguises a *second* clear implication that priests were accustomed to sell the sacrament of Extreme Unction for money (see No. 146, here above). Moreover, it stops short just at the point where the bishop describes the curious semi-pagan superstitions which impelled some parishioners to refuse Extreme Unction altogether. (Wilkins, II, 135; cf. p. 295.)

148. p. 203. "It was, moreover, a positive law of the church that every priest should go at once on being called to a sick person, no matter what time of the day or night the summons might come." Not only does the actual text of the Exeter synod, thus garbled by the Cardinal, suggest that this law was imperfectly obeyed; but in the almost contemporary Chichester synod we find the bishop fulminating against transgressors who "*as some [priests] have hitherto presumed to do*, send their deacons to the sick with the Holy Eucharist, while they themselves are busied with potations or with other delights of the flesh" (Wilkins, II, 170, sect. 16: see also No. 151, here below).

149. p. 205. "What this ['cyphus pro infirmis'] may have been is not quite clear, but probably it was the dish in which the priest purified his fingers." The same Exeter synod which prescribes this *cyphus* describes its use clearly also; it was for giving the sick, at their last communion, a draught of unconsecrated wine, in place of the consecrated wine which Catholic practice now denied to the laity.

150. p. 204. The references to "two lanterns instead of the one" shows equal ignorance of this Exeter synod, which clearly prescribes *two* lanterns.

D 151. p. 206. Bishop Grandisson "had heard that *some carelessness* had been noticed" in carrying the viaticum to the sick. Compare these words underlined with the tone of Grandisson's actual letter (*Reg.* p. 787). He writes: "we are shaken with pain of heart, and filled with bitterness of horror;...many (*plerique*) rectors...as we are made aware by daily scandals....bear themselves with the extremest irreverence" (*nimis irreventer se exhibent ultra modum*). We must never, of course, fail to allow for medieval vehemence of speech; but it requires some courage to claim this letter of Grandisson's as proving the care ordinarily bestowed upon this sacrament in the Middle Ages. (See No. 148, above.)

152. p. 245. "Labour was lightened and the burdens of life eased by co-operation on an extensive scale. A common mill

ground the corn, and the flour was baked into bread at a common oven." The ignorance which can plead the common mill and oven as instances of beneficent popular co-operation is simply astounding. They spelt not popular co-operation, but capitalist monopoly; mill and oven were not the people's, but the lord's, who too often used his monopoly to grind the faces of the poor. Among all the grievances which the French peasantry enumerated before the Revolution, this of the common mill and common oven came quite in the front rank.

ENGLISH MONASTIC LIFE (1904)

The whole book is vitiated by the author's habit of describing the theory rather than the ascertainable facts. Quotations from disciplinarians, who describe what monastic life should be, are too often substituted for the evidence of chronicles and visitations which tell us what it actually was. And here, as in his *Parish Life*, the Cardinal scarcely vouchsafes a single reference from beginning to end, even where he could have actually economized space by referring to a definite page of a definite book, instead of tantalizing us with "according to one English Custumal", "says a writer in a late number of the *National Review*", "one sixteenth-century authority states", etc., etc.

M 153. p. 23. "A smaller hall, called...the 'spane', at Peterborough." This word *spane* is simply a blunder adopted from earlier writers; the hall was, in fact, called *le seyny*: see *Lincoln and York Arch. Soc. Reports*, XXXII, 92, n. 300.

M 154. p. 24. "The soup or pottage, which formed the foundation of the monastic dinner." This is wrong; the *generale*, and not the *potagium*, formed the *pièce de résistance* of monastic dinners.

D 155. p. 70. "The sacrist, as one of the English Custumals has it, 'should be...careful in *keeping* the brethren to traditions'." The original has *revocatione*, 'recalling' (*Chron. Abendon*, II, 374), a word of very different significance; and the difference is fully borne out by such monastic records as have come down to us.

156. p. 75. "'The pudding-wife' on great days to make the pastry." The medieval pudding had nothing to do with pastry, as a reference to the *N.E.D.* will show. The institution of "pudding-wife" was in fact one of the channels through which monasteries utilized even the refuse of their kitchens, instead of giving it to the poor. Just as the very bones were sometimes sold and accounted for, so the entrails were made up into puddings, for

home consumption or for sale, by these women. The Cardinal
seems dimly aware of this, however, on p. 211, where he quotes
a case from St Edmundsbury but gives no reference.

D 157. p. 79. "A *caritas*, or extra glass of wine." The *caritas*,
like the pittance, was only occasionally an extra allowance of
wine; and, even then, the quantity was not such as could fairly
be described as "an extra glass". So far as the Cardinal's slipshod want of references permits us to judge, he is speaking on
this page of the Abingdon customs. At Abingdon, we are
expressly informed, the *caritas* measured nearly three quarts;
and on high festival days each monk had half this amount of
wine (nearly three pints) for dinner, and the same amount of
mead for supper. At Evesham, the *caritas* was of exactly the
same capacity. (*Chron. Abendon*, I, 346; II, 399; Dugdale-Caley,
II, 30, col. 2.)

V M 158. p. 146. "The monk, it must be remembered, was in
no sense 'a gloomy person'.... In fact, the true Religious was
told to try and possess *angelica hilaritas cum monastica simplicitas*."
Apart from this startling Latin, the whole implication conveyed
by these sentences shows an equally startling ignorance of the
writings of monastic disciplinarians. See c. vi of my *From St
Francis to Dante* (second ed. p. 63), and the quotations from
medieval sources in the eleventh of my *Studies* (Book II, c. vi).

159. p. 148. "Of course manual labour, that is, the working in
the gardens, or fields, or workshops of the establishment, always
occupied at least a part of the working hours of every monastery,
and frequently a large part." This is quite false, except at
exceptional times of fervour and discipline. It is idle to quote
the ancient Cluny constitutions, when we have the direct
evidence of Peter the Venerable that they had fallen into desue-
tude even before 1150 (Migne, *P.L.* tom. 189, col. 1036–7), and
when even Peter's reforming energy contented itself with
reviving them "to a certain extent". It is very rare, indeed, to
find evidence for Benedictines or Austin canons working in the
fields after the twelfth century; yet these (with the friars, who
never pretended to do manual work after the first few years of
Franciscan fervour) formed the overwhelming majority of
medieval Religious. A frequent entry in monastic accounts is
"to John So and So for mowing the cloister-garth"; or "wages
to the hired gardeners"; and monastic apologists of the later
Middle Ages are sometimes found arguing away the rule of
manual labour altogether; cf. my eleventh *Study*, Book II, c. ii;
or Thomas Waldensis, *Doctrinale Fidei*, lib. IV, art. ii, cc. 24, 31.

D 160. p. 156. The next twenty pages profess to sum up the evidence derived from a nunnery account-book—Grace Dieu, A.D. 1414–18. Without references, it is almost impossible to trace all his assertions; but the following cases seem certainly wrong:

p. 171. "Made under good sound cloth by their own hands, or at least under their own direction." None of the entries which I have found in the manuscript bear this out (P.R.O. *Minister's Accounts*, 1257–10): and certainly the more definite repetition of the same implication on p. 175 is false: "they grew the wool and spun it and made it into cloth". In the third year the nuns pay for spinning, just as anyone else might do; in the fourth they buy sackcloth ready-made; in the fifth, they pay for the weaving of cloth, and buy some, at any rate, of their spun thread. Indeed, it would be startling, if we had not other evidence of the kind, to note how little manual work these nuns of Grace Dieu did. They hired women for their harvesting (first year), hired a clerk to write their accounts (fourth), bought, instead of making, purses and gloves (second and third); had a man to make their tallow-dips. The Cardinal even copies down some of these items, but sums up in the teeth of the general evidence. The cope which they sold for £10 probably was made by some at least of the fifteen nuns; but we cannot assume this for certain, in the face of frequent records which tell of valuables sold to relieve financial straits.

D 161. p. 175. "They lived, too, within their income." This is flatly contradicted by more than one passage of the account-book, referring explicitly to their debts (*e.g.* third, fourth, and fifth years). Between the first and second years comes a long list of debts still owing, some of it "ancient" (*de veteri debito*).

M 162. p. 175. The corrodies which they paid are spoken of as a work of charity. Yet the Cardinal can hardly be ignorant that the majority of corrodies, in the later Middle Ages at any rate, were frankly pecuniary transactions, the monastery receiving a lump sum or some similar consideration, in return for which it granted to the corrodian a pension in kind, or even in money. There is similar economy of truth in his remarks on p. 170 about the "clothes-money" (or "salaries" as the accountant calls it in another place) of the nuns. This covert form of pocket-money was expressly forbidden by Benedict XII; but the abuse flourished notwithstanding.

163. There are also several blunders of transcription or translation in the few direct quotations printed by the Cardinal. The ten lines on pp. 165–6 contain three mistakes in the sums

of money, and an omission of three lines; one of the two proper names is misread; *dī. last albi allecis* is translated "house food"; and *in feryncicis aquis*, "at the sluice". The Cardinal was evidently nonplussed by this spelling of *forinsecis*, which, however, is not so very uncommon. On p. 169, again, what the Cardinal transcribes as "woofing and warping" cloth stands quite plainly in the manuscript as *weyfyng and walkyng—i.e.* "weaving and fulling".

164. p. 177. "John Aubrey, too, writes almost as an eye-witness of the Wiltshire convent." John Aubrey was born in 1626 and wrote in 1659 at the earliest; that is, his book is as far removed from the actual facts which he professes to describe as Cardinal Gasquet's is from the younger Pitt's first ministry in 1784. The whole of this legend about the Wiltshire nunnery is fully discussed in the tenth of my *Studies*, pp. 16–17.

D 165. p. 187. The abbot did not claim exemption "on the ground that he had been appointed by the Holy See". The actual letter (Grandisson's register, p. 395) shows that he made a claim far more damaging to the bishop's disciplinary authority: "quod *consuevit* esse nostrum monasterium totaliter exemptum et ab omni jurisdictione episcopali fuisse immune". Again, compare the Cardinal's whole version of this Tavistock case, which he gives as an example to prove that "the episcopal powers were very great and were freely exercised", with the extracts and references to the actual documents which I have already given above in the first of these *Studies* (pp. 8–10). A comparison of his account of the Bodmin visitation on p. 188 with Grandisson's register (pp. 980 ff.) will be equally instructive. It must be borne in mind that no references are given by our author, so that it is not easy for a student to check these cases unless he knows the registers fairly well.

M 166. p. 194. "Not only did the monks furnish the ranks of the secular priesthood with youths who had received their early education at the Cloister School or at the almonry":

Very few children were educated in these almonry schools (which did not usually contain more than a dozen scholars), or at the choir schools, which were still smaller and less numerous. "Cloister schools" for outsiders (as so high a Roman Catholic authority as Père Mandonnet admits) were "rare and short-lived" at all times, and "no trace of them remains" in the later Middle Ages (see his testimony in the tenth of my *Studies*, p. 36). Against this handful of pupils who thus owed their education to the monks, we must set the complaints of the Oxford Chancellor, Gascoigne, in 1450. It is (he says) the appropriation of so many parish churches to the monks, who render no services proportionate to the income thus absorbed, which lies at the root of "the destruction ...of learning, and good counsel, and good example, and hospitality, and providing poor youths with the means to go to the university" (*Liber Veritatum*, p. 3). The same complaints are repeated with equal emphasis on pp. 106, 195, and Gascoigne ends up: "thus perisheth learning and true clergy!" It must be remembered that Gascoigne is one of the best and most accessible authorities for fifteenth-century Church life, and that his statements are borne out by official documents, which the Cardinal altogether ignores in this context.

M 167. *Ibid.* "But the churches and vicarages of places impropriated were the special care of the religious." On the contrary Gascoigne asserts (p. 114) that, through the appropriation of parish churches to monasteries, "the churches are ruined, the cures are ruined, and the value of the living is ruined". The author of *Piers Plowman* speaks with bitter scorn of "Religious, that have no ruth though it rain on their altars" (B. x, 313). In that visitation of parishes in Exeter diocese, to which Cardinal Gasquet appeals as saying what in fact it does not say (*Parish Life*, p. 84; see here, above, No. 137), the *appropriated* churches reported on by the bishop's visitations show just *twice* as many dilapidations as the *non-appropriated* churches; and, in two cases, it is actually reported that rain falls on the altars of these churches from which all the great tithes went to the monks (*Eng. Hist. Review*, Jan. 1911, pp. 112 and 120, nos. 8 and 52). Mr A. Hamilton Thompson has arrived at a similar result from an independent study of the existing church fabrics. He writes: "It is noteworthy that, of the numerous beautiful chancels of the early fourteenth century which are to be found in Lincolnshire, Notts, Derbyshire, and the adjacent counties, not one is to be found in a church which, during this period, was appropriated to a monastery" (*Lincoln and York Arch. Soc. Reports*, xxxii, 65).

M 168. p. 212. "All these [women-servants for monks] were selected with care." Here, again, the Cardinal only indicates the theory as expressed in the Custumals, without making any attempt to estimate the practice, as indicated in the records of official visitations. These records show that the women-servants frequently gave occasion for scandal. They crept into the monastic system when the monks gave up their earlier ideal of handiwork—that is, at least as early as the thirteenth century. From that time forward we find laundresses and other women-servants within the precincts, until at last the Cistercian houses found it almost hopeless to struggle against this "ingressus et frequentia mulierum" (*Eng. Hist. Review*, Jan. 1914, p. 39, n. 62).

M 169. p. 242. "[The Pied Friars] had but one house in England, at Norwich." They certainly had one in London also; see Stapeldon's register, Introduction, pp. xxx and xxxi: cf. *Piers Plowman's Crede*, line 65.

ABBOT WALLINGFORD (1912)

An attempt to clear Wallingford and the monks of St Albans from the accusations rehearsed against them by Cardinal Morton in 1490; accusations which may be found fully and correctly translated (except that the weary catalogue is a-bridged towards the end) in Froude's *Henry VIII*, c. x.

170. pp. 2, 3. The Cardinal asks us to stand before the great altar-screen of St Albans and think of "the man who built it, Abbot Wallingford", and take it as our "leading principle" "that art is a finer and more subtle expression of the inmost soul even than words". Yet very little knowledge of the Middle Ages is needed to remind us that Wallingford "built" that screen only in the sense that he ordered it and paid for it. The latter part of the argument would, to St Bernard or St Francis, have seemed frankly pagan; if we are to canonize Wallingford on the strength of the altar-screen, we must attribute still greater sanctity to nearly all the petty tyrants of the Renaissance, who did incalculably more for art than he.

D 171. p. 3. "Quite recently we have been asked to change our estimate of William of Wallingford." This is flatly false. Some years before 1490, a fellow-monk deliberately handed him down to posterity as a liar, perjurer, and thief. The Cardinal tries to prove that this accuser was not really Abbot Whetham-stede, though the document not only bears his name but is also marked with his very peculiar mannerisms; and, here, he can plead the authority of Riley, no great scholar. But this cannot touch the main point; the fact remains that Wallingford was (rightly or wrongly) written down a rascal four centuries before any of us were born.

172. These instances, just cited from the first few pages, give a measure of the whole book: it is written for a particular public, which looks no farther than whatever the Cardinal chooses to say. We are twice referred pedantically to "MS. Cotton. Nero. D. VII" for well-known documents which have often been printed, and which the Cardinal quotes elsewhere from those

printed sources (pp. 14, 17). Giraldus Cambrensis is referred to by page without the volume (p. 3); three notes on pp. 15 and 24 refer us to the wrong books altogether.

V 173. The Cardinal twice mistranslates a very easy sentence, giving the manuscript source as his reference, though he has evidently been misled by the mispunctuation of the printed copy (pp. 56, 65). Riley prints: "Iam vero hic dicam, palamque monstrabo, quonam, scilicet, pacto per Spiritus Sancti viam in Abbatem postea electus fuerit". The Cardinal, deceived by this punctuation into separating the well-known phrase *quonam pacto*, translates the former word as *that*, and connects the second with the latter half of the sentence. Wallingford, he writes, was elected abbot "by unanimous agreement (*pacto, per Spiritus Sancti viam*)" and again "elected as abbot by acclamation (of the Community, *pacto per viam Spiritus*)" (pp. 56, 65). For Latin scholarship, this is almost as great a curiosity as the *expertes* of No. 109 above.

D 174. But, as usual, his worst offences are in suppressions of facts. While professing to summarize the evidence against Wallingford, he omits altogether the damning accusations contained in Innocent VIII's Bull, which accompanied Cardinal Morton's monition to St Albans. In this Bull the Pope recites how the monks, "in certain [monasteries of the Province of Canterbury] giving themselves over to a reprobate mind, and putting the fear of God behind their backs, are leading a wanton and exceedingly dissolute life...to the evil example and scandal of very many folk" (Wilkins's *Concilia*, III, 630).

D 175. pp. 42 ff. Moreover, in dealing with Cardinal Morton's monition itself, he prefaces and follows it by gross misrepresentations. The document is not a mere "warning to Abbot Wallingford of his [Morton's] intention to apply this [visitatorial] authority to the case of St Albans". Still less is it true that the accusations contained in the monition are "suggestive of...common form" (p. 45); "rather reports" than "charges" (*ibid.*), or that "their face value is, at the worst, that they remain to this day 'not proven' by any evidence whatsoever" (p. 48). All these statements are as false in canon law as the instances which I have already given in Nos. 26 and 128 above.

A *monitio*, such as this of Cardinal Morton's, was a regular method of intimating to any cleric that the outcry against him was so strong and considerable as to create a legal presumption of his guilt; and that it now lay upon him to bring sufficient evidence to clear his character (cf. Lyndwood's *Provinciale*, ed. 1679, p. 127, f and r). That is why Morton, in this present monition, speaks of the *scandalum plurimorum*; that is why he interlards it with the legal expressions *notorie, diffamatus, publica fama* (words which, as will be presently seen, are consistently omitted or distorted by Cardinal Gasquet). In canon law, a man solemnly stigmatized by his superior as *diffamatus* or *infamatus* of any offence was a man who had already been condemned by public opinion. He was offered a very lenient process of establishing his innocence by "compurgation"; if he refused, judgment went against him by default. For these sufficiently well-known facts the reader may consult President Tanon's *Tribunaux de l'Inquisition* (pp. 270 ff and 285 ff) or the well-known medieval manual of canon law called *Summa Angelica*, s.v. *Infamia*, sect. 2. As this *Summa* puts it, "*Fama*, in the proper sense, is when the whole city or neighbourhood, or the greater part thereof, agrees as to a certain fact....It is necessary, in the first place, that it should be founded upon probable conjectures; for otherwise it is not *fama* in the effective legal sense, but mere popular gossip" [*vanae voces populi*]. Let us take a concrete instance from one of the earliest pages of a series of records published (with numerous textual errors in the earlier volumes, it may be noted) by a society of which Cardinal Gasquet is a prominent official—the Canterbury and York Society. On p. 97 of the register of Bishop Hugh of Wells occurs the following entry, dated between 1215 and 1220: "Roger the Chaplain, presented by the Abbot and convent of Leicester to the church of Eastwell, after an inquisition held by the Archdeacon...was admitted and instituted to the same church, on condition that he should serve the said church personally, and that henceforth he should not keep the concubine of whom he hath been hitherto *diffamatus*, or any other concubine". This was in exact accordance with canon law. *Fama*, in the legal sense—not *vanae voces populi*, but the sober judgment of responsible men—had condemned Roger; and the accused had not even ventured to throw himself upon the notoriously over-lenient methods of purgation allowed by the Church. He was, therefore, enregistered to all time as *diffamatus*, and consequently (in default of legal purgation) as condemned: but the offence was pardoned for this one occasion. Medieval records swarm with such passages; they are especially common in those episcopal registers to which Cardinal Gasquet appeals so frequently and emphatically, yet for which he declines to give specific references when challenged. Wallingford also was *notorie diffamatus*, Wallingford also made no attempt to establish his innocence from these very definite charges; therefore, in canon law, he was a condemned man.

D 176. pp. 42 ff. But canon law is not history; however certain it may be that Wallingford was, in the legal sense, a condemned criminal, we are bound also to consider his case on its own merits; and the Cardinal professes to pass on to this consideration. He gives a summary of Morton's monition far briefer and less accurate than what Froude gave long ago; the comparison is easy to any reader, and will prove most instructive. At the very outset, he garbles Morton's words in a fashion which no ignorance of canon law can excuse. In the first sixteen lines, which profess to be an actual translation, he omits altogether, without the least warning, the decisive legal term *diffamatus*, the strengthening adjective *multorum*, and again, on two separate occasions, reinforcing sentences of nearly two lines each. In other words, he has taken the liberty of silently omitting 10 per cent. of his text, and in many ways the most significant percentage; moreover, he softens down *enormibus* into *great*. The rest, which only professes to summarize, proceeds after the same fashion. He writes: " ... Then follow a series of the gravest charges against the moral character of *one* of the nuns of Pray", where the word I have italicized stands for "moniali*um* stupro"; "ad *eam et alias* ibidem et alibi, tanquam ad publica prostibula". At Sopwell the Cardinal summarizes only the financial, omitting all mention of the graver moral mismanagement recorded by Morton: "whilst thou [Abbot Wallingford] dost depose good and religious women in both convents [of Pray and Sopwell], and dost therein promote the evil and sometimes the corrupted (*vitiatas*) to the highest dignities, Religion is cast aside, virtue is neglected...so that those convents, once very[1] religious, are now rendered and reputed as it were profane and infamous".

D 177. Moreover, he pays no attention whatever to those words of Morton's which most clearly contradict the theory that the charges rehearsed in this monition were "common form". Once again Morton uses the technical term *diffamatus*; thrice he uses the almost equally damning word *notorie*; but of this the Cardinal gives us no hint. And he even omits the sentence in which Morton complains of the terrible scandal which these things are causing among the general public, so that "we are daily besieged and distracted by fresh clamours for the reformation of these things". Lastly, his summary obscures the fact that Morton called on the abbot to give him, within thirty days, a *detailed* account of such amends as the abbot might have made: of "what thou hast meanwhile bent thyself and striven to effect for the reformation of thine own person, and the persons and morals of thy fellow-monks, and of the priories of Pray and Sopwell and

[1] *Satis religiosa.* This is often a puzzling word; we cannot always distinguish between its classical meaning and the frequent later medieval signification which survives in the Italian *assai*.

other dependent houses, and for restoring them to the true
pattern and rule of thine Order, in accordance with the laudable
ordinances and institutions thereof". As if this were not definite
enough, let us remember the extreme precision of some of
Morton's charges—the very name of the adulteress, with a still
living husband, who had been made first nun and then prioress
of Pray—the very value (8000 marks) of the woods cut down and
sold, so that "the worldly possessions [of St Albans], both in
real property and in moveables, are *notoriously* tending to
desolation...to the scandal of very many people; wherefore thou
[O Abbot] *art clearly seen* [*dignosceris*] to stand in the greatest
need of my office of correction and reform...and so are many
of your brethren the monks therein dwelling". And, bearing
this in mind, let us pass on to the words in which Cardinal
Gasquet sums up his own brief and garbled version: "This
is the *monitio*, or warning; and on the face of the document it
professes to be merely the statement of reports, of the gravest
nature it is true, but merely of unproved reports against the good
name of the Abbot and Convent".

M 178. p. 62. The Cardinal argues: "If the condition of the
Abbey was really as bad as these rumours would have us believe,
the blame must fall quite as much upon Ramridge [the prior]
as upon Wallingford [the abbot]". This is contradicted not only
by St Benedict's own Rule, which clearly treats the abbot as the
primarily responsible person, but also by frequent records of
monastic visitors. For instance—to quote almost at random from
a book which the Cardinal ought to remember something about—
two of the earlier visitations in his own *Collectanea Anglo-
Premonstratensia* might have taught him better (II, 70, 77).
And, strangest of all, this very monition of Morton's, which he is
professedly discussing all the time, supplies even plainer evidence.
It is *from the abbot*, says Morton, that God will require at the
Last Day the blood of these monks who are sinning with his
connivance; there is no word in this context of the *prior*.

M 179. Equal ignorance, or equal bad faith, underlies the
Cardinal's desperate plea that the whole story is too bad to be
true. "They [the accusations] are so sweeping and terrible that
the whole is suggestive of the equally sweeping common form
in which the 'pardons' previously referred to are couched",
etc., etc. (p. 45). He goes on to argue from similar premisses on
pp. 46, 59, etc.; and these assumptions are so important and so
demonstrably false that I will deal briefly with them here.

Next to Jocelin of Brakelonde, the Evesham chronicle is
perhaps the best known of English records, unquestionably
authentic, dealing with the more intimate side of monastic life.

It was written in an age of comparative fervour (early thirteenth century) and by a model abbot, Thomas Marleberge, who had himself played the principal part in bringing to justice the criminous Abbot Norreys. The value of his chronicle for our present purpose is increased by the facts that Evesham, like St Albans, claimed exemption from episcopal jurisdiction, and that the main visitor in both cases was a Papal legate. Let us, therefore, enumerate the points which Cardinal Gasquet would put aside as scarcely credible, and parallel them from the solemn record which Abbot Marleberge has left to posterity.

(1) Wallingford is defamed of having systematically wasted and embezzled the Abbey property. But Norreys had done so even more thoroughly and openly for twenty-two years, and might have gone on for as long again if he had not quarrelled with his monks. (2) Wallingford is possibly accused of adultery, and certainly of conniving at unchastity in his brethren. Norreys had had children by two married and six unmarried women whom Marleberge was able to specify by name, from among a far longer list of persons unknown; he also (we are told) would have been glad to see his monks imitate his example. (3) We are asked to discredit Morton's *monitio* because it merely calls upon the accused Wallingford to reform his own abbey, instead of calling in an outsider to interfere. Yet the legate had done just the same to Norreys; and the very book from which Cardinal Gasquet most frequently quotes, the so-called Whethamstede register, tells us how Brother John Langton, disgraced and removed from Tynemouth by Wallingford in 1478, was by that same abbot appointed visitor in 1480, to correct the short-comings of the Tynemouth monks! (4) But Wallingford (it is argued) received a testimonial from his brother-monks, who supported him in his resistance to Morton. The document quoted in support of this argument contains at least one plain mis-statement and one self-contradiction, and leaves its main purpose a matter of pure conjecture; moreover, it is astonishing how Cardinal Gasquet can describe it as "a categorical denial of many of the evil reports" (p. 58), in face of the fact that it scarcely touches Morton's accusations at any important point. Yet, even if it had been all that he describes and all that he conjectures, it would still be insufficient for his argument. Few pages in medieval history are more startling than that page 121 of this most unexceptionable Evesham chronicle, wherein the model Marleberge coolly relates how he and his fellow-monks swore to stand stoutly by the octogamous villain Norreys, and to hold their tongues even under the bishop's threat of excommunicating them for their silence, if only Norreys would stand as stoutly

by them in resisting the bishop's authority. If Norreys had kept his part of the bargain; if he had merely possessed the proverbial measure of a thief's honesty, he might have gone down to posterity with scarcely a spot upon his reputation; and other visitatorial documents of the Middle Ages simply swarm with similar evidence of deliberate conspiracies to conceal the facts from a visitor. The Cardinal's argument *ab incredibili*, like his suppressions and falsifications of documents, can only help him with readers ignorant of medieval conditions and content to enquire no further than the Cardinal chooses to take them. The real question is, not what modern monks and modern visitors would do, or what modern dilettantism would expect them to do, but what medieval documents of unexceptionable authority record them to have done in the Middle Ages. Certain psychological riddles suggested by the Cardinal's habitual treatment of medieval documents need not concern us here; but the fact that he does habitually garble these documents must very closely concern every student of that period. We may successfully misrepresent even the plainest documentary evidence to certain readers, and for a certain period of time; but, in the long run, a cause which relies upon such misrepresentations must become a cause which appeals only to the thoughtless or the ignorant.

ENGLAND UNDER THE OLD RELIGION (1912)

A collection of old essays, of which only the first and the last deal with the Middle Ages. "We have fortunately ample material", writes the Cardinal in the first; and presently wanders off into a series of unvouched quotations, of which less than half are from the "ample material" of actual pre-Reformation documents, the rest being from modern writers often of dubious authority. But the last essay is most interesting, in view of the fact that the Duke of Norfolk has lately claimed as one of the Cardinal's main characteristics "a distaste for controversy" (*The Times*, June 27, 1914). That last essay was published in 1902, and deliberately republished in 1912. It is, from first to last, a gratuitous and savage attack on certain authors who were in no sense professed medievalists, and of whom the Cardinal might be pretty certain that they would never reply. The *Spectator* reviewer, in an obsequiously favourable notice of the book, confesses that "most of the essays included are of a strongly controversial nature", and that this final essay, especially, makes the reviewer "take up his pen and his parable in fear and trembling" (April 26, 1913).

The Cardinal has in fact never shown any great dislike to controversy where he had no reason to fear retort and exposure. Readers, therefore, must now judge for themselves why he was so voluble in 1902 against two amateur editors who had never attacked him, and why he has remained so silent in the face of repeated accusations of ignorance or bad faith at other times, from critics who have rested their attacks upon plain documentary evidence.

APPENDIX III

(From the *Catholic Times*, May 29, 1914.)

THE CEREMONY OF THE BIGLIETTO ADDRESS BY CARDINAL GASQUET

Immediately after the Secret Consistory, says a Reuter's telegram, a small ceremony took place which is called *Il Biglietto*, or Notice of Appointment.... This committee of three handed to each of the new cardinals in Rome his biglietto, the recipient, in accordance with tradition, appearing much surprised.

Amidst great attention, Cardinal Gasquet delivered a brilliant address in reply, in which he said that he had received the "immense honour", as Cardinal Newman called it, without having held the usual positions leading to it, and remarked that he understood that the Pontiff conferred the dignity because of his (the Cardinal's) lowliness. He then continued:

To judge from the letters and telegrams that have poured in upon me during the past few days, my election has been received with pleasure in all English-speaking countries; and it has been a source of the greatest satisfaction to find that this feeling is not confined to the Catholic body. My old friends at the British Museum and the London Record Office—non-Catholics, I think, to a man—and some of the societies like the Royal Historical and the Bibliographical, have expressed their pleasure at an honour given to one whom they regard, so they kindly say, "as one of themselves". From a professor of history in one of the German universities, a Lutheran Protestant, I have heard that in that country they have regarded my elevation as an honour to the historians of the world.

APPENDIX IV

PROPORTION OF CRIMINALS AND THEIR PUNISHMENTS IN "COLLECTANEA ANGLO-PREMONSTRATENSIA"

The Cardinal deals with both questions in his Preface to vol. II, pp. xxii ff. He there professes to sum up fully the visitors' records of incontinent Religious, and writes:

In all, then, *during the last five-and-twenty years* of the fifteenth century over which these visitations extend, the records show some sixteen cases of admitted or proved incontinency, and possibly two more doubtful cases. In this period *no fewer than* 1806 canons presented themselves, including, of course, several occasions of different visitations, and were examined and interrogated by the visitor during his visitation. Of these 1806, in the quarter of the century, eighteen at most—that is, barely 1 per cent.—were charged with any crime whatsoever against morality.

That is, of sexual morality. Yet, even so, the words which I have italicized give a very false presentation of the facts. The records are far from complete for the whole "five-and-twenty years", as the Cardinal himself knows: he has noted in another context (p. viii) that a large proportion of the visitations are altogether missing; and, indeed, this is one of the first facts that must strike any careful student. Moreover, the lists of banished canons published by the Provincial chapters—fragmentary as these confessedly are—are sufficient to indicate that the missing visitation records were as unfavourable as those which have survived; or, if anything, more unfavourable.[1] Again, it is palpably absurd to count each canon afresh, every third year, as a different man, when the records enable us to estimate their numbers almost exactly. In the houses visited in this second volume (to which the Cardinal arbitrarily confines his calculations), about 470 canons were domiciled at

[1] *E.g.* the visitation record of Newbo in 1478 is imperfect, but the chapter of 1479 sentenced two canons of that house to banishment (I, 148). Of the twenty-six serious cases thus mentioned in these chapter records, twelve are unrecorded in any other part of the surviving documents; this shows how many accusations recorded by the visitors must have perished among the records which have not come down to us.

different times during these twenty-five years: therefore not
1 per cent. but 4 per cent. of these men were formally accused
of incontinence.

But, instead of thus confining ourselves arbitrarily to the
first half of the houses taken alphabetically, let us take a survey
of the whole. Twenty-nine monasteries were visited in the
twenty-five years, containing at any given time about 420
inmates, but, during the whole twenty-five years, about 950.[1]
Out of these persons, forty-eight at least were seriously accused
of incontinence. The guilt of twenty-nine of these is placed
beyond doubt; the large majority were formally convicted,
and in the five remaining cases the visitor treats the evidence
as conclusive without further formalities. In twelve other cases,
though the records convey a very strong implication of guilt,
the visitor does not press the case to its legal issue, but punishes
the accused, or solemnly warns him, as he feels inclined. Only
seven of the forty-eight were able to "purge" themselves by
those very lenient canonical processes which (as the Oxford
Chancellor, Gascoigne, was publicly complaining at this very
time) afforded "an occasion of intolerable wickedness" at
Oxford, and often resulted in the acquittal of the most notorious
culprits.[2]

Moreover, this list necessarily omits such a significant case
as vol. II, 211, where the visitor forbids that, in future,
"women suspected of incontinence or of theft should frequent
the cloister or other parts [of the monastery], or have speech or
association (*concursum*) with the canons, especially those from
the town of Barnard Castle". Again, I have taken no notice
of the half-dozen cases where the visitor accuses a canon of
"multa enormia" or "abominabilia", without specifying their
exact nature. Finally, a large number of other canons are

---

[1] Talley, in Wales, was never actually visited: the abbot was simply
summoned on one occasion to come and give his own report. The
number of inmates may be counted from the Index, with allowance
for cases where the indexer has made a single canon into two.

[2] *Munimenta Academica*, II, 536. The cases are as follows:

Condemned, II, 36, 66, 76, 78, 97, 117 (two cases), 121, 130, 182
(two cases), 241, 258 (abortion); III, 7, 16, 18, 38, 112, 115 (the same
offender again), 113, 143, 185, 187, 200, 207.

Assumed to be guilty, III, 30 (two or more), 41 (cf. 39), 162 (two or
more).

Not pressed further, II, 254, 259; III, 68 (five cases), 104, 115, 185
(two cases).

Purged, II, 7, 19, 131, 242; III, 35, 41, 150.

recorded as "apostates"; and there is reason to believe that a considerable proportion of these were living an entirely unmonastic life.[1] Altogether, considering the fact that so many of the visitations of these twenty-five years have perished, it would be utterly unhistorical to treat the forty-eight cited cases as even a remotely exhaustive record; yet, even if we confine ourselves to these, we get a proportion of nearly 5 per cent. accused of incontinence, instead of the Cardinal's 1 per cent. It is important, in this context, to remember that Cardinal Gasquet represents Cromwell's visitors as accusing only 3·1 per cent. of the Religious, and that he refuses to accept even this as a possible proportion. I have pointed out elsewhere that the records of Nicke's first visitation of Norwich diocese give an unimpeachable record of 6·1 per cent. (*Monastic Legend*, p. 3). If we add to the forty-eight cases actually recorded by the visitors those twelve other cases of banishment which, in defect of visitatorial records, we happen to know of only through the chapter records, we shall get sixty cases, or rather over 6 per cent. And when we remember further that chapter records fail us altogether, and visitatorial records to a very great extent, for the periods from 1475 to 1479 and again from 1497 to 1500, it will be difficult to conclude that these Premonstratensian houses were in a much better state than the monasteries of Norwich diocese.

Again, let us take the question of the punishment of detected offenders. To the historian, this is even more important than the question of the numbers detected, since it enables us to take a measure of the visitor's energy and authority. If we find him treating the *convicted* offender with reasonable severity, we shall have some right to infer that he has previously showed a similar spirit in *discovering* the offender; if, on the other hand, he shows himself embarrassed in his dealings with detected crime, we may rightly suspect him of equal weakness in the preliminary work of bringing hidden crimes to light. There can be no stronger evidence against any system than the record

---

[1] No less than fifty-one are at different times so noted, excluding about twenty more who are accused of "apostasy" in the narrower sense, *i.e.* of having illegally broken bounds for a more or less brief period. Moreover, a large number of these canons spent their lives in country cures away from the monastery, and were therefore considerably more free from direct visitatorial observation than the rest. It is significant that some of the worst offenders drifted into such country cures.

of its helplessness in the face of wickedness and open indiscipline. Bishop Redman, the visitor in this case, was certainly above the average of his fellows during the years immediately preceding the Reformation; we have, therefore, in these records, a favourable picture of the visitation system. How, then, did Redman deal with his black sheep?

"On the face of the documents" (writes the Cardinal, p. xviii) "which are the official records of the results, it is impossible for the most prejudiced mind not to admit that wrongdoing was never tolerated by the authorities, and that the punishments meted out were sufficiently drastic at least to prove their honesty of purpose." And again (p. xxiii): "those found guilty *were punished with exemplary severity*...generally the culprit was *actually sent at once* to some other monastery for three, seven, or ten years, to live there *without any of the rights belonging to a member of the community*....In the face of these documents, then, it is impossible to suggest that the Superiors did in any way tolerate serious abuses".

It would, indeed, be difficult to suggest this, if the crucial words which I have italicized were true. Dr Gairdner, in the days before he had learned the habit of verifying the Cardinal's references, took for granted the truth of these italicized words, coming as they did from an editor who claimed to be dealing with facts so easily verifiable; and, trusting implicitly to this assertion, Dr Gairdner (as I happen to know) was much impressed by this part of the preface. Yet the Cardinal's assertions are grotesquely, and almost incredibly, false.

I. "*Punished with exemplary severity*." The total list of grave faults dealt with is about seventy-five; this includes not only incontinence, but such offences as theft, embezzlement, assaults with murderous weapons, apostasy,[1] rebellion, etc. In at least eighteen cases, the punishments inflicted are almost childish: *e.g.* a single recitation of the Psalter is inflicted (*a*) upon three canons who got out at night to haunt taverns, and "returned as dogs to their vomit" instead of amending their ways; and (*b*) upon a far worse offence to the medieval mind—actual dabbling in witchcraft. A canon who had illegally pawned three books (which would probably represent a serious embezzlement) was let off with the recital of seven penitential psalms (III, 79, 117; II, 212). Another who was "always intent upon consorting

[1] Only a fraction of the apostates were actually available for punishment; the majority were evidently beyond the visitor's reach, and are therefore not counted here.

and talking with women at recreation-time" had to recite the Psalter seven times during the ensuing year (III, 190). An abbot, convicted of incontinence and malversation, was indeed deposed from his office, but at the same time handsomely pensioned for the rest of his life (III, 18). Another even worse abbot was deposed, but no further punishment is recorded (III, 185). Of the third, John Newynton, worst of all, we do not even know that he was deposed, though his canons (apparently without exception) accused him of wholesale malversation of property, drinking and filthy speech in taverns on Sundays and holy days, and "great incontinence with divers harlots and suspected women" (III, 105). For one case of simple embezzlement, no punishment was inflicted (III, 115); none again for persistently consorting, after solemn warning, with a suspected and forbidden woman (III, 115); none again upon a canon who, after a bad record for six years past, is now acting as vicar of a parish, where "the common report spreads and proclaims on all hands that he has lived in an abominable and disorderly fashion, and has run into debt with many persons; from which accusations, when we brought them more fully against him, he was unable to clear himself" (III, 196). In consequence of a fatal brawl, the visitor forbade the canons of Eggleston to wear daggers at their girdles, as Church law had long since forbidden it. Three years later, he found some still wearing their daggers, but there is no hint of punishment (II, 218, 220). Finally (to omit other examples which might be cited) a whole batch of apostates and incontinents are, on one occasion, left by the visitor to the abbot's correction (III, 162).

II. "*Actually sent at once.*" This statement is, if possible, even more false than the first. In all, about thirty-eight persons were sentenced to different terms of banishment to other abbeys; but in twenty-eight cases, or nearly 75 per cent., these sentences were mitigated on the spot, the visitor himself (*a*) adding the proviso "unless, by way of mercy he be dispensed from this", or (*b*), more frequently, yielding to the tears of the culprit and his friends, and following up his sentence with a "continuavimus"; *i.e.* holding over the punishment a year, or perhaps for three years, in the hope of amendment. Moreover, the lists of canons given at each visitation enable us to trace their movements fairly accurately; and these lists prove that the visitor's sentence was often not carried out, even when he had not previously suspended it himself. For instance, the first of these unconditional sentences is that passed on W. Bentham, of Cockersand, who was convicted of "multiple" incontinence, and sentenced to Croxton for three years. This was December 13, 1489; yet on April 26,

1491, he is not only still at Cockersand, but has actually risen to the post of sub-prior! The next recorded instance is James Skipton, also of Cockersand, sentenced for incontinence to seven years at Sulby. Yet he also is still at Cockersand in 1491, and promoted to cellarer; in 1494 he is still there, and in an equally responsible office; and in 1502 he became Abbot of Cockersand! (II, 117 ff; *Vict. County Hist., Lancs.,* II, 156). A few minutes' search would have convinced Cardinal Gasquet that these offenders were not actually banished; yet he serenely takes his bill and writes down as a summary of this very record: "*two* canons found guilty of incontinence *and punished severely*". It is true that the visitor also sentenced them to forty days of penance; but what reason have we for supposing that this part of the sentence was not privately disobeyed, when we know that the major part was so unblushingly neglected? After going through all these lists myself, with something of the thoroughness with which the actual editor should in conscience have gone through them, I can testify that the evidence points strongly towards the escape of at least three-quarters of these culprits from the banishment to which they were sentenced. Things went a little better with the Provincial chapter sentences (which the Cardinal, by the bye, does not notice). Out of the eleven sentences of banishment which we hear of only through these chapter decrees, five seem to have been actually carried out.

Not only has the Cardinal blinked this, which would have been revealed by a few days of careful comparison between his different documents, but he repeatedly falsifies even the facts which lie on the very surface of each separate record. He prefaces each report with a summary of its contents in English. To take these again in order from the beginning. W. Hymmers, of Alnwick, is condemned to Dale *pro perpetuo*, but with the usual mitigation *nisi alias*. The Cardinal quietly omits this *nisi alias*, and records "is severely punished", though in fact the documents show that Hymmers remained at home (II, 19 ff.). So with the next case (II, 36), where the *nisi alias* is again blinked. In the next (II, 36) the bulk of the punishment was remitted on the spot, and even the remaining twenty days of penance were left to the abbot's discretion; yet here again the Cardinal summarizes "is severely punished". In the next (II, 66) an unmitigated rascal was sentenced to six years of banishment; execution, however, was at once formally deferred, and in fact the documents show that he never went. The Cardinal summarizes "is punished severely, *and removed to another house*". In the next again (II, 76) sentence was deferred, as usual, in the same breath in which it was pronounced; but the summary runs "is *sent* to another monastery". Nor can this be explained by ignorance of the technical term *continuavimus*; for the Cardinal occasionally lapses into a correct and conscientious translation of this word.

III. Thirdly, it can be proved that some even of the worst offenders did not "*lose their rights belonging to a member of the community*". Here, again, even the most cursory study of the actual documents reveals an enormous gap between theory and practice. We have already seen how the two Cockersand criminals, instead of being degraded, were actually promoted. Let us take another instance from the monastery of Sulby (III, 112–16; I, 176). In 1491, Robert Bredon, sub-prior, was found guilty of very gross immoralities, and sentenced to forty days of penance, and banishment to Alnwick for seven years; but, in consideration of his tears and promises, the punishment was deferred, to give him a further chance. In 1494 we find him still at Sulby, not only sub-prior but also sacrist, and still wallowing in his sins. Again, Richard Ralston, of Welbeck, confessed, in 1488, to "multiple incontinence". He was sentenced to forty days on bread and water and three years' banishment; but there is no trace of his name on the lists of any other monastery. He was not at Welbeck in 1491, but he may well have been wandering about outside in apostasy, as so many others were. When next he appears, in 1504, he is Abbot of Wendling! (III, 197). Finally, John Newynton, of St Radegund's, was excommunicated once again, at the visitation of 1488, as an apostate who had been "frequently" excommunicated already. In 1491 we find this John Newynton actually Abbot of St Radegund's; in 1497 "the whole monastery alleges the greatest enormities against him", but in 1500 he is still abbot, and the convent again accuses him of the adulteries and other crimes already detailed above (III, 105). It is useless to put forward any psychological theory which might explain how, in the face of these facts, Cardinal Gasquet can write as he does, even under cover of his imperfect system of references. The facts stare us in the face from the original documents; but what percentage of readers ever travels beyond an editor's preface and summaries?

FALSE SUMMARIES

The following instances will give an idea of the liberties which the Cardinal has permitted himself in these summaries.

Vol. II, p. 26. "*Publica* aures nostras propulsavit *fama*, eo quod fratres dicti monasterii frequentius usque villam de Alnewik vadunt, et presertim ad *loca suspecta*." This the Cardinal renders: "There was a report that the canons frequented the town of Alnwick too much." Yet the words I have italicized and which he has omitted are the stock legal phrases used in visitation documents; *fama publica* means legally "the general consent of trustworthy witnesses in the district" and *suspectus* means "disreputable"; cf. II, 78, "ad loca suspecta et ad mulierem suspectam".

Vol. II, p. 55. "Item, in noctibus, post Completorium, fratres exeunt claustrum, et tandiu vigilant et potationibus utuntur, quod in mediis noctibus, tempore matutinarum, vigilare non possunt."
G. "The canons sometimes give themselves to potations at night."

Vol. II, p. 76. *G.* "A canon, *accused* of incontinence...is *sent* to another monastery for punishment and threatened with perpetual imprisonment." As a matter of fact, the canon was not only accused, but convicted; he failed in his attempted compurgation. The banishment was not inflicted, but suspended, *continuavimus*, a word which the Cardinal translates quite correctly in other places.

Vol. II, pp. 107, 110. This summary entirely suppresses the fact that the Abbot of Cockersand had been accused by the visitor of things which, *propter suorum* (sic) *enormitatem*, had been reserved for the General chapter to deal with; and that the abbot, *dissimulatione exquisita*, had managed to suppress this part of the report. This may be added to the cases already cited in which grave offences are not recorded to have been punished.

Vol. II, p. 177 (Dale). *G.* "One canon found guilty of disobedience."
Text. "De vicio inobediencie...*et multis enormibus aliis et excessibus*, impetitus."

Vol. III, p. 25 (Langley). *G.* "Bishop Redman, on strictest enquiry, finds the reports of incontinence against the abbot to be untrue." Yet the summary omits to add that there is "maxima infamia...per circuitum diffusa", and that the bishop commanded the abbot, under pain of excommunication, never *again* to admit the suspected woman to the monastery, *or permit her to dwell in any place thereunto appertaining.*

Vol. III, p. 80. The summary mentions that one canon had thrice apostatized, but omits that another canon and a nun were also in apostasy. Similarly, vol. II, p. 35, though three are named in the text as apostates, the Cardinal only sees one.

Vol. III, p. 104. *G.* "The *suggested* offences." Compare the word which I have here italicized with the actual text on p. 103

and the two paragraphs at the top of p. 105, where it is recorded that *the whole monastery* joined in accusing the abbot of these offences. Compare, similarly, the summary on p. 68 with the actual text.

Vol. III, p. 146. *G.* "One canon convicted of apostasy, rebellion and theft."

Text: "Super apostasia, *incontinentia*, furto, et manifesta rebellione *multipliciter* diffamatum et convictum."

This list is far from exhaustive, but it will suffice.

INDEX

NOTE. All Saints will be found under St

Abbess, immoral, 76

Abbey, bankrupt, 9; books in, 94; dairy in, 6; debts of, 9; income of, 94

Abbot, bad, 6, 8, 10, 18, 19, 226, 254, 259, 267; banished, 9; chaplain of, 9, 18, 216; children of, 9; criticized by own monks, 270; deposed, 9, with pension, 266; dilapidation by, 215, 259; dress of, 9; election of, 9, 252, 255; excommunicated, 9, 268; and flesh-eating, 8; good, 259; on horseback, 51; litigation by, 127; and mortuary, 127; murder by, 19; pawning monastery jewels, 215; responsibility of, 258; rights claimed by, 127; St Gregory on wandering, 95; squire of, 19; suppression of truth at visitation, 214; suspended, 10; and women, 51. *And see* Visitation and conspiracy

Abingdon, *Chron. Abendon*, 249, 250

Absolution, before execution, 192; bought, 247

Acre, 197

Adam, Brother, 54

"Advocators", 244

Aesop, 99

Agag, 56

Agen, 68

Agriculture, 151; cowherds, 119; day-labourers and Church dues, 129; friars and crops, 168; ploughing with oxen, 32; tithes and, 124; wages in, 127. *And see* Animals, Monks (labour), Peasants

Aldby, Prior of, 5

Alexandria, 191

"Alleluia, the Great", 30, 31

Almonry, 252

Almsgiving, and infidelity, 78; and tithes, 124 n. *And see* Clergy, Monks

Almshouses, founding of, 116

Alnwick, 267

America, American, 87, 132; Gasquet in, 2; *North American Review*, 30 n.

Ancien Régime, 128

Andrew, Brother, 60

Anger, Richard, 213

Anglia Sacra, 229, 231

Anglicanism, Anglicans, 1, 18, 58, 59, 86

Animals, bell-wethers, 185; birds, 64; cats, 36; Church's attitude to, 54; cows, 128; dogs, 21, 55, (hunting), 93; flies, 54, 61, 67, 168; Franciscans and, 54; geese, 124; goats, 35; hawks, 54; hounds, 10; medieval attitude towards, 54; on monastic farms, 93; oxen, 32, 93, 118; pigs, 54; rats, "drunk as", 153; serpents, women as, 185; sheep, 70, 93; sparrows, 54; swallows, 54; swine, 93; toads, 36. *And see* Mortuary

Antiquaries, Society of, 86

Antoninus, Marcus, 74

Apocalypse, 116

Apostate, *see* Nuns

Apostles, 32, 128; Creed, heretics and, 119

Appropriations, *see* Churches appropriated

Ap Rice, 210

Aquila, 64

Aquitaine, 8

Archaeological Journal, 153

Archbishops, and bribery, 133; duties of, 163; good, 128; and money (probate fees), 136; in plague, 229

Archdeacons, 124; duties of, 164. *And see* Visitation

Architecture, art, artists, destroyed before Reformation, 68; frescoes in churches, 65, 66; in town-hall,